not
here

# COLLECTED POEMS

COLLECTED WORKS

A MAP OF THE UNIVERSE ISSUED IN 1909. THIS MAP IS ONE BEGINNING OF THE GOLDEN BOOK OF SPRINGFIELD.

"THE QUEEN OF BUBBLES" WAS FIRST DESIGNED IN 1904, AND THE VERSE WRITTEN TO FIT THE FIRST DESIGN, IN 1904.—THIS IS A FAIR REPLICA OF THE IDEA. THE POEM APPEARED IN "THE CRITIC" FOR MARCH, 1904. MY FIRST APPEARANCE IN PRINT. THE RIGHT HALF, ONLY, OF THIS DESIGN APPEARED NOW THE WHOLE DESIGN IS PRESENTED.

OUT OF THE DESIGN AND VERSE CAME "THE MAP OF THE UNIVERSE." IN THE SUMMER OF 1904 IT WAS FIRST PRIVATELY PRINTED IN "THE TRAMP'S EXCUSE," ISSUED IN THE AUTUMN OF 1909.

THE MAP HAS DOMINATED ALL MY VERSES SINCE IT IS A MERE KINDERGARTEN MAP, AND MAKES NO PRETENTIONS TO PROFUNDITY

BEGINNING IN THE UPPER RIGHT-HAND CORNER OF THE MAP, WE SEE THE BUBBLES WHERE "THE QUEEN OF BUBBLES" RIDES. WE SEE THE BOATS OF THE PROPHETS AND THE ANGELS, ABOVE THE THREE THRONES OF THE TRINITY UNDER THE THRONES ARE THE JUNGLES OF HEAVEN

UNDER THE WALLS OF HEAVEN WE SEE THE AMARANTH-VINE GROWING FROM EARTH TO HEAVEN. THIS IS BUT A DIAGRAM OF THE VINE, NOT A PICTURE. THE PICTURE IT IS IMPOSSIBLE TO DRAW NONE OF THE PICTURES ARE POSSIBLE TO DRAW

## THE AMARANTH—THAT WILL COME TO THIS CITY

NOW, IN THE NIGHT ALL MUSIC HAUNTS US
HERE.
IS IT FOR NOTHING HEAVEN CRACKS AND
YAWNS
AND THE TREMENDOUS AMARANTH DESCENDS,
LOADED WITH GLORY OF TEN THOUSAND
DAWNS?

THE AMARANTH MEANS:—GOD WOULD HAVE
US SAY:—
"WHETHER YOU WILL OR NO, O CITY YOUNG,
HEAVEN WILL BLOOM LIKE ONE GREAT
FLOWER FOR YOU,
FLASH AND LOOM GREATLY ALL YOUR STREETS
AMONG."

FRIEND, I WILL NOT STOP HOPING, THOUGH
YOU MOURN
WE SEE SUCH FLOWERS, AND SOME OF THEM,
SHALL COME,
THOUGH NOW OUR STREETS ARE JAZZED, OR
SADLY GREY,
AND THOUGH OUR BOYS ARE STRIDENT NOW,
OR DUMB.

FRIEND, THAT FLOWER-TOWN, THAT WONDER
TOWN SHALL COME,
NAUGHT CAN PREVENT IT THOUGH IT MAY
NOT BE
WHAT WE MAY PLAN, IT COMES, AT LAST—WE
KNOW
WITH STREETS LIKE CHANNELS OF AN IN-
CENSE-SEA,—

WITH TWILIGHT MISTS FROM HEAVEN'S JUN-
GLES DEEP,
OR WHERE THE BUTTERFLY'S GREAT SOUL
STILL FLOATS ASLEEP—
BENEATH GREAT HEAVEN'S GRANITE
STEEP;—
IT COMES, AT LAST WE KNOW,
WITH MUSICAL BELLS, FROM THE GREAT WEST-
ERN TREE,
FROM THE FAR STAR, OR GOLDEN MAIDS THAT
COME
FROM EVE'S GREAT EASTERN PALACE OF THE
SKY
WHERE GREAT GOLDEN WONDERS NEVER DIE

BESIDE THE VINE, ABOVE EARTH, BETWEEN EARTH AND THE WALLS OF HEAVEN, JUST ABOVE THE MOON IS THE SOUL OF A BUTTERFLY NAMED: "BEAUTY." WAY TO THE EAST, ON THE EDGE OF THE UNIVERSE AND ACTUALLY EAST OF THE UNIVERSE, IS "THE PALACE OF EVE" WHERE ALL THE BRIGHT BEAUTIFUL GIRLS COME FROM. BETWEEN THE SUN IN THE MIDDLE OF THE PICTURE, AND THE FLAMES OF HELL JUST BELOW IT ARE THE SAME BOATS OF THE PROPHETS AND ANGELS THAT HOVER ABOVE THE THRONES OF THE TRINITY

ON THE EDGE OF THE UNIVERSE, BELOW THE PALACE OF EVE, IS THE SOUL OF A SPIDER, CALLED: "MAMMON."

THE DOTTED CIRCULAR LINE, EQUI-DISTANT FROM THE SUN ON EVERY SIDE, IS THE EDGE OF THE UNIVERSE

BELOW THIS CIRCLE IS THE TOMB OF LUCIFER, WHO WAS CURSED BY THE ANGELS FOR SINGING TOO WELL. OVER THE TOMB FLOWS THE RIVER OF HATE. JUST ABOVE THE TOMB, JUST INSIDE THE EDGE OF THE CREATED UNIVERSE, IS THE HARP OF LUCIFER STILL FLAMING, AND THE FLAME OF THE HARP LEAPS TO THE JUNGLES AND THRONES OF HEAVEN BUT THIS IS A FLAME OF MEMORY RATHER THAN SONG. AROUND THE HARP ARE THE GULFS OF SILENCE

WEST OF THE UNIVERSE IS THE TREE OF LAUGHING BELLS, WHICH GROWS ON THE STAR OF LAUGHING BELLS, THE FARTHEST STAR OF ALL. THE WINDS OF CHAOS BEAT UPON THE TREE, AND SHAKE DOWN THE BELLS ON THE SIDES OF THE STAR AND INTO THE SEAS OF CHAOS

THE DARK MASSES ON THE UPPER LEFT HAND CORNER ARE THE CAVES ON THE COAST OF THULE, FROM WHICH THE UNIVERSE CAME LIKE A BUBBLE. HERE OFTEN MAY BE FOUND THE SPOKANE WONDERS:—"THE MOHAWK," "THE LOCOMOTIVE" AND "THE BUFFALO," (OF WHICH MORE ANON)

THE BORDER OF EGYPTIAN BOATS, IN HIEROGLYPHICS, REPRESENTS THE TWENTY-FOUR HOURS' JOURNEY OF THE SUN; AND OF THE VARIOUS SUN-BOATS OF THE SOUL IN WHICH, ACCORDING TO LEGEND, THE SOUL RODE WITH THE SUN, IN THE DAY-SKY AND THEN UNDER THE UNIVERSE, IN THE NIGHT THE SOUL RODE THROUGH LIGHT AND SKY AND RAIN AND SEA AND NIGHT, THROUGH EACH IN TURN

SEE PAGES 346 THROUGH 309 FOR MANY FEATURES OF "THE MAP OF THE UNIVERSE" SEE, ALSO, "THE LAST SONG OF LUCIFER," PAGES 111 THROUGH 118, AND "THE TREE OF LAUGHING BELLS," PAGES 212 THROUGH 219 SEE ALSO PAGES 18, 19, AND 197.

SEE "THE GOLDEN BOOK OF SPRINGFIELD," PAGES 229, 230, 231, 262, 265, AND PAGES 305 TO 329. THESE ARE DISCOURSES ON EVERYTHING FROM THE PALACE OF EVE TO THE BOATS OF THE PROPHETS.

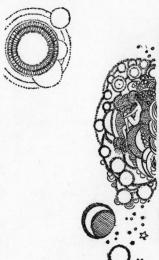 

# COLLECTED POEMS

BY

## VACHEL LINDSAY

REVISED EDITION WITH ILLUSTRATIONS
BY THE AUTHOR

THE MACMILLAN COMPANY

THE MACMILLAN COMPANY

PRINTED IN THE UNITED STATES OF AMERICA

THIS BOOK IS DEDICATED TO
SARA TEASDALE, POET

For permission to reprint some of the poems contained in this volume the author is indebted to the courtesy of the editors and publishers of the *Metropolitan, Poetry: A Magazine of Verse,* the *Independent, Tuck's Magazine, Reedy's Mirror,* the *Little Review,* the *American Magazine, The Outlook, The Chicago Herald, The Masses, The Red Cross Magazine, The Bookman, The Seven Arts, The Forum, The Chicago Daily News, Contemporary Verse, The New Republic, "Books and the Book World"* of the New York *Sun, Others, Youth,* William Stanley Braithwaite's anthology entitled *"Victory," The Yale Review, The American Miscellany* of 1920 and 1922, and the University of Virginia's *"Enchanted Years."*

Harriet Monroe awarded the Levinson Prize to "The Chinese Nightingale," as the best contribution to *Poetry: A Magazine of Verse,* for the year 1915.

# TABLE OF CONTENTS

# SECTION II—ORATIONS, COLLEGE WAR-CRIES, AND OLYMPIC GAMES . . . . . . . . 109

# TABLE OF CONTENTS

# TABLE OF CONTENTS

# TABLE OF CONTENTS

## TABLE OF CONTENTS

# TABLE OF CONTENTS

# COLLECTED POEMS

## ADVENTURES WHILE PREACHING
## HIEROGLYPHIC SERMONS

Being about to start on a new national tour, it is my petition to my prospective audiences that they provide themselves with the illustrated edition of my COLLECTED POEMS before I arrive in town. I urge them to bring it to the lecture hall, not only to follow the texts as I recite them, but to follow the forty designs as I here discuss them. Begin with "The Village Improvement Parade," front and back end-pages, and also page 204; and follow it up with a careful study of "The Map of the Universe," frontispiece, and the poems which grew out of it.

The preface to the first edition of the COLLECTED POEMS is entitled "Adventures While Singing These Songs." This *might* be called "Adventures With the Bottle Volcanic" (see drawing next to page 202), *might* be entitled "Adventures While Designing These Hieroglyphics." The first preface says that I am about to start on another reciting tour. I made the tour while the book was in the press, and being published. Later I toured the Western Capitals of Canada, as far north as Saskatoon, Saskatchewan. In the late winter the swing around the circle finally ended at Gulf Park, Gulfport, Mississippi, about which I have written many songs. This very preface is written at *The Studio of the Driftwood Fire,* at Gulf Park.

At Gulf Park College I have been teaching "The New

Poetry Anthology," by Harriet Monroe and Alice Corbin Henderson, reading it through to my classes with the greatest joy. I have been revelling in poems most of them written by personal friends under circumstances fairly familiar. It has been a great luxury thus to pause and with the help of such shrewd editors as Harriet Monroe and Alice Corbin Henderson, make a reappraisal of all things that have happened in the United States and British Languages in Poetry since that mystic date of 1912. I anticipate interpreting for many years, to picked classes, these verses, and newer songs, for I am sure that the New Poetry Movement has but begun, and that this anthology will need to be enlarged again in a few years. These singers are young.

Harriet Monroe says in her preface:

"Indeed, many critics feel that poetry is coming nearer than either the novel or the drama to the actual life of our time. The magazine, *Poetry,* ever since its foundation in October, 1912, has encouraged this new spirit in the art, and the anthology is a further effort on the part of its editors to present the new spirit to the public."

I am always urging upon my classes the valor and efficiency and worth of Harriet Monroe and Alice Corbin Henderson.

But my present story is far from that story and almost all of it dates from before 1912, way back, when I drew "The Map of the Universe." Between October, 1912, and July, 1914, an astonishing number of events in the Poetry World can be chronicled. And to this general interest in poetry I attribute the fact that I, a speaker to whom not six persons were ever known to listen with patience, became a conventionalized "reciter" of my own verses almost instantly, and have since that time recited to about one million people.

I have put as much energy into reciting as a National League baseball player puts into grand-stand plays. It is not a bad fate, but this illustrated edition is a weapon in a strenuous warfare against that fate.

By the conservative estimate of all magazines that have a circulation of one million, I have a constituency of three million. I now address, as a body, my three million. May they enjoy it. The magazine of one million subscribers has a tragic limitation: which I am resolved to escape with the aid of this, my book of forty pictures,—forty mysterious ways for the grand-stand player to escape through the fence.

We will go back to the *Saturday Evening Post* of that much announced day when it reached one million subscribers and three million readers. Suppose on that occasion it had changed its entire formula, and taken on the aspects of *The Atlantic Monthly*. That million would, in two months have shrunk to one hundred thousand. Or suppose that it had taken on the aspects of a magazine I admire much more than either of these esteemed mediums. Suppose that it had suddenly become *Poetry, A Magazine of Verse,* published by Harriet Monroe, in Chicago?

Or suppose that the magazine *Poetry* with its present creditable circulation should suddenly publish forty poetical drawings, pen and ink experiments by a young artist. Probably many friends would be vexed. Yet life is an adventure with me, not a matter of professional standardization. I refuse to be put into uniform paraffin packages for the trade, like Uneeda Biscuit. Let me meet you, dear audience, as though you were an individual.

I want to come to your town. But I want to be judged, not by my speaking tours, but by what I did before October, 1912, even before *The Poetry Magazine* began, and before those tours began. So look at "The Village Improvement Parade" and "The Map of the Universe."

I have the notes on a long chant about my first long speaking tour. That tour was one of the great panoramas of my life. Never will I forget it. When I reached England and all the time that I was there reciting I was still remembering the thrill of California. When I was again in California, the

English memory came in splendor. Life has been like a movie turned too fast, but even then a thrilling movie. Now I find the whole touring scheme hardening around me like a steel Pullman car, in the minds of the friendly committees. Even my oldest friends seem to want two expeditions to be as much alike as two bound volumes of *The Saturday Evening Post*. Against this deadly fate I now wage my warfare with these forty pictures. Also let me insist that I am teaching the Monroe-Henderson anthology steadily.

So look at "The Village Improvement Parade" and "The Map of the Universe."

The Mystic Springfield in which I always live, wherever I may happen to be, is not a place of recitals, of Pullman Car Welcomes and Pullman Car Farewells. It is a place dating before 1912 where one walks alone, from childhood, among historic structures (see text and hieroglyphic, page 9) a place of clear visions. It is a place dominated in my mind by one harmonizer of all its history to the present hour, and a tiny group of devotees quite alien to her in their essential mood, but her practical allies. The friend was my English teacher in high school, Susan E. Wilcox. The group is a circle of the followers of Swedenborg.

Susan E. Wilcox is still the head of the very distinguished English Department of the Springfield High School. Half the poems in this book show her stern hand. Leaving out the members of my own family, she is, without doubt, both as a person and a teacher the noblest and most faithful friend of my life. She stood by me for years when I went through the usual Middle West crucifixion of the artist.

Early Hierloglyphics, like "The Shield of Lucifer" (page 110), and early songs like "Lucifer" (page 111), I submitted to her many times while she corrected everything. She worked on Johnny Appleseed with me the same way, much later. She will rise and testify that I am no improviser. By the time we were through with any one piece of writing

she had not only the verse by heart, she had the comma
by heart. My alleged theory of the jazzing of poetry,
which I have never endorsed or agreed to, amounts to just
this: I submitted the "Hieroglyphic," and then read and
re-read the poem to Susan Wilcox. Week after week for
six months I would read the verse till she was sure it was
clear, grammatical and reasonable. Some of the British
critics like neither my hieroglyphics, my spelling nor my
punctuation. I refer them to the wrath of Susan E. Wilcox.
She has a reply, if they care to write to the Springfield
High School.

The Swedenborgian circle we found for friends much
later, darkly suspected poetry and the reciting of poetry, as
a work of the evil powers. Those who look for scraps of
my alleged ragtime, vaudeville or jazz theory, in that
circle, are doomed again to disappointment. But those
Swedenborgians had ideas. Those critics who say that I
have no ideas are casting reflections not on me but those
Swedenborgians, for I listened to them with all my ears
for years. I loved them because they could always talk
me down. An egotist always likes an even stronger egotist
to make him imagine he is humble. What did we have in
common? We had in common what might even be called
a "Swedenborgian Springfield," the Springfield of the
"Map of the Universe"; a Springfield of Visions. But with
the visions I was given the benefit of their intense hereditary intellectual Swedenborgian discipline, which let no
man pass over hurriedly. It counts greatly in our villages.
So look at "The Village Improvement Parade" and "The
Map of the Universe."

The great and admirable Robert Frost said in *The New
York Times,* in reference to his new work in Amherst: *"Philosophy, that's another subject I am going to teach. Philosophy of what? Of life. Of people about you. What's my
philosophy? That's hard to say. I was brought up a*

*Swedenborgian. I am not a Swedenborgian now. But there's a good deal of it that's left with me. I am a mystic. I believe in symbols," etc.*

Springfield, without knowing it, was *"brought up a Swedenborgian,"* by this circle. Wherever I go I want to bring with me what might be called "The Swedenborgian Springfield." Johnny Appleseed, whom I recommend to all men who love visions, was a man of lonely walking, a literal Swedenborgian all his days, distributing tracts when occasionally he met a settler. For the most part he was consoled by his personal visions in the wilderness. I am for Johnny Appleseed's United States. Up to 1912, while I walked in Springfield for the most part silent as to literal vocalization, I tried to express this United States in cartoons. This Johnny Appleseed mood was our common ground.

The exquisite, sharp-edged Swedenborgian culture, though confined to an almost invisible sect, has brought some beautiful fruit that has been accepted the world over.

Howard Pyle was a literal Swedenborgian. His place as an old Master of American illustration is continually growing. William Dean Howells and Henry James and William James came of Swedenborgian stock. Their disposition to choose and fulfill a lifetime task with great severity to themselves and great kindness to their neighbors was typically Swedenborgian. The final act of the mind of Swedenborg was far from these three. They were unwilling to see their thoughts as splendid visions in the air. The most ordinary movie magnate goes further into this than Howells and Henry and William James. Swedenborg should be re-written in Hollywood. We want to know the meaning of all those hieroglyphics that they are thrusting upon us, for the present as unsolved, in many phases, as the hieroglyphic ruins of pre-historic Mexico and South America. The American mind has become an overgrown forest of unorganized pictures.

And this may be said to be true of the whole world, controlled in the end by the political cartoonists of *London Punch*, and the like. So look at "The Village Improvement Parade" and "The Map of the Universe."

The Christian Century for September 27, 1923, says: *The members of the New Church, Swedenborgians, are much encouraged by the publication recently of a book called "New Light Upon Indian Philosophy." In this book D. Goupal Chetty, late editor of "The New Reformer," takes the position that it is the writings of Swedenborg which will make the necessary connection between Hindu Philosophy and Christianity. Mr. Chetty is a Tamil, and there are twenty millions of his race. His book will be given wide circulation in the English-speaking world by the Swedenborgians of England and of America.*

Howard Pyle always saw his pictures in the air, first, before he drew them. I see myself as the draughtsman of my own ideas only, and of those of my oldest and most intimate friends of our Swedenborgian Springfield before 1912.

These ideas I have had so long, I necessarily see them as pictures in the air. No doubt if they were all worked out they would be as poor philosophy to a real philosopher as Griffith's "Intolerance." Still they are with me in fancy, perhaps five hundred hieroglyphics, big and little, all of them differing from one another and all of them differing from anything that I have ever been advertised in the newspapers as doing. After I have written songs for them, you may pronounce these songs as being akin to the song of John L. Sullivan, if this is the truth. But I want the songs to have an even chance to be in contrast to that song, and the picture to be in contrast to the best liked drawing in this collection. I want it to be liked because it is a surprise. I claim the privilege of this versatility.

Up to 1912 I had been first, last and always, a cartooning adventurer and a cartooning preacher.

I consider all my cartooning in some sense hieroglyphic in the old Egyptian way. The principal towns of Southern Illinois are Cairo, Karnak and Thebes, and the swamp-bordered river moves southward past Memphis, Tennessee, named for the town of King Menes, first King of Egypt. There is a parallel between the psychology and history of the Mississippi delta and the famous delta of the old Nile. Africans roll cotton bales to steamships on wharves of both rivers. They sing the same tunes, ten thousand years old. Once I sang the Congo. Long before that I sang the Nile. The forty pictures in this book, most of them dated before 1912, are in their own way, a part of the Egypt that is in me forever. And I beg all my readers to look into Swedenborg's theory of Egyptian Hieroglyphics. No one can read it without getting the notion that some fate is swinging us around to the moods of Egypt.

In anticipation of publishing this illustrated edition of my Collected Poems, I distributed in the summer of 1922 to many literary friends throughout the United States two grammars of Egyptian Hieroglyphics. One was Margaret A. Murray's delightful Elementary Grammar, published by Bernard Quaritch. The other was Gunther Roeder's Book, translated by Samuel F. B. Mercer, and published by the Yale University Press. Both grammars are simplified from Adolph Erman.

I thrust these books upon my friends as though they were candy. The while the Macmillan Company were reading the manuscript of the first edition of these "Collected Verses," and while my friends were carefully scrutinizing these grammars, and while I was way off in Saskatchewan, reciting for the British as well as I could, I read in the Saskatoon paper that Tut-Ankh-Amen's tomb had been opened by an Englishman and an American in friendly alliance. Such a roar went up to the sky that it swept from the hot Nile to the snow-buried plains of Canada.

Even the Egyptian Kings are on my side.

My friends opened their grammars again. It reminded me of the time in the "Adventures While Preaching the Gospel of Beauty," where the old "Duck-Pond-Diviner" told me I was a "Child of Destiny," and *also fond of sweets.* Part of my destiny is to issue "The Village Magazine" at intervals of years.

"The Village Magazine" is not a Monthly Magazine. It is a "destiny" magazine.

There is a new issue almost like the others for October, 1924.

I used "The Village Magazine" of 1910 and "The Village Magazine" of 1920, and all tracts allied to them in my Gospel of Beauty campaigns. These campaigns, begun in my days as a New York Art Student, became more intensive as I went back to my home town, expecting to settle and hide there forever.

I was suddenly hurled into a more conventional life almost against my will. In consequence of my having recited for a million people in their Sunday clothes, most of my friends have insisted on "jazzing" the motive of my life.

I have been looking out standardized windows of "The Flat-Wheeled Pullman Car." I have been living in standardized hotels, have been eating jazzed meals as impersonal as patent breakfast-food. It has been an amazing experience in "The Flat-Wheeled Pullman Car," "jazzed" and jerky.

But I suspected, when at the tender age of twelve, that the incessant orator blunts the edges of his brain. I have suspected it all along. I have tried to fight off all jazz. I have great sympathy with all those who share this same misgiving.

There is a secret to my travelling, oratorical life. So I begin to travel again with joy. The unstandardized thing is the overwhelming flame of youth that swept up and sweeps up from those thousands and hundreds of thousands of faces. It is a changing flame of far more subtle colors than the

xxv

critic knows, a flame that still possesses me from this ten years' memory and eleven years' memory and twelve years' memory, and still burns on through my heart and mind and body and bone and soul. The critic hears my voice. He does not look down into those faces, into an audience of one thousand different dazzling hieroglyphics of flame, differing from one another as one star differeth from another star in glory. My mystic Springfield is here, also, in its fashion.

I have travelled so long it seems to me I have seen all young America and young Canada face to face. And each face is as it were a new word from Egypt, written by Hathor, goddess of young love.

I see the "Springfield Hieroglyphic," something akin to "The Village Improvement Parade," with the "Amaranth" above it, and "The Map of the Universe."

All touring appeals to me as a splendid and unending drunkenness, in spite of the flat-wheeled cars. But touring is not the innermost serious plan of my heart unless you help me bring "The Mystic Springfield" with me. What I want and pray for is a Springfield torn down and rebuilt from the very foundations, according to visions that might appear to an Egyptian or Shaw's Joan of Arc, or any one else whose secret movie-soul was a part of the great spiritual movie.

I believe that civic ecstasy can be so splendid, so unutterably afire, continuing and increasing with such apocalyptic zeal, that the whole visible fabric of the world can be changed. I believe in a change in the actual fabric, not a vague new outline. Therefore I begin with the hieroglyphic, the minute single cell of our thought, the very definite alphabet with which we are to spell out the first sentence of our great new vision. And I say: change not the mass, but change the fabric of your own soul and your own visions, and you change all. See "The Soul of the Spider," and "The Soul of the Butterfly," page 366. This very precise new beginning of our life is something far more than the mere drunkenness of addressing enormous assemblies.

Every new high school auditorium is built to receive the whole school at once, generally two thousand students. It generally has a stage, almost as wide and high as the length of the auditorium the longest way. This is standardization with a vengeance. But there is an innocent and happy glory that goes with it. And there is a secret here, also, that remains unadvertised.

As he meets me in the office for the preliminary chat, nearly every principal says:

"We had eight hundred students in the old high school building. We built this new school and auditorium for fifteen hundred, and two thousand young men and women came the first day. Therefore they are sitting on the platform, stuffing the balcony, and in the aisles and standing up in the back, and crowding in there at the open doors, and some are out there in the yard trying to find a place to listen. We are now erecting a Junior High School building on the other side of town."

And so he continues in a matter of fact strain.

Yet I see the "Amaranth," the special "Springfield Hieroglyphic," in the air above him. This is the secret. It is a secret something akin to "The Village Improvement Parade."

Students who were leaving high school in 1912 and heard me then were university seniors in 1916 and heard me then, and are now the people sending for me as the heads of responsible faculty committees in universities. That is, I have seen these young Americans grow up, hundreds of them, all over the United States, unharnessed young Americans.

Those I spoke for, once, in one State, I meet again and then again in other audiences in other States. They are growing in gorgeousness and power. And they seem at first generalized types. But I see the special Springfield Heiroglyphic above their heads, and things like "The Soul of the Butterfly," and their own Hieroglyphics above their heads.

The fact that I am a part of this generation is a wonderful gift to me from the sky. The fact that I have had a voice physically loud enough to hold them, has spoiled their critical judgment, almost spoiled mine. Like the rest of the literati, they have at first a wholly jazz and oratorical notion of my ideas. But always a dozen of them speak to me about Springfield, in the handshaking afterward. As to the actual text of this volume, Percy Grainger has made the best appraisal of its intention (æsthetically). The composer of "The Irish Tone from County Derry," and "Country Gardens" and "Colonial Song," approaches the verse as musical and not jazz composition. Please send for him, and add to his appraisal, "The Map of the Universe," the forty hieroglyphics of this book, "The Soul of the Butterfly," and "The Village Improvement Parade." My business is not jazzing, but Springfield and hieroglyphic and vision-seeing adventure. I claim the privilege of this versatility. I claim the privilege of issuing tracts, drawings of censers, such as are here in this book.

Even my enemies in Springfield know I want that city rebuilt. First of all I want a cathedral there. To that extent Theodore Maynard is right in saying I am a *"Catholic with a few fads."* But I doubt if Theodore Maynard or G. K. Chesterton would consent to have the statue of Johnny Appleseed or Prince Siddartha put up in their Cathedral, or that they would endorse the other prophecies of the Springfield Cathedral in "The Golden Book."

He is a Great Hieroglyphic, Prince Siddartha, seen in profile against the clouds of the ages. My Springfield will not be complete without him. His first virtue was humility. I hope in a thousand years to approximate his first teachings on that virtue. But I can say at least this thing humbly: That he is to me the supreme personality of history. There

xxviii

is something of this conviction back of my song of "The Rose and the Lotus," and the design—page 211.

I have been accused of having many heroes. Certainly the hero of the climax of the "Litany of Heroes" is Socrates, immediately approached through Wilson. Wilson is used as a modern follower of Socrates.

But setting that poem aside, remembering private studies of a lifetime, never put into rhyme, the hero having for me the greatest personal fascination is Prince Siddartha. And anything in any orthodoxy or high school ideal that runs counter to that admiration must be sacrificed. And this is but a hint of my cathedral, and the "Springfield Hieroglyphics," in which it is drawn for me.

Moving on toward my Cathedral, though maybe ten thousand years off, I started the march of "The Village Improvement Parade." I drew that series of panels in 1910. The marchers follow one another in varied succession and rhythm, as one might conjugate the Egyptian verb: *"To strut, or march."*

One need not have the Hieroglyphic grammars that I have mentioned to go into the understanding of such drawings. One need not have a phonetic theory. One need not to have read Swedenborg.

Another series, that might be compared to the conjugation of the Egyptian verb, "To Illumine," is the set of moon designs. See pages 239, 240. The moon pictures have been scattered everywhere among my friends, done in many mediums. Practically all the moon-poems began with the simple picture of the moon, drawn with an ordinary high-school compass. But each one was separately developed by pen and ink or other medium to show a separate action of the moon. Some I did in Japanese embossed style, with cut-out papers of various hues and textures. I claim the privilege of this versatility. And the design called "The Moon Worms" (page 240), was issued in Springfield about

1913, printed on a three-foot panel of gold and white. Some citizens liked these as an awful warning, some did not.

Next, let us look at the drawings of nine Springfield buildings, with censers swinging over them. These varying censers, shown in the pictures as though lowered by the hands of the angels, might stand for the conjugation of the verb: *"To have vision,"* see pages 9, 10, 13, 53, 207, 306, 354, and the pages near them.

This set of drawings was first issued separately printed in gold, and these golden pamphlets I issued by the thousands in Springfield, Illinois, putting my last cent into them, as I did for every pamphlet, going broke over and over again for my pamphlets quite ostentatiously, greatly to the vexation of the wise. There were two seriously organized and promoted assemblies, nevertheless. One was given by the Avonian Club in the Library, and I addressed them on the meaning of these designs. Later, upon a Sunday evening, I was invited to preach my evangel in the largest church building: The First Methodist. The place was packed to the doors. A copy of the pamphlet was put into the hands of every person to look on, while I discussed the drawings, much as now, in your town, dear reader, this book will be open to those same drawings, and on the knees of those who welcome me, and want to know precisely my message. (Dear reader, either bring the book, or stay away!)

This Methodist evening was by the generous invitation of the pastor, A. C. Piersel, and I shall ever be grateful. He brought the book!

I have just read a brief biography in an Indianapolis paper which says: *"He has spent most of his life lecturing for the Anti-Saloon League."* I have spent most of my life doing most everything else.

Once I spent three months pushing a truck in the wholesale toy department of Marshall Fields, Chicago. Once I worked three months for a gas-tubing factory in New York City.

Once I spent two weeks digging for the Springfield Illinois Department of Public Property, where they were installing a new boiler at the Water Works. Once I spent three days south of Springfield cutting corn for a silo, with as rare a gang of dollar-a-day thugs as ever remained unhung. Once I was offered the job of assistant town sanitarian (as it were) for the town of Raton, New Mexico, seventy-five cents a day, but I did not take the job. Once I spent a day painting signs in Tampa, Florida. It is a mistake to make me out a steady, orthodox established official Anti-Saloon-League worker. My precise experience and views on that subject may be found in the Chapter on "The Substitute for the Saloon" in "The Art of the Moving Picture." There is a certain type of dulcet and affetuoso Bacchanalian who would make me out the one and only dry in the United States, mentioning it rather bitterly in passing. But that imputes to me entirely too much personal influence on the constitution. I doubt if there is a Y. M. C. A. Secretary, member of the Salvation Army or Anti-Saloon-League worker who has ever opened one of my books. And when my pamphlets began to fly in Springfield, certainly those institutions were cheerfully hostile. I was dropped instantly from the rolls of the Y. M. C. A. and the Anti-Saloon League. They would not allow me any of the privileges of that versatility for which I am even now battling. Nevertheless I issued without their consent or approval, temperance tracts, such as the one inserted (page 336). There is one consistent thread in my life. From first to last I have been an Art Student. I have spent the big part of my life in Art Galleries, Art Schools, and Art Libraries. From all the various adventures I returned to this study, and still return. No Y. M. C. A. man or Anti-Saloon-League worker likes an Art Student, even if he floods the town, gratis, with tracts like that on page 336.

The merry war with Springfield respectability, with the stereotyped United States in general, which any artist has to wage till death, is not a tragedy, but akin to one hundred Gilbert and Sullivan Operas, in long line, in continued performance, like Chinese plays that go on and on. Springfield is still a place of lifetime intimates who regret everything I have ever done, even the tract (page 336), and everything up to October, 1912. They are sure I should pretend to have been born 1912, and so ignore all my painful past. They are continually spatting me on the wrist, even yet, for things like the tract on page 336. They deceive the stranger by talking as though they had written my books. And all this without opening the books, they are so sure that they contain statements deadly obscure, highbrow as German Philosophy at its worst, or else plain *"Russian Bolshevism."* This is the exact reverse of the jazz slander. This type of old neighbor is one of the most valuable, infinitely better for my conceited soul than any advertiser with an ax to grind. Strangely enough, I see above his head "The Amaranth," the Springfield Hieroglyphic, and many solemn and splendid visions hover above the merry war.

I have definitely in mind a series of *"United States Follies"* in the mood of Percy Grainger's most light-hearted compositions, on the theme of the present essay, Gilbert and Sullivan affairs but with a Mohawk flavor, built on Middle West and Far West United States ideas, artistic, and anti-artistic. A friend of mine, of the old art student days on Fifty-seventh Street, New York City, is destined to do them if I do not. And these will contain the special Springfield Hieroglyphic in various outline, and fancies like "The Soul of the Butterfly," page 366, will hover above it all.

I am overwhelmed by people rising and testifying in New Towns that they are my intimate friends, just before I arrive. The papers are so full of jazz that my friends are forced in the end to believe, it comes in such a stream. I am now going to appoint official "old friends" familiar with drawings, hieroglyphics and tracts. Every fact should have their O. K. before it reaches the point of a jail offense. One of them is the aforementioned Susan E. Wilcox of Springfield, Illinois, who really knows what I am about and has known since I was a very small boy. Another is this friend from Springfield with whom I first went to New York, Willard Wall Wheeler. He is full of plays and light operas, and the like. Both of us were boys together and chums when we were eight years old in Springfield. Both of us took lessons in English in high school under Susan E. Wilcox. We are still waiting in vain hope to deserve her stern praise. But we are still loyal, and glad that there is one firm and accurate standard of excellence in the world. A third is John Price Jones, of New York City and the world.

Willard Wall Wheeler is now a most active citizen of Cleveland, Ohio. But once upon a time, namely about 1904, we laid siege to New York City as though we were one Macedonian Phalanx. He had graduated from Williams College. I had spent the same period of time in The Art Institute, Chicago. We undertook to push the Flatiron Building over with the help of John Price Jones. It still stands. But we were in the same boarding houses on Fifty-sixth and Fifty-seventh Streets. The same crowd of newspaper men, artists, singers, actors, musical students and young writers were around us. Bill was the local center. He dug them out from everywhere. The pageant of the *"younger generation"* poured before us and past us.

We are going to write a "United States Follies" with John Price Jones, about the people of this period. Many of our crowd were rallied round a restaurant we decorated "The Pig and the Goose" (see page 2). The two were cub reporters. I was a cub art student. Some of the cubs are tigers now; some of them fat bears. Many of the ideas Wheeler brought up from Williams College and I brought from the Art Institute were in the drawings and tracts I scattered in that region of New York. A member of the gang who has followed my work, every inch of it, till now, is George Mather Richards, still in New York. I accept his censorship absolutely.

It was with a head of steam still up after five years of grand free adventuring in New York with these that I went back to Springfield to continue my tracts and hieroglyphics.

In August, 1918, avowedly back in Springfield for good, renouncing "Babylon" forevermore, I began to issue certain "War Bulletins." They assembled all the heresies of the Columbus Circle region, the "Greenwich Village" of that time. According to my doctrine, which I had proclaimed in that "Greenwich Village," I had gone back to "Preach the Gospel of Beauty" in the admired home town. Akin to these "bulletins" was one of my first tracts, scattered in every yard in the town "The Building of Springfield" (page 74), and I brought out my bulletins till Christmas, then declared a "Christmas Truce." I did it by handing out to any one who would take it on the street "The Sangamon County Peace Advocate."

The opening poem was:

"In this the City of my Discontent,
Sometimes there comes a whisper from the grass:—
*Romance, romance,* is here. No Hindu town
Is quite so strange. No citadel of brass
By Sinbad found, held half such love and hate.
No picture palace in a picture-book,
Such webs of friendship, beauty, greed and fate.'"

The closing poem was: "The Springfield of the Far Future," page 347. (See also page 62.) I mailed "War Bulletins" and "Peace Advocate" back to Willard Wall Wheeler, George Mather Richards, Gertrude Lundborg Richards, Earl H. Brewster, Ascha Barlow Brewster, Marjorie Torre Hood (now Torre Bevans), Leighton Harring Smith, John Price Jones, and others. I was at first happy with cheers from New York. Springfield did not hear those cheers. It was at this point that I was dropped from such Y. M. C. A. work and Anti-Saloon-League work as I was doing in the Springfield region. I was as near to the hieroglyphic as I will ever get, but far from the Sea at Sunrise. The rigors of that loneliness I will never again achieve, unless I consent to go to jail with Debs. And I do not agree with Debs. But there is a certain final clarity for the elect in tracts written amid stern conditions. I expect to fish out those tracts from the bottom of the Sangamon, one at a time, and republish them. Verses that paraphrase them may be found, pages 335 through 369. And I refer the reader to "Adventures While Preaching the Gospel of Beauty," and such copies of "The Village Magazine" (privately printed) as are in the hands of the literati to indicate the mood of the tracts and see also the hieroglyphic and parable, page 205—"The Fairy from the Apple-Seed."

There is just one way to convince citizens of the United States that you are dead in earnest about an idea. It will do no good to be crucified for it, or burned at the stake for it. It will do no good to go to jail for it. But if you go broke for a hobby over and over again the genuine fructifying wrath and opposition is terrific. They will notice your idea at least. I flooded Springfield with free pamphlets incessantly. And so I began to relish home-town controversy on its absolute merits: being conceited beyond all mortal toleration, being also *a child of destiny and fond of sweets.*

Critics are still instructing me in elementary matters they would find summarized in the bulletins if they went on the hunt. I, too, have been instructive (sarcasm).

"War Bulletin Number Four," brought out that fall of 1909, had for a sub-title: "The Tramp's Excuse." For appalling sentiments in this book I was proscribed by the Country Club and glared at by the Chamber of Commerce. It contained the drawings or ideas, on pages 94, 334, 366, 358, 219, and similar designs.

And so, for years, no one would have anything to do with me in Springfield, but Willis Spaulding and the Swedenborgians; Frank Bode and the Liberal Democrats; George and Maydie Lee and their daughter Virginia and the Single Taxers; Mr. and Mrs. Duncan Macdonald and the Socialists; Rabbi Tedecshe and the Jews; Rachel Hiller and Susan Wilcox and the English teachers; and the Honorable James M. Graham and the Knights of Columbus.

I have never been in the least a literal Swedenborgian. But I back Willis Spaulding. All this time he was the Commissioner of Public Property, therefore the most powerful citizen in the City Hall. He was re-elected many times. He was continually trying to hunch the city nearer to Single Tax. The pleasant things said about him at The Country Club I will not here put down. I doubt if my tracts won a single vote for Willis. They won for me the opponents that fought him always in vain. They fought me to the point of getting the aforesaid "Peace Advocate" out of me and poems such as those on pages 62 and 347.

Stephen Graham is a lifetime friend of mine, but he has made one mistake. He says in one place that I am not for the Irish. I may have dropped a more impatient word in regard to the Irish than any Britisher is accustomed to drop. All of us are apt to show impatience with the theme at times. But, thinking it all over, I must say that I am for the Irish. I am for Padraic Colum *among* the Irish. And then I am for the *United States* Irish. Willis Spaulding could not carry a single Springfield election without them. Certainly I am for the *Springfield, Illinois,* Irish. I will never forget how Joseph Farris, a Single Taxer, as Irish as ever lived, stood by my "War Bulletins," in Springfield, when even some of the Swedenborgians were appalled. All things being equal, I get all my national and international views from Joseph Farris, out of pure gratitude. I like every political cartoon that he likes. His views, as man and politician, are close to the hieroglyphic, and close to the sea at sunrise. For years we were the two hottest readers in Springfield, of Reedy's St. Louis *Mirror*.

But to speak, even more seriously—the one ever-open church in the United States is built by the Irish. I am profoundly grateful for this Church. There it is waiting for me, the stranger, in Tucson or New Orleans or Bangor. I can step into that door from my hotel. There is instant peace and seclusion. There I can go back to my mysterious Springfield, even to my Swedenborgian Springfield, if you please. Other churches are marked most sentimentally *"Enter, rest and pray."* But generally the door is locked of a summer time. The only way to *"enter, rest and pray"* is to enter a church with the door open. And there I am a million miles from the Pullman car, the glittering hotel lobby, the loud lecture platform, the howling newsboys, the automobiles, the magazines. There Mary, Star of the Sea, always waits for the contrite. There too, I am close to the hieroglyphic, and close to the sea at sunrise.

Springfield surely will sometime have a great World University, and surely will take on the aspect after immemorial years of a great "University World's Fair." It will all go back to one cosy Swedenborgian cottage of that glowing and adventurous time that followed shortly after the period of the bulletins. The cottage that suddenly shone so brightly in our town was the home of George and Maydie Lee.

"Maydie" was only a pet name. Her solemn Swedenborgian name was Mary Thankful Spaulding Lee. Her consecrated heart was the mysterious heart of our mysterious Springfield. Twice my brother-in-law and my sister, Dr. and Mrs. Paul Wakefield, went to China and twice returned. Each time they joined the circle on their furlough. They found under that roof the seemingly contradictory ideas of the whole of active American citizenship, assembled in a tiny conclave. To this group the Wakefields brought news of Asia. They were a part of the circle 1908, and then again, on a second return, five years later.

The heroes of Maydie Lee's circle, among the living, were Joseph Fels, Herbert Quick, Woodrow Wilson, Robert La Follett, Brand Whitlock, Frederick C. Howe (then newly famous for his book of disguised Single Tax—The City, The Hope of Democracy), Newton D. Baker, Mayor of Cleveland, Mr. and Mrs. Raymond Robbins, and Jane Addams. Dr. Caroline Hedger was a close associate of Maydie Lee. Of our heroes was William Allen White, author of the series of bulletins entitled "The Old Order Changeth," which did more to make the fundamental thought of the Progressive Party, then forming, than any word or act of Theodore Roosevelt. White was the soul back of the Kansas chapters of "Adventures While Preaching the Gospel of Beauty."

The heroes of our circle, among the recently departed, were Tom Johnson, the great Single Tax Mayor of Cleveland, Golden Rule Jones, Mayor of Toledo, John P. Altgeld, Governor of Illinois, the most fearless user of the privilege of free speech since Jefferson. Among the great further back were Henry George, and, of course, Emmanuel Swedenborg.

These last two men seem to go together in the minds of many more Americans than our great universities realize. They furnish more austerity, fire, vision and relentless lifetime resolution to those who would make over our cities, than the heathen have ever dreamed. Thousands of folks of our purest, most valuable, oldest stock, go to the Swedenborgian church on Sunday and work steadily and silently for the Single Tax all week.

Catholic and Protestant, Jew and Greek were all brought to fine speaking terms by our great hostess. Her consecrated heart was indeed the very heart of Springfield. After his obvious victories, she kept her brother Willis Spaulding at the actual battle of bringing her ideals before the folks of the city, in some form that they could understand.

She it was who kept open house for the radical lobby that came down season after season to the State House, Agnes Nestor, Margaret Haley and the rest. She was the leading spirit of the local branch of the Woman's Trade Union League, and Mrs. Robbins' devoted lieutenant. Incidentally George and Maydie Lee gave one year of their lives to a state-wide campaign for "The Initiative and the Referendum," in which we all helped.

They circulated Progress and Poverty like a new Bible.

The spirit of this tide in American life is well set forth in Waldo R. Browne's "Altgeld of Illinois," published by B. W. Huebsh.

It was while all these activities were at their height that the *Mirror* brought out the "Spoon River Anthology." It was read instanter in Springfield. We followed its victories across the world as though they were our own. The father and mother of Edgar Lee Masters were old residents of Springfield. This of course greatly sharpened our interest.

Ours was what might be called "The Old Court-House America" (see hieroglyphic, inserted page 53), what might be called: "The Old Horse-and-Buggy America," the America that first put Woodrow Wilson into the Presidential chair. It was among this circle that I scattered my pen and ink drawings and cartoons and war bulletins with the most welcome. I fought my best to add to genuine Gospels of Democracy, my Gospel of Beauty, gathered in Life Classes and in Art Museums, and among Art Students, for many a day. And I had to fight every inch of the way with very stubborn, very earnest, very admirable minds. Wherever I go, as a lecturer and evangelist I find myself most wrongly interpreted, *and inconveniently fibbed about.* If you want to know the meaning of my life, my tracts and hieroglyphics from the beginning to the end, to the extent of three or five columns, interview my worst enemy in Springfield with whom I flooded these tracts, rather than my best friend discovered after October, 1912, from some other town.

The morning of June 1, 1912, when I started out on the "Adventures While Preaching," with a pack full of "Village Improvement Parade" posters, and "Rhymes to be Traded for Bread," George E. Lee was the man who walked out alone with me. He told me good-by and gave me his blessing. Ask those who hated and loved us just what we meant to the town. It was out of our warfare for Beauty and Democracy that most of the forty drawings in this book were born. It was out of the drawings and others like them, that the verses were finally born.

"The Map of the Universe," in the front of the book, was one feature of *War Bulletin Number Four,* a "bulletin" which was actually a booklet which I called, *The Tramp's Excuse.* If examined closely the map will be discovered to be Miltonic: —as orthodox as Milton, certainly. It was the basis of a book that I wrote about the Millennium in Springfield. I afterwards destroyed it without publication, it seemed to provoke such amazing wrath. I called it *Where is Aladdin's Lamp.* The book was later reborn as *The Golden Book.* Sometimes I think the Millennium will come in ten thousand years, sometimes in one hundred thousand years. I have never had the delusion it will come immediately. But it is worth working toward. There is no sense in assuming we are hell-bent. I feel also, that the world war will somehow be made up to us by the powers invisible, and that civilization is on the edge of a new flowering that is far indeed from the millennium, but is a flowering, nevertheless. My hope in this matter has been called credulity. Still, please look at "The Village Improvement Parade," and remember that Florence, Athens and Venice once flowered. They flowered quickly, in one generation. The very edges of the Universe are nearer together than were the outer walls of Florence in her splendor; such is wireless and such is commerce to-day. It is not absurd to suppose the world will suddenly take on glory, as one city, as one compact Springfield, as one heroic village. "Hieroglyphic Marchers Here We Bring." (See text and Hieroglyphics, page 204.) And this will not be the millennium. Falstaff will riot in the taverns, when the world becomes for the first moment of its conscious life, one little Springfield, Athens, Florence, Venice.

If my friends will again examine the "Map of the Universe," in front, along with the history of our Springfield circle, just outlined, they will have some of the material out of which *The Golden Book of Springfield* was written.

All my tracts have their bearing on *The Golden Book of Springfield*. They are, of course, out of print, or in the hands of Springfield people who hated or loved the circle that was around Maydie Lee's home. I have said in the preface: "Adventures While Singing These Songs," much about Lincoln (see text and hieroglyphic, page 10), much about the South, Kentucky, Campbellism, and my own peculiar experiences as a tiny child in the Lindsay family. All this is far indeed from the Swedenborgian refrain I have now been singing. Between the events of my first preface and this there is the period of fifteen or twenty years of experience completely skipped. But already that first preface is being hardened into a plaster cast for me. So I write a new one. May the kind reader make the most of it. I claim the privilege of this versatility. And if this is not enough, there are other gods between my tenth and my thirty-second year I can invoke to overthrow any tyranny of Campbellite or Swedenborgian.

I was once introduced to a Canadian audience as having come from "humble and poverty-stricken antecedents." Then I said:—

"I am not only sophisticated, but all my ancestors were sophisticated. My people were not only important but they were self-important. The family conceit is hereditary from

xli

a long way back. It is the hardest thing I have to over-come."

"The Rose and the Lotus" is associated in my mind with one of the thrilling memories of my life when I was enter-tained in Washington by the Honorable and Mrs. Carl Vrooman. Carl Vrooman was then Assistant Secretary of Agriculture. The song I sang that seemed to mean the most in Washington was that of "The Rose and the Lotus." Franklin K. Lane, the then Secretary of the Interior, did me the honor to print it and send it to both Houses of Congress and to all those interested in a special way in the opening of the Panama Canal and the opening of the Panama-Pacific exposition at San Francisco. It is the nearest that my life has ever come to politics.

I drew the present design of "The Rose and the Lotus" from a sketch made when the poem was written. This I circulated on my own in Springfield, Illinois. The tract was issued with great faith in the good-will of the whole wide world. This faith I still maintain. The masses of mankind are in good-will toward one another. Only the old and silly are venomous.

Obviously the drawing of "The Rose and the Lotus" has a hieroglyphic and not a jazz meaning. I offer it here again as a visible symbol of good-will between all the races of man-kind. It can be painted on the wall of every temple, shrine, tomb, state-house, court-house, and hut of the world, without destroying or interfering with any government, race integrity, religious prejudice or philosophic dogma of Buddha or Swedenborg or any saint between.

As to the Lotus:—

The lotus-eaters were the dreamers of classic allusion. They were those who had what might be called "The Asiatic Mind." The Egyptian used the lotus for revel, as we use the rose, and so it was used in India. Yet the lotus in great *solemnity* dominates Egyptian design. In India the

xlii

lotus symbolizes the highest philosophic attainment of self-conquest. All the seemingly contradictory things that mean Asia are poured into the lotus-cup. The Thibetan invocation to the prayer-wheel that a Thibetan missionary once taught me: *"Om mane, padme hum:* 'O the jewel in the lotus!' " is a phrase that in its very reiteration shows the potency of the flower in the Asiatic mind. We have seen jades and crystals from China carved in lotus patterns. We have seen beautiful pictures of the Kamakura Buddha sitting on the big lotus flower. The lotus means all the million contradictory things which stand for Asia from the beginning. All those that mourn, all those that rejoice, in the East, turn to the lotus.

In like manner, the rose means Europe and America from the beginning. Christ says: "I am the Rose of Sharon and the Lily of the Valley." Dante found that Paradise was one great rose. A medieval romance was "The Romance of the Rose." Then the "Wars of the Roses" were the tragedy and song of certain days in England. The most beautiful thing in the Gothic Cathedral is the rose window. Anywhere in the world the humblest Catholic home has a picture of Mary with a wreath of roses around her heart. And she is prayed to with the rosary. All those that mourn and all those that rejoice, in the West, turn to the rose.

So, long before the opening of the Panama Canal, as I walked alone in Springfield, I was thinking of those flowers and their separation from the beginning of time. My first song about them is "The Canticle of the Rose of Tennessee," written after my first begging trip. See the story, "Lady Iron Heels," in *A Handy Guide for Beggars.*

I kept thinking of those flowers, and their separation from the beginning of time. I thought of the rose as a vine climbing westward, Europe slowly moving away from Asia, apparently forever. Then I thought of "The Rose and the Lotus," meeting across the Pacific, and destined to face one another forevermore. Grainger says: "America, instead of being the most westerly interpretation of Europe, is the most easterly interpretation of Asia." Hal Bynner has returned from China, translating the Chinese classic poems. Eunice Tietjens has returned from China with her wonderful song of "The Most Sacred Mountain," and her "Profiles from China." Amy Lowell has translated much from the Chinese. The recent great Japanese earthquake proved every heart in the world could love and pity Japan. The whole world sent help.

On a recent Sunday I heard my sister, Mrs. Paul Wakefield, at the Euclid Avenue Christian Church, make a speech to the Sunday School children, in the capacity of a returned missionary. She championed, at least for free argument's sake, the Confucian order of society, with the scholar and the sage ranking the highest in the caste system, because they give the most to the world. And the soldier she described as ranking lowest, according to Confucius, because he only destroys. She said that which is a commonplace, anywhere but in Sunday School, that Confucius existed as a great sage and teacher many hundred years before Christ, that Confucius had a great deal to teach every Christian. I felt the chill going up and down the spines of some of the hundred per centers as she spoke. Nevertheless she continued to teach the children the Confucian proverb: "Under Heaven, all one family." She taught them to say it in Chinese. She showed them how shameful race prejudice is, in the eyes of a good Confucian. She showed that the best Chinese Christians understood Christ better than the average nominal Christian of the West, because of inherited Confucian training. She said that open-minded missionaries went to China as much to learn as to teach. Representing a medical mission, she could speak thus boldly. Also, I remember her sending me a picture of the Kamakura Buddha with words of great admiration as she was passing through Japan for the first time. And these are some of the things that I meant when

I drew the hieroglyphic of "The Rose and the Lotus." Others may be found in "The Jingo and the Minstrel," page 375.

I want the reader of this article to assume that I hope to be called to the platforms of art schools as much as any, or be backed by the art departments of the universities, the high schools and the local clubs. I hope we may offer programmes seldom discussed in the papers. We come, looking for those who desire the beautiful and holy city, and the visible arts in their most spiritual aspect. We want the art schools and the art teachers to make themselves the radiating centers of The United States Gospel of Beauty. Thus, my dear friends, will you permit me to keep close to the hieroglyphic I knew in Springfield before 1912, and close to the sea at sunrise as well, to keep all the elements of my mysterious Springfield around me, and make my "Map of the Universe" a Universal Universalist University indeed.

Mine has been a college and university circuit. There is only one art school to each hundred colleges. Yet those schools stand out to me as the most worth winning from the hieroglyphic standpoint. I hope all my friends will enter into conspiracy to win them on my behalf.

They will find in the opening pages of *The Art of The Motion Picture,* the account of an affair put on in Fullerton Hall, The Chicago Art Institute. They exhibited the film "The Wild Girl of the Sierras, as acted by Mae Marsh." I tried to point out the possible æsthetics of the future movie, as that glorious film moved along. It is my especial pride that I am the first person to have done such a thing in an Art School. These and similar questions I want to talk over with you in your town. I do not want to recite "The Congo." You can recite it yourself as well as I can. I do not want to recite "General Booth."

This essay has turned much on the date 1912. In June, 1912, I started West from Springfield, Illinois, with

*Rhymes to be Traded for Bread,* and copies of the panels *The Village Improvement Parade.* People talk about my distributing my rhymes. They do not remember that I distributed these pictures with an equal zeal.

I wrote letters back to Springfield, to my father, mother and sister, and to Susan E. Wilcox and others. These letters, covering the period up to October, 1912, are all assembled in the book *Adventures While Preaching the Gospel of Beauty.* That book can be read at one sitting, and I most earnestly urge that it is a summary of all I have to say in your town for audiences, especially the proclamations at the front and back. Please read this book because it was written. This is the book I myself buy in quantity and give away as a tract. It is not even a rhymer's book. It is an art-student's book, from first to last. I consider it the final test, the central point of my work. All these pictures are implied in it. Closely related to it are: *The Village Magazine, The Art of The Moving Picture* and *The Golden Book of Springfield.* None of these are books of the jazz idea. They are all of them the books of an Art Student. My life is not an attempt to recite, but an attempt to re-apply in various ways till I find the right way, the sharpest sentences of the proclamations in *Adventures While Preaching the Gospel of Beauty.* The pouring crowds since 1912, though many of them would have none of this, have not in the least altered this fundamental purpose. I can *easily renounce the crowds forever if they seem to imperil the ultimate purpose of my crusade.*

Let us return to *The Village Improvement Parade.* Note the circle of the sun, drawn with the same compass as the circle of the moon, in the moon-plates. Note how it is really the central decorative theme of "The Village Improvement Parade." This same circle, drawn with a compass, is the central design of the "Litany of Heroes," page 187, for which, once upon a time, I did twenty-six big panels in colors.

with a separate symbol for each hero. I used to put all twenty-six panels around the lecture hall, and expound the twenty-six designs around which the twenty-six verses were written. I am planning now to issue the panels in a large portfolio, eighteen by twenty-four inches. The point is that there, as here, the central symbol is the circle of the sun. And that is not a jazz device, but a sound principle of picture-writing. Turn to the article on Egypt in the *Encyclopaedia Britannica*, to the hieroglyphic page of that section. There, as here, you will find the central symbol is the circle of the sun.

And what are the signs we read against the sun, written as it were by our banners on the very face of the sky:

*"To begin, we must learn to smile.*

*Fair streets are better than silver, green parks are better than gold.*

*Bad public taste is mob-law, good public taste is democracy.*

*A crude administration is damned already.*

*Let the best moods of the people rule.*

*A bad designer is, to that extent, a bad citizen.*

*A hasty prosperity may be raw and absurd, a well-considered poverty may be exquisite.*

*Without an eager public, all teaching is vain.*

*Our best pictures should be good painting, our best monuments should be real sculpture, our best buildings should be real architecture.*

*Ugliness is a kind of misgovernment."*

Among other things of which I have been accused, by friends who should know better, is that I am a millennialist, that I think the millennium will arrive to-day.

I have recently spent one week with my Gulf Park class in *Modern American Poetry*, reading, straight through, the "Revelation of St. John the Divine," King James's version. We read it as a sort of test and measure of all poetry, ancient and modern. Men will differ forever on that book, but all will agree that it is full of splendor and hope, the very heart of the Christian future. Reading with these eager young Americans, it seemed to me that they were also a living Apocalypse, close to the sea at sunrise, close to the Ultimate Divine Hieroglyphic, the Alpha and the Omega, the soul of America. Yet the magnificence of which they are a prophecy, will have no sudden achievement. I see the glow of century after century in their eyes. *For youth does not prophesy to-morrow so much as the hundred thousand years after to-morrow upon this earth.* This America will take long to ripen. It will be longer to our goal than from Adam to Mary of Bethlehem. If we are millennialists, we must be patient millennialists. Yet let us begin to-day as though the Millennium were to-morrow, and start our "Village Improvement Parade" down Main Street, and turn the corner east toward the rising sun to a land of clear pictures and young hearts. Close, indeed, to the hieroglyphic, and close to the sea at sunrise, close to the Percy Grainger "Colonial Song."

My publishers have decided on "The Map of the Universe" as the frontispiece of this book. So I here insert, in the latest revision of this copy, poems relating to this map. Many of them are from my very oldest, privately printed pamphlets, "War Bulletins," and the like, others reprinted from the middle of this book to show the relation.

But first please re-read "Lucifer" and "The Tree of Laughing Bells," with the map before you.

## INVOCATION FOR "THE MAP OF THE UNIVERSE"

(Showing how none of the pictures are possible to draw and can only be indicated in diagrams and hieroglyphics)

Would we were blind with Milton, and we sang
With him of uttermost Heaven in a new song,
That men might see again the angel-throng,
And newborn hopes, true to this age, would rise,
Pictures to make men weep for paradise,
All glorious things beyond the defeated grave.
God smite us blind, and give us bolder wings;
God help us to be brave.


## TO EVE, MAN'S DREAM OF WIFEHOOD
## AS DESCRIBED BY MILTON

Darling of Milton—when that marble man
Saw you in shadow, coming from God's hand
Serene and young, did he not chant for you
Praises more quaint than he could understand?

"To justify the ways of God to man"—
So, self-deceived, his printed purpose runs.
His love for you is the true key to him,
And Uriel and Michael were your sons.

Your bosom nurtured his Urania.
Your meek voice, piercing through his midnight sleep
Shook him far more than silver chariot wheels
Or rattling shields, or trumpets of the deep.

Titan and lover, could he be content
With Eden's narrow setting for your spell?
You wound soft arms around his brows.  He smiled
And grimly for your home built Heaven and Hell.

That was his posy.  A strange gift, indeed.
We bring you what we can, not what is fit.
Eve, dream of wifehood!  Each man in his way
Serves you with chants according to his wit.


## JOHNNY APPLESEED'S WIFE OF THE MIND

Johnny Appleseed dreamed that because of his monastic
self-immolation in the depths of the frontier forest, he would
be rewarded in the next life with two very beautiful wives.

### I

Come let us pray to the Lord of the sky
        For revelry,
        Fair revelry,
For a marble porch on a threshold old
Where the swan-white flowers of fantasy
Poised in the twilight wondrously,
Come to the eyes like songs to the breast,
While we drink and we conquer gloriously
The fountain springs of Alchemy,
The watercups of the Sons of God
        In high Archangel Revelry.

Friendship is that heavenly drink,
Friendship builds those palaces;
What have the angels more than this—
Than friendship, in their chalices?
Oh God! For the crystal wine we call
Forever strong as the water-fall,
Forever cold as the snowbird's wing,
Forever dear as the desert spring,
Dearest above all;
In a porch called "Beauty," crumbling not,
In the heaven all men have forgot,
We will sing our praise in the heights of the sky
  With revelry, fair revelry.

## II

The slender maiden found me sleeping,
 Stirred my breast by her wings and her singing,
Lifted me to the place of feasting
 While the water-falls in the court were ringing.
There we ate of the crust of knowledge,
 There we drank of the water of kindness.
The cups were simple, formed of silver,
 Vermillion banners waved behind us.

Her eyes were round with noble wonder,
 Deep her songs from her sweet throat throbbing;
Wise her words and fine her laughter
 While the water-falls of the court were sobbing.

The lamps were low when we turned all sated
 To view the streets in their moss-hung glory:
The heaven jungles stretched before us,
 The nodding trees were weighed with story.

51

**I** scarce dare say what the dark groves told us,
  Their whisperings of grim, dim sadness,
Over rotted harps and rusted gold
  In the treasure-pits, and the bold lithe gladness

Of the moon-vines cold on the ivory chariots.
  Of the ivy-vines round the fallen fountains
Of the magic amaranthine flowers,
  Lighting the jungles and the mountains.

We were alone; that, that was Heaven,
  And when she left me, not forlorn,
But praising God, in my beggar's hut—
  I watched the coming of the morn.

## JOHNNY APPLESEED'S HYMN TO THE SUN

Christ the dew in the clod,
  Christ the sap of the trees,
Christ the light in the waterfall,
  Christ the soul of the sun,
Innermost blood of the sun,
  Grant I may touch the fringes
Of the outermost robe of the sun;
  Let me store your rays till my ribs
Carry the breath of lightning,
  Till my lips speak the fullness of thunder
To waken world-weary men:
  Till my whisper engenders lions
Out of the desert weeds.

Give me your eyes, O sun,
  To watch through the universe
Where other suns speed on,
  Brothers, children of God,
Making the great deeps fair.

Take me unto yourself.
  My flesh is a sacrifice,
If only my soul may go
  As a flame to the edge of the sky
Where the sin-born stars come forth
  From the black strong chaos-sea,
From the infinite widths of night.

Grant I may die in a star
  As the chosen of God all die
Rising again in the dreams
  Of sinning, star born men,
Destroying their sins forever.

Give me your hidden wings,
  That I may go to the heights
Of the gold-built cliffs of heaven,
  Where jungles in silence reign.
Where the streets, knee-deep in moss
  And the mansions heavy with trees
With Cedars of Lebanon
  With olive and orange and palm
Are silent but for the wind,
  Empty, mysterious.

Give me your strength, O sun!
  Give me your hidden wings,
Till I climb to the holiest place,
  That highest plain of all,

With its glassy shallow pools,
    That desert of level fear
Where three great thrones stand high
    Hewn from three ancient mountains,
Blind thrones of a fair lost land.
    You have left your thrones for the suns,
Great God, O Trinity,
    With all your marvelous hosts,
Cherubim, seraphim.
    You blaze in our eyes by day.
They gleam from the stars by night.

Give us your life, O sun!
    Body and blood of Christ,
Wafer of awful fire
    Give us the contrite heart,
Take out the death from us.

Either the dead are dead,
    Or to-day is eternity,
Your face is eternity,
    Your rays are our endless life.
You are girt with a golden girdle,
    You are with all your crucified
Angels and saints and men
    Who die under clouds in the stars:
You are bringing them back from the dead.
    They breathe on my face as I pray.

Give me your innermost life.
    Come quickly, Alpha, Omega,
Our God, the beginning and end!

## JOHNNY APPLESEED'S SHIP COMES IN

This is the night my ship comes in.
The wine comes pouring down.
Glory and pain! The Angel's blood
Anoints the teeming town.
And the mighty flagship sways and dips,
And I thank my God with fevered lips.
My prophet brings a thousand ships
And the dream of a thorny crown.
He will lead these empty ships like sheep,
He will sail the hills of air,
He will find bold sailors, young as I
Who will love the scars of care—
The care that comes with crimson hands,
From pouring of the wine;
The wine of angels crucified,
The wine of demons crucified,
Brothers of Christ, all crucified
In the stars, and made divine.

We will lead our fleets through newborn skies,
We will scour each rebel world—
Till every lonely deck shall see
Strange prophet-scrolls uncurled
Till every lonely mast shall see
Strange prophet flags unfurled—
Till cataracts from the cups of God
Upon the stars are whirled.

# JOHNNY APPLESEED SPEAKS OF THE APPLE-BLOSSOM AMARANTH THAT WILL COME TO THIS CITY

Now, in the night, all music haunts us here . . .
Is it for nothing heaven cracks and yawns
And the tremendous amaranth descends,
Loaded with glory of ten thousand dawns?

The amaranth means:—God would have us say:—
"Whether you will or no, O city young,
Heaven will bloom like one great flower for you:
Flash and loom greatly, all your streets among."

Friend, I will not stop hoping, though you mourn.
We see such flowers, and some of them shall come,
Though now our streets are jazzed, or sadly grey,
And though our boys are strident now, or dumb.

Friend, that flower-town, that wonder town shall come,
Naught can prevent it. Though it may not be
What we may plan, it comes, at last—we know
With streets like channels of an incense sea,—

With twilight mists from heaven's jungles deep,
Or where the butterfly's great soul
        Still floats asleep—
        Beneath great heaven's granite steep;—
It comes, at last we know,
With musical bells, from the great western tree,
From the far star, or golden maids that come
From Eve's great eastern palace of the sky
Where great golden wonders never die.

## JOHNNY APPLESEED'S WIFE FROM THE PALACE OF EVE

(See Harper's Monthly Magazine for November, 1871)

The crickets call through the long, long night
    And the clouds are grey and the wind goes down,
And I wonder and wait in the moonlight white
    For the maid from the Chaos Town. . . .

For the maid from the Palace of Eve to come,
    Soul of my body, blood of my arms,
By love made blind, by fear made dumb,
    A bride, with a bride's alarms:

A girl with the bridal glory red
    From her quivering face to her rosy feet,
With her heaven-made bridal vows all said,
    And mine on earth complete.

O Mother Eve in your deathless power,
    By Adam's throne in the crumbling years,
Send her one murmuring perfect hour
    Of fear and passionate tears!

Let her love be wild as a cataract,
    The storm you knew when the morning came;
Or ever you felt the drouth of noon
    Or the drouth of sin or the drouth of shame.

Make her of bread from out of your hand,
    Make her of honey from your board,
Make her kiss like the lightning brand
    That shall pierce my soul as a sword:

lvii

Her breath of songs from the east and west
    And every fragrant wind that blows;
Her splendid knees from the lily's breast
    Her tender feet from the lips of the rose.


Make her a sacrificial fire
    Where noble friendship shall be slain
On the spice-flamed wood of dread desire,
    Stronger in glory and joy and pain.


Make her blood of the grapes of delight,
    A cup of your shadowy garden-wine;
Her breasts of the asphodel so white,
    Her face of the amaranth divine!


\*    \*    \*    \*    \*    \*


The crickets call through the long, long night,
    And the clouds are grey and the wind goes down.
And I wonder and wait in the moonlight white
    For the maid from the Chaos Town:


From the Chaos Town in the furthest East
    Beyond the edge of the things that are,
Built from the broken rock and mist
    Of many a dead titanic star.


And the hours go on and on and on
    And my empty arms are iron and lead,
And the skies are blue, for the dawn has gone,
    And I wait by a weary bed.

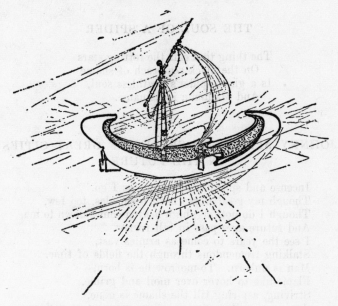

## THE EMPTY BOATS

Why do I see these empty boats, sailing on airy seas?
One haunted me the whole night long, swaying with every
     breeze,
Returning always near the eaves, or by the skylight glass:
There it will wait me many weeks, and then, at last, will
     pass.
Each soul is haunted by a ship in which that soul might
     ride
And climb the glorious mysteries of Heaven's silent tide
In voyages that change the very metes and bounds of Fate—
O empty boats, we all refuse, that by our windows wait!

## THE SOUL OF A SPIDER

The thing that eats the rotting stars
On the black sea-beach of shame
Is a giant spider's deathless soul,
And Mammon is its name.

## JOHNNY APPLESEED SPEAKS OF GREAT CITIES IN THE FUTURE

Incense and splendor haunt me as I go.
Though my good works have been, alas, too few,
Though I do nothing, high heaven comes down to me,
And future ages pass in tall review.
I see the years to come as armies vast,
Stalking tremendous through the fields of time.
Man is unborn.  To-morrow he is born,
Flame-like to hover over moil and grime,
Striving, aspiring till the shame is gone,
Sowing a million flowers where now we mourn—
Laying new, precious pavements with a song,
Founding new shrines the good streets to adorn.
I have seen lovers by those new-built walls
Clothed like the dawn in orange, gold and red.
Eyes flashing forth the glory-light of love
Under the wreath that crowned each royal head.
Life was made greater by their sweetheart prayers.
Passion was turned to civic strength that day—
Piling the marbles, making fairer domes
With zeal that else had burned bright youth away:
I have seen priestesses of life go by
Gliding in samite through the incense-sea—

## JOHNNY APPLESEED IN THE JUNGLES OF HEAVEN

Innocent children marching with them there,
Singing in flowered robes, "The earth is free":
While on the fair, deep-carved unfinished towers
Sentinels watched in armor, night and day—
Guarding the brazier fires of hope and dream—
Wild was their peace, and dawn bright their array!
And scattering dreams, and glory,
Prophets' boats sailed in from far away,
And angels' boats sailed in
From chaos-seas and many a stormy bay.

## HOW JOHNNY APPLESEED WALKED ALONE IN THE JUNGLES OF HEAVEN

Oh, once I walked in Heaven, all alone
Upon the sacred cliffs above the sky.
God and the angels and the gleaming saints
Had journeyed out into the stars to die.

They had gone forth to win far citizens,
Bought at great price, bring happiness for all:
By such a harvest make a holier town
And put new life within old Zion's wall.

Each chose a far-off planet for his home,
Speaking of love and mercy, truth and right,
Envied and cursed, thorn-crowned and scourged in time,
Each tested death on his appointed night.

Then, Resurrection Day from sphere to sphere
Sped on, with all the POWERS arisen again,
While with them came in clouds recruited hosts
Of sun-born strangers and of earth-born men.

lxi

And on that day gray prophet saints went down
And poured atoning blood upon the deep,
Till every warrior of old Hell flew free
And all the torture fires were laid asleep.

And Hell's lost company I saw return
Clear-eyed, with plumes of white, the demons bold
Climbed with the angels now on Jacob's stair,
And built a better Zion than the old.

.    .    .    .    .    .    .    .

And yet I walked alone on azure cliffs
A lifetime long, and loved each untrimmed vine:
The rotted harps, the swords of rusted gold,
The jungles of all Heaven then were mine.

Oh mesas and throne-mountains that I found!
Oh strange and shaking thoughts that touched me there,
Ere I beheld the bright returning wings
That came to spoil my secret, silent lair!

## PARVENU

Where does Cinderella sleep?
By Heaven's jungle-river,
A secret place her burning Prince
Decks, while his heart-strings quiver.

Homesick for our cinder world,
Her low-born shoulders shiver;
She longs for sleep in cinders curled—
We, for the jungle-river.

# COLLECTED POEMS

# COLLECTED POEMS

## ADVENTURES WHILE SINGING THESE SONGS

### AN AUTOBIOGRAPHICAL FOREWORD

I have had many adventures while singing these songs. Now I have had the adventure of collecting them, and deciding for the first time the natural sequence of them all.

Section One of the collection, called *Nightingales,* and Section Two, *Orations, College War-Cries and Olympic Games,* are obviously in contrast, as songs differ from orations, and I have put the songs first, because I somewhat prefer them. In these two sections, as in the whole book, many sentences may be found which run parallel to the opening chapter of *The Art of the Moving Picture* (1922). That book, as this one, champions my favorite notions of Painting, Sculpture, Architecture and Hieroglyphics. I have been an art student all my life, in the strictest sense of the word. I have been so exclusively an art student, I am still surprised to be called a writer.

Section Three, *Litany of the Heroes,* is an "Outline of History," written in 1906-7-8, still in process of development. The litany was projected with the active aid and choice of heroes, and other accompanying discussions by a

1

group of fellow-students of art. We decorated a restaurant together, and the restaurant used this song for a souvenir. We gloried in that place. It was there we held some of our midnight arguments. We were grander than Greenwich Village, long before there ever was such a thing on the art map. We were Paul Burlin, George Mather Richards, Pierre Laird, Earl H. Brewster, Leighton Haring Smith, and some brilliant girls, among whom were Margery Torrey Hood, now Torrey Bevans, and Achsa Barlow, now Mrs. Earl H. Brewster. The restaurant was called *The Pig and the Goose,* and has since disappeared. Brewster is painting the lives of St. Francis and of Buddha, in Sicily and Ceylon, and winning his due meed of laurels and friends. Those two heroes are in the song. The rest of our group are following our various gods over the world, and I have added a few new heroes and villains since we scattered. I hope some day to write the delectable story of our Pig and Goose Restaurant, which was half-way between history and tradition, being on Fifty-ninth Street, between Columbus Circle and the beautiful Paulist Fathers' Church.

Section Seven, *Runes of the Road,* runs parallel with the prose work, *Adventures While Preaching the Gospel of Beauty.* This might also be said of Sections Four, Five and Six. And the last two sections of the book run parallel to *The Golden Book of Springfield.*

In the Table of Contents I have made a running commentary that the unity of thought, such as it is, may now have a better chance.

I have just completed two national reciting tours, and am this month starting on another, covering again every state in the Union. If to my fellow-art-students and fellow-larks, with whom I have spent much time for many genial years, there seems an over emphasis on some points in the present method of editing, please let them remember that this whole book is a weapon in a strenuous battlefield; that practically

2

every new copy will be first opened on the lap of some person in a new audience of mine, trying to follow me as I recite, as one follows the translation of the opera libretto. Let them remember that these new friends are stuffed with hasty newspaper accounts of what it is all about. Night after night I step forth, a gently but altogether misrepresented stranger, and therefore separated from new audiences that I love at sight, and dearly desire to win, for a simple lifetime friendship.

My favorite long poem in this collection is "The Chinese Nightingale," and therefore the first section is named for it. My favorite short poem is, "My Fathers Came from Kentucky." This answers the question I am oftenest asked in new towns.

If there is one fact in regard to my verses of which I am proud, it is that they have been danced. "The Chinese Nightingale" has been used for several seasons in a special production evolved by the students of English at the University of Chicago. When she was twelve years of age, I petitioned Miss Ruth Lovett to undertake the matter. She was even then a wonderful dancer, severely trained, no mere improviser pinned up in a sheet. It was not long till I had heard that that infant Pavlowa had grown up, and had danced the poem in the spacious Mandel Hall, with all the University of Chicago in her train. This production has been reproduced and imitated in other parts of the country.

The singing and dancing of poetry is based on the twenty-six letters of the United States and British alphabet, and on the way they are pronounced in the dictionary and in clear conversation. Poems to be danced are to be made musical in the same sense that classic dramas are to be made musical by good actors. The exact pronunciation of the letters of the alphabet should prevail over the tune. It always disturbs me when people write asking for permission to set my verses to music. It shows such a misapprehension of the

3

point of view from which they were written. It is like asking permission to rewrite the poems entirely, while pretending they remain the same. Sheet music, piano music, orchestras and the like should not be in the same room with verses, as a general rule. No musical notation ever invented can express the same musical scheme as the twenty-six letters of the alphabet. Stringed instruments destroy the value of vowels. Music might be played between lines or stanzas.

But back to the University of Chicago version of "The Chinese Nightingale." Having had faithful friends in that University for years it was easy, even before the "Nightingale" event, to try an experiment there on a large scale. The first "Poem Games" were given with the aid of Miss Eleanor Dougherty, a graduate of the University of Chicago, who had there an enviable record in the acting of the Elizabethan drama. She also was a dancer, trained in severe schools, and equally a careful technician with her brother, Paul Dougherty, the marine painter, and Walter Hampden, the Shakespearian actor.

The Eleanor Dougherty "Poem Games" were first put on, on a large scale in Mandel Hall, at the University, in the autumn of 1916. This work was accomplished in many of its stages with the moral support of active promoters of the *Poetry Magazine* in Chicago: Mrs. William Vaughn Moody, Miss Harriet Monroe, Carl Sandburg, and others. Llewellyn Jones of the Chicago *Evening Post* Literary Review called the affair a rhythmic picnic. Maurice Browne backed us at the Chicago Little Theatre, and gave suggestions.

And with the whole Chicago Poetry group I had argued pro and con for several seasons the question of dancing poetry.

The substance of the Mandel Hall event was this: I chanted the poems, by the side of the stage, and Miss Dougherty occupied the entire stage for the evening, dancing to the syllables of the verses. She used her own interpretations of "The

4

King of Yellow Butterflies," "The Potatoes' Dance," "Aladdin and the Jinn," "The Rose and the Lotus," "King Solomon and the Queen of Sheba," and others. The stage directions of King Solomon are hers. Miss Lovett and her group, having witnessed Miss Dougherty's dancing in public and in private many times, evolved the present University of Chicago production of "The Chinese Nightingale."

Every English Department that I visit insists that I discuss the matter of rhythm. I have chosen my old "Song of Lucifer" as the key to such rhythm as I understand. I wrote this chant at Hiram College in 1899 when I was re-reading John Milton. I presume I read "The Last Song of Lucifer" to fifty fellow-students throughout that year, correcting immediately by their suggestions, making it all casual and conversational. It was one of the Hiram courtesies to read orations to one another, and take criticism endlessly, much as in art school we criticise each other's drawings systematically and with interest. The Hiram custom goes back all the way to the famous orator and statesman, James A. Garfield, who was a student of Hiram, and President thereof, and creator of its spirit. The Garfield influence so prevailing, the college undertook to make every student a trained public citizen, capable of holding for the length of an oration the student and village and faculty assembly, four hundred strong. We had great speaking field days with all the victors heroes. There was as keen oratorical competition as there is athletic competition in less classical schools. Yet Hiram had the astringent New England mind, with the astringent, non-rhetorical standards of speaking. I submit the poem as one which has suffered if not survived this test, and being as full of the rigid Hiram rhythms as I and my fellow-students knew how to fill it and also as containing all the tunes and rhyme-schemes which are supposed to have first appeared in later work.

I have paid too great a penalty for having written a few

rhymed orations. All I write is assumed to be loose oratory, or even jazz, though I have never used the word "jazz" except in irony. I knew and loved in infancy the lines of Keats:

"Heard melodies are sweet but those unheard
Are sweeter; therefore, ye soft pipes, play on."

I, who have spent scraps of many winters lecturing on the Doric and Ionic elements in the evolution of the Parthenon, and the austere prehistoric gold ornaments and cups of Greece, I, who have drawn endlessly and with great admiration the casts of the Elgin Marbles am assumed to hate the classics and champion their destruction. I, who have spent delightful years alone in the corridors of cool museums, am assumed to love noise and hate quiet. I read it in every newspaper in every town to which I go.

"How then? How about the Kallyope Yell?" asks the skeptic. We will now discuss the Kallyope Yell.

In my speaking tours I appear almost altogether before high-school, university or college assemblies, and I adore them. They are The United States in its gorgeous youth, and I love them like my own soul. I love their customs. They generally welcome me with the high-school, university or college "yell" and I generally reply with the Kallyope Yell. The literati of Great Britain do not seem to have realized it, but yell-writing is as steady an occupation of bright youths here, as the writing of sonnets was in England in the Elizabethan age. I take it that "sonnet" is Sanskrit for "yell," and "yell" will some day be Sanskrit for "sonnet." It can be music, just as is the music of bagpipes or flutes, or the Shouts of the Valkyries in Wagner, and is in fact the beginning of a Natural United States Opera, and United States Russian Dancing. Many of the yells are already danced, especially after victory.

But let it be noted that the *Kallyope Yell* is marked to be given in the manner of the University of Kansas or Jay Hawk

6

Yell. Let all students of the University of Kansas teach the tune of the Jay Hawk Yell to the world, especially to those inclined to true United States poetry. That yell, as all who have heard it know, contains no strain, jazz, spasm or vulgarity. It is actually whispered, slowly and beautifully, by about four thousand students, in spiritual unison, all soul-children of William Allen White of Emporia. It sounds like a glorified editorial from the Emporia *Gazette*. The least whisper of that village paper may creep over America like a wind or leap like wireless.

All my verses marked to be read aloud, should be whispered, however contradictory that may seem. All poetry is first and last for the inner ear, and its final pleasures are for the soul, whispering in solitude. Even the University of Kansas war cries have not served their full use till the graduate takes his walk alone through the wheat, whispering to himself its secret battle-cry, in meditative warfare arming himself for the soul's long solitary Pilgrim's Progress to the sun.

As the best comment on Section Four, *Verses of an Especially Inscriptional Character, Being Songs of My Art-Student Days,* let me say that, of course, my early drawings are of no interest except as a matter of record and a statement of method. Any one interested in full sets can get them secondhand, from Coe's Book Store, Springfield, Illinois, or Barker's Art Store, by writing a letter. Each of my acquaintances in Springfield has one or three copies of my portfolio humorously named *The Village Magazine.* There was an issue of 1910 and an issue of 1920, it being a decade magazine, instead of a monthly magazine. There will probably be a 1930 issue. The 1920 and 1910 issues were generously reviewed by the late Edward J. Wheeler, creator and long president of the Poetry Society of America. It is one of the many debts I owe that generous spirit that he took more interest in this portfolio than it deserved. I dedicated the second issue to him. *The*

7

*Village Magazine* is expounded by him in *Current Litera-ture,* March, 1911, and in *Current Opinion,* September, 1920. Those reviews are preliminary to what I would now more emphatically point out, the difference between poems to be danced and chanted, and poems written for pictures. Poems written for pictures are to be judged by a Philosophy of Hieroglyphics. If the friends of this book care to go further into my notions here, I invite them to glance through the Egyptian chapters in *The Art of the Moving Picture.* Poems to be danced and chanted are to be judged by stand-ards of oratory and music, and come in through the imagina-tion, of the inner ear, rather than the imagination of the inner eye.

I have had many adventures while singing these songs One type has been straightening out extraordinary biog raphies, such as the statement that I have spent all my life as a box-car tramp. An interesting life, but alas, not mine.

I was stuffed with family history in my helpless infancy The last of my tribe to reach this land arrived in Balti-more in 1800. An aunt of mine once told me she suspected that there was one Red Indian among the ancestors, and if that is true, there were millions of them, of course, if one goes far enough back. I take an increasing interest in my aunt's suspicion.

I was born in Springfield, Illinois, in the house where I now live. Everything begins and ends there for me. Ours happens to be an old house. When it was new, long before my people bought it, it was owned by Mr. and Mrs. C. M. Smith, early builders of Springfield. Mrs. Smith was a sister of Mrs. Abraham Lincoln. As I knew from my earliest days, our front parlor was a place of distinction. Parties had been given to Abraham Lincoln there by his sister-in-law, especially one grand party, before he started for Washington.

My uncle, Johnson Lindsay, lived next to the Lincoln home, four blocks away from our house. His daughter,

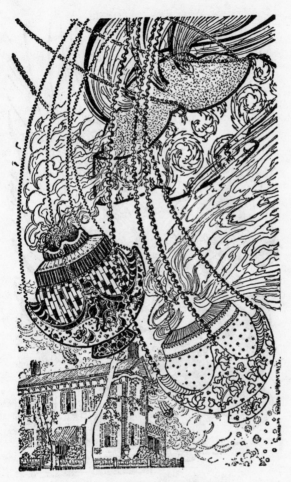

THE LINCOLN RESIDENCE
SPRINGFIELD, ILLINOIS

**THE LINCOLN TOMB**
SPRINGFIELD, ILLINOIS

Ruby Vachel, was my favorite playmate. We made a Christmas tree of the lilac bush in the shadow of that home, and we kept it up all the year round. At that time the well-known collector, Mr. Oldroyd, was the custodian of the "Lincoln House," and he was on good terms with all the children. I used to play through the rooms of the "Home" with Ruby Vachel, while the G. A. R. veterans who were entertaining out-of-town visitors from all over the world, conducted them from picture to picture. The walls were covered with the Oldroyd collection of Civil War cartoons, since removed to Washington, D. C. These cartoons were from Northern and Southern papers, immediately preceding the Civil War, and from London *Punch* and the like. Those who hate the George Gray Barnard statue of Abraham Lincoln seem to think their hero has always been a steel engraving of a man in a Prince Albert coat and decorously trimmed whiskers. They have seen this so often on the back of the dollar bill that they believe it. But Ruby and I knew better than that about Lincoln. He was a profound volcano, producing, incidentally, ferocious debate. We saw the cartoons of his enemies, showing the alleged rank, slack, ungrammatical, sweating, thieving person. We saw the cartoons of his friends which expressed every kind of devotion to the rail-splitter and lawyer from the vast prairie circuit. But there was no Prince Albert dollar-bill hero dominating the devotion of his friends. Meanwhile Ruby at her school and I at mine were taught "The Battle Hymn of the Republic," and "Marching Through Georgia," and "John Brown's Body" and "Shouting the Battle-Cry of Freedom." We loved these songs, and marched to them in our games.

And the Grand Army of the Republic, the American Legion of that time, was marching through the streets to these songs, on all occasions, carrying the elections for the Republican Party under John A. Logan, and investing the State House of our little capital like a fortification. Visitors to the city were taken to the State House Memorial Room, dripping with Northern trophies, captured "rebel" battle flags, and the like.

And the same visitors who were taken to the Lincoln residence, and the State House, were taken to the Lincoln Tomb. The Lincoln Tomb is a little north of the town, at Oak Ridge, where all the Springfield dead are laid away. The Lincoln Tomb is cold and strange as the legendary tomb of Osiris at Abydos must have been. And there is an obelisk over it, to give us Egyptian thoughts.

Ruby and I, though personal acquaintances of the Oldroyds, remained Southerners. The inexplicable Mason and Dixon line, deep-dyed and awful, ran straight through our hearts. We were made conscious of this by all our Lindsay kin. They were Breckenridge Democrats, remaining for the most part in Kentucky, but they came visiting us in our Ishmaelite loneliness in this flaming and arrogant G. A. R. state capital. Ruby and I told fairy stories, most of the time. We made them up, Ruby one sentence, then I one sentence, till Aunt Emma made us quit. But when we were not telling fairy stories we were having Democratic parades among ourselves, since the G. A. R. seemed to monopolize the streets most of the time. Our fathers helped manfully in the event when Grover Cleveland was first elected. My father went to the nominating convention, and on the night of the parade ratifying the election the streets were really ours for the first time. Our papas rode in that torchlight parade that was millions of miles long. Our papas had on big sashes, and the Democratic hats of that time, and their horses cavorted splendidly. Next day Ruby and I were still called rebels by the other children in the school yard. Springfield is still a Republican state capital, and I am still a kind of intrusive Kentuckian, though it was long before I saw Kentucky.

At home my mother's favorite tale was how one of her

10

pioneer grandfathers in Kentucky taught Daniel Boone's children to read. She was full of such stories as are found in the autobiography of Peter Cartwright, but she told them with the literary accent of her idol, Jane Austen. But if you think we followers of Alexander Campbell and the Methodists were the same, read Peter Cartwright and get yourself enlightened. Our precise, pedantic, frigidly logical Campbellite scholars were the dearest foes of the wild Methodists. The "Campbellites" were the enemies of all the religious ecstatics of their time, and I still resent being called a Methodist. I remember my mother's frequent report of the legends of the "Cane Ridge Meeting." Imagine them told by a disciple of the much-mentioned Jane Austen, and then read Peter Cartwright's report. There was always a cold second thought, a double consciousness, among the "Campbellite" theologians. They breathed fire, but they thought in granite. Scotch heads, Red Indian and Kentucky blood.

In infancy I never heard of New England. I heard of Europe every day. History, tragic and awful, was a straight path in war and cartoon and politics and pioneering and preaching, and fighting the Methodists in debate, and University building and all similar activities along the Daniel Boone trail, from a Scotland we left millions of years ago. One of the multitude of books brought from Kentucky was the little blue volume of the Poems of Edgar Allan Poe. Another of my personal treasures was a gift from my father of Rawlinson's *History of Egypt,* two thick volumes, of which I knew every picture by heart, and the substance of every line, when I was very young indeed. I was even then moved to awe and curiosity by the strangely cartooned face of Amenophis Fourth, that archeology has of late so glorified and refined. He has been made a hero of antiquity like King Asoka. It is a matter of outrageous pride with me that I knew him, even in his cruder

11

guise, when I was very young. Another heavy treasure was a battered *Chambers' Encyclopædia of English Literature* that did not mention any Americans, and stopped about 1830. From it I knew Chatterton and Shelley and Byron and Coleridge and Dryden as very special discoveries, like the Kings of Egypt.

Poe was always a kind of Egyptian to me. In the gorgeous bridal chamber of Ligeia there is in each corner a great coffin, "From the Tombs of the Kings Over Against Luxor." There was not even a picture of Poe in the histories of American Literature taught in the High-School when I entered it. There was nothing to be found but the full-page portraits of a famous mutual-admiration society. I knew exactly Poe's opinion of these whiskered worthies. I had read his complete works, criticism and all, through and through, before I was fourteen. I could use his whip. I could quote his critical headlines, that brought blood. I was a kind of literary outcast, because I championed Poe and his view. I knew also George E. Woodberry's *Life of Poe.* In my egotism I thought that I and George E. Woodberry were the only people north of Kentucky venturesome enough to estimate Poe as a sage, and a high priest of every form of beauty, and not a jingle man. One of my great days was when the *Century Magazine* published a picture of the Zolnay bust which is at the University of Virginia.

But back to a far more remote infancy: My mother destined me, from the beginning, to be an artist. This seemed reasonable, for those were days of splendor. For instance, my mother staged two miracle plays, which were apocalyptic in color. These she had written and staged in a Kentucky college where she had taught painting and English literature.

These plays were written in a similar style to the *Litany of the Heroes,* and I suppose that is where I found the idea. Women's clubs write me a letter a day, asking me just where I get my ideas, and insist on something confidential, not

12

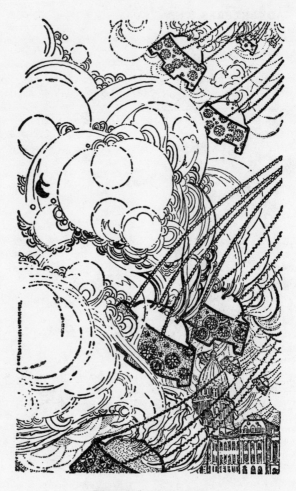

**THE STATE HOUSE**
SPRINGFIELD, ILLINOIS

imparted to the vulgar throng. Now there is something confidential.

One of my mother's plays was "Olympus," with the well-known characters, from Mercury to Father Time. My uncle, Johnson Lindsay, was Neptune, since he had a wonderful, long, beautiful red beard, and was exceedingly tall and handsome besides; a Neptune of Neptunes, when draped in seaweed. The Sunday School superintendent impersonated Bacchus. How they let him get into the pulpit with all those grapes on him I do not know. But he laughed hard, and Peter Paul Rubens would have been proud of him. I was too young to know what the church elders said about him. My mother was a riot in those days. How she did it in the midst of that rigor I do not know. Possibly she persuaded the elders it was like a Christmas or Easter Entertainment, which had by that time been accepted as primitive, Biblical and orthodox, and in no way violating the conditions of Saint Peter's platform on the day of Pentecost.

I know my mother called her show "Colloquy." It takes an epic poetess to call a heathen show a "colloquy" and have the associated elders and deacons openly approve. But my mother was already flushed with victory. She had recently read a famous paper on the great Italian Madonnas. This had been before the Illinois Art Association assembled in annual conclave in the State House I have mentioned. She was flaming with many such great days in her youth, including many oratorical triumphs, which were, in their fashion, spoken epics, in frank imitation of her forensic and senatorial Kentucky and Virginia ancestors. It now becomes plain that I was pumped as full of ambition by this aggressive lady as my silly little hide could hold. But back to that colloquy. My mother was, in a way, like Woodrow Wilson, and trained me early to respect such a type of mind. Anything of which Wilson is accused, is to me a point for admiration rather than reviling. My mother wrote all the speeches

13

for all the gods. She did it deftly enough, I have no doubt.
Impersonating deity, or writing shrewd speeches for various
divinities comes naturally with a certain ecclesiastical strain.
My Sunday School teacher was chosen by my mother to be
Venus in this colloquy. Venus was as voluminously robed
and as magnificently crowned as is the Statue of Liberty in
New York Harbor, and in my memory, would resemble that
figure, if the bronze of the New York idol could be changed
to perfect ivory.

I was six or seven years old at this particular time, and
I was Cupid. To silence the thunders of my Grandfather
Nicholas Lindsay, who was blind, and hated effeminacy in
his namesake, and reviled my long curls every time he put
his hand on my head, my mother had recently cut off those
curls and cried all over me. But now she let my hair grow
again. She put it up in papers for all one night, and when
she took out the papers, I did not know myself. She took off
most of my clothes. She put a pink slip on me, and sewed
dove's wings to the back of it. I was given silver pasteboard
arrows, and a silver pasteboard bow, and a silver quiver on
my shoulder, under the wings. I climbed into that pulpit
hand in hand with the beautiful Venus, my Sunday School
teacher. She had discussed with me, heretofore, the story of
the suffering saints of the Old Testament and what they
endured in Egypt from my friend Pharaoh. She had spoken
of the virtuous adventures of Joseph, and of Moses, and
such-like matters. But now, in silence through most of the
"Colloquy," she let her beauty speak for her. And when,
at last, she addressed implacably the awestruck throng, it
must have been something like a verse from the "Song of
Songs" in which the Church, the Bride, speaks devoutly of
the Bridegroom.

I said nothing, but held tight to one hand of Venus. In
her other hand she carried a beautiful golden apple.

At this time my mother staged another colloquy, in which

14

nations, rather than gods, were impersonated by the best and handsomest actors in Springfield. It was ostensibly to celebrate Washington's Birthday. It was given once in the Church of the Disciples, once in the Y. M. C. A. Hall. My mother was epic poet enough to write the speeches for the nations. She went on through her life, writing oracles and speaking them to audiences of thousands in the Middle West, oracles for the gods and for the nations. In a great many places where I go my crowds are rallied by those who once heard her. Sometimes even the nations and the gods seemed to listen to her oracles. Oftener they did not. If they would only live up to her "Speeches" as she humbly called them, it would be a kinder, a more literary, a more sapient, a wittier, a more motherly and a far more resplendent world.

As I have said, my mother destined me from the beginning to be an artist. My Grandfather Frazee had spoken rather contemptuously of poets in my self-important infant presence. He said they were clever men, and we liked to memorize long passages from their works, and it was eminently desirable we should do so. But almost all of them had a screw loose somewhere. He said this in the midst of his much-read books, which began with Shakespeare and Addison, and ended with all of Mark Twain. And then, incidentally, there were all the established authorities on short-horn cattle.

My Grandfather Frazee was a great man, so I stored this matter away in my infant mind, and decided, if one wrote poetry, one did it as a side-line, and agreed with my mother I was to be an artist. All the elegant young ladies in our family had always painted pictures. Some few could draw well. But in general their kind of craftsmanship has been characteristic of the accomplished daughters of pioneer families since the Daughters of Noah embroidered superfluous bibs for the elephants in the ark.

Before I went to the usual public school and met for lifetime friendship all the youngsters in our end of town, I was sent to a breathlessly exclusive private school, and was "taught drawing." My exercise book was called *The Aurora Drawing Book,* and on the back of it was an engraving of Guido Reni's Aurora. My mother and I were both quite fond of the picture. It was the fresco delineating Apollo and his chariot. The chariot is drawn by the horses of the dawn. The muses are dancing behind and around on lovely clouds, and Cupid or some other dimpled infant is flying before them with a splendid torch. Aurora herself, leading the pageant, is scattering flowers on the sleeping cities. It is a picture I still love, despite any cubists in the world, or drunk, disorderly and obscene painters and beach-combers, from the Pacific islands.

At Miss Sampson's drawing class I filled this book with pictures of peacock feathers, and of clover red and white, and all the strange grasses I could gather in the vacant lots of South Sixth Street. I am fond of clover and wild grass and peacock feathers to this day, and no man shall shame me out of it.

The way the easier gods had won authority over my father and mother was the romance of their lives. He, Doctor Vachel Lindsay, and she, school-marm, Kate Frazee, had done their courting in the galleries of Dresden, Saxony, and Florence, Italy, and in the gondolas of Venice. Between times Doctor Vachel Lindsay was taking a season of study at the Vienna hospitals. He had practiced medicine about nine years near Springfield. He was in Europe to brush up and perfect himself in the hospitals most approved by all the world for learned young physicians of his time. My mother and her chum, Eudora Lindsay, fellow teachers from the same Kentucky college, were taking their European year in art galleries and cathedrals and pagan temples from Scotland to Sicily. My Aunt Eudora subsequently put the studies into a book, *Wayside Notes and Fireside Thoughts.*

which is one of the household gods of the tribe. Both girls were corresponding with Kentucky literary weeklies.

So all the stories of this trip were a thousand times retold and re-measured in my infancy. And my father and mother returned throughout their lives to Europe and came back with new improvised unwritten poems about the architecture and the pictures, reappraising the favorites of their youth. They divided their summer holidays between this sort of thing and camping like cinnamon bears on Mount Clinton, Colorado, and admiring the views from every peak within a day's climb. And once they went to China.

So it was natural that my infancy should be crowded with oracles about the nations, and the Italian painters, and when I was told I was to be an artist, that was final. Literature was taken for granted. For instance all we children were drilled in memorizing choice verses from King James' Bible. We had to recite three verses apiece before we could have our breakfast. Thus we memorized every Sunday School lesson, having it letter-perfect by the end of the week, for fourteen years. My mother took an especial pleasure in those poets who dealt also in art, and filled me full of the Brownings and the Pre-Raphaelites.

My little world still insists I am a student of phonetics. But it seems to me reasonable that, as one of my new adventures while singing these songs (if the technique of my verse is to be discussed at all from town to town by committees) that my verse be judged not as a series of experiments in sound, but for lifetime and even hereditary thoughts and memories of painting. Let the verse be scrutinized for evidences of experience in drawing from life, drawing architecture, drawing sculpture, trying to draw the Venus of Milo, and imitating the Japanese Prints and Beardsley, and trying to draw like Blake, and all such matters. Unless I am much mistaken, I shall sooner or later evolve a special type of United States Hieroglyphics, based

17

on a contemplation of the borderline between letters and art, and the bridges that cross it. The theory of these hieroglyphics is already embedded in the text of *The Art of the Moving Picture*.

I have now, for eighteen years, walked the corridors of the Metropolitan Museum of Art, for the most part alone. Each room echoes like a mausoleum. Of all the university thousands I address in the winter, and have addressed since 1915, none turn up in that Museum that is my Princeton and my University of California. An art student is far more separated from the United States Civilization than is a speaker or writer. And this brings me to a curious story, which may serve as a symbol of this assertion.

When I was in the New York School of Art, William M. Chase gave us a lecture on drawing the beauties of the nude figure from memory. I had already drawn from life four years. I could put up the usual life drawing, and have it exhibited on the line in due place. So, bearing the words of Chase in mind, I made the conventional charcoal record of a most Olympian model, a most exquisite model, of whom I made a dull, accurate map.

That evening, far from school, and the thought of the day's work I pinned to the wall a sheet of the same size of paper as I used at school, and to my astonishment drew from memory a better picture of that model in an hour than the one it had taken a week to draw in class. It was one of the great adventures while singing these songs, to find it could actually be done. I brought the two drawings together next day and found that the memory drawing was as well measured, but more Greek than the other.

Then, again from memory, I did the picture in miniature, in pen and ink. Then I added, beneath the feet of the lady, a bubble-chariot, in which she was riding. Around her were stars and moons, turning to bubbles, and bubbles turning to stars and moons. Then I gave her a crown of bubbles, and

18

the whole picture seemed to be ascending. Ascending to what? I put in the final bubble, a gigantic one, in the top corner of the picture. Then I gave it sunrays, and made it a sun. Then, and only then, did the poem occur to me, which was later accepted by Ridgely Torrence for *The Critic,* and has gone, with his generous endorsement, into anthologies. The picture of the Queen was turned down by *The Critic,* through the austere insistence of Miss Jeannette Gilder, Mr. Torrence's co-editor. She hated the nude, even when it was flying to the sun in blazing sunshine. In a perfectly friendly way, as it were, for argument's sake, I blame Mr. Torrence for not fighting like a desperate wild-cat for the picture.

Miss Gilder was the first of a long series of people in the world of letters quite sure a poet should not draw pictures. Now the newspaper editors that never scrutinize my books and who send their reporters to get hasty impressions at my recitals, are vowing I can recite, but cannot write. All that some newspapers are willing to leave of my infant and prenatal destiny is the Kentucky Orator. It is "Too Much," as Artemus Ward said, "Too, Too Much." At the risk of being accused of every kind of lavishness, I say "Back to the *Aurora Drawing Book,* and the pictures of Peacock Feathers and Clover."

Newspaper reporters of the sort who never read any man's books, and who do not expect to begin with mine, are fond of filling column after column, in town after town where I recite, with stories of how I have spent the most of my forty-three years in some form of deeply degraded beggary.

The reason my beggar days started talk was that each time I broke loose, and went on the road, in the spring, after a winter of Art lecturing, it was definitely an act of protest against the United States commercial standard, a protest against the type of life set forth for all time in two books of Sinclair Lewis: *Babbitt* and *Main Street.*

After I had been twice on the road, and proved my inde-

19

pendence in a fashion, there were days in my home town when the Babbitts and their friends in the Country Club were about ready to send me to jail or burn me at the stake for some sort of witchcraft, dimly apprehended, but impossible for them to define. One of my crimes was a course of lectures at the Y. M. C. A. on Ruskin's famous chapters on the Nature of Gothic, from the second volume of the *Stones of Venice.* I went on lecturing, approving all Ruskin said, in spite of mutterings.

After I had been twice on the road, still the Babbitts insisted on my drawing purely commercial pictures, or quitting the business of drawing altogether. They insisted that I write purely commercial verse, that could be syndicated like crackers and cheese, and they brought their views to bear in every direct and indirect way. The only way out was a clean-cut defiance. I was told by the Babbitts on every hand I must quit being an artist, or beg. So I said, for the third time, "I will beg."

But I made this resolve after having had my pictures and verses turned down by every art editor and literary editor of New York for two years. And on two other desperate occasions named above, I thus broke loose.

It was because it was a three-times-loudly-proclaimed act of defiance, not the time spent on the road, that made the stir. As a matter of fact I came back temporarily beaten each time, at the end of less than four months. But each time I was fortified to try it again. I am not yet through, either. I have spent a total of only two springs and one summer as a beggar, less than a year. Because it was an act of spiritual war, I have written many bulletins and reminiscences.

As to my fourth extensive experience on the road, it was as a pedestrian, not as a beggar, as a companion, as a Franciscan'pf the more liberal observance. This is all too generously recorded by my good friend Stephen Graham in that book of his own verses and his own prose :—*Tramping with a*

*Poet in the Rockies.* So here I give my poor thanks, and it comes with a full heart.

The United States Men of Letters in general have experienced a similar fraternity from other British Men of Letters, and they all appreciate it as a God-given thing. I hope that forever and a day, writers will walk with writers, politicians with politicians, statesmen with statesmen. I venture on the strength of this hope to suggest that British and United States Universities explore the world abreast. I urge students of California, Washington and Oregon, contemplating a University career, to go to England. With even more emphasis I urge the British to send all the sons they can spare, not to any eastern school, but to the University of the State of Washington, the University of Oregon, the University of California.

The poem called "General Booth Enters Heaven" was built in part upon certain adventures while singing these songs. When I was dead broke, and begging, in Atlanta, Georgia, and much confused as to my next move in this world, I slept for three nights in the Salvation Army quarters there. And when I passed through Newark, New Jersey, on another trip, I slept in the Salvation Army quarters there. I could tell some fearful stories of similar experiences. I will say briefly, that I know the Salvation Army from the inside. Certainly, at that time, the Army was struggling with what General Booth called the submerged tenth of the population. And I was with the submerged.

In the spring of 1912 the news went around the world that the great founder of the Army had gone blind. Every Sunday newspaper had a full-page picture of the blind General. Later came the announcement of his death, with elaborate biographies. Later in these same newspapers, all over the world, came the story of his life as told by himself. So much has happened since, such rivers of blood have run under the bridges of the world, that this succession of newspaper

21

features has been forgotten. Meanwhile the fanatical Salvation Army, that was like the Franciscans of the Strict Observance in the very earliest days of St. Francis, has emerged as a prosperous rival of the Y. M. C. A.

By General Booth's own story, quoted incessantly by the papers the year of his death, he went into the lowest depths of London, with malice aforethought, with deliberate intention to rescue the most notoriously degraded, those given up by policeman, physician, preacher and charity worker. He reiterated in his autobiography that he wanted to find those so low there were none lower. He put them into uniform. He put them under military discipline. He put them in authority over one another. He chose their musical instruments, and their astonishing tunes. The world has forgotten what a scandal to respectable religion the resulting army was when it began. It was like the day St. Francis handed all his clothes to the priest, or the day he cut off the hair of St. Clara. In my poem I merely turned into rhyme as well as I could, word for word, General Booth's own account of his life, and the telegraph dispatches of his death after going blind. I set it to the tune that is not a tune, but a speech, a refrain used most frequently in the meetings of the Army on any public square to this day. Yet I encounter a great number of people who are sure they have never heard of the General, the army, or the tune, or who ask me if I wrote the poem to "make sport."

The verses in the section of this book called *Politics* remain as promises of more elaborate efforts in the future on that theme.

About the same time I was the tinseled infant Cupid that I have described in the early part of this discourse, my father had filled me with the notion that, way down in Kentucky, once upon a time a certain Abraham Lincoln came, with many soldiers. According to this tale they stole all the horses from my Grandfather Lindsay's estate, drove off

22

all the negroes forever (my grandfather's personal property and mine), burned the crops, and then, in a way not mentioned, stole the farm, and left us all to begin again by studying medicine by a solitary candle. And as for Harriet Beecher Stowe, any one who would read her book was worse than an infidel. This general view of history was challenged by my mother, who, though having many Southern ideas, was all for Lincoln. And I have in many ways agreed with her, but not enough to alter the fact that Mason and Dixon's line runs straight through our house in Springfield still, and straight through my heart. No man may escape his bouncing infancy. I do not expect to get ten feet from my childhood till I die.

Elegant ladies ask me hundreds of times as I come to their towns as a reciter: "How did you get your knowledge of the 'neeegro' ?" They put *e* in the word three times over. After profound meditation I now give my answer to them all. My father had a musical voice, and he used to read us *Uncle Remus,* and he could sing every scrap of song therein and revise every story by what some old slave had told him. He used to sing the littler children to sleep with negro melodies which he loved, and which negroes used to sing to him, when they rocked him to sleep in his infancy. We nearly always had a black hired man and a black hired girl. My father took us to jubilee singer concerts from Fisk or Hampton, and came home rendering the songs authentically, and from boyhood memory. Moreover, our negro servants did not hesitate to sing. One-fifth of the population of the town of Springfield is colored. I played with negro boys in the Stuart School yard. I have heard the race question argued to shreds every week of my life from then till now. We have so many negroes that we had race riots for a week in 1908. I took time off for months to argue the matter out with a good friend, a local negro lawyer, Charles Gibbs, who was just then beginning to practice law. Springfield is as far

23

south as Maryland, Delaware and northern Virginia. Mason and Dixon's line goes straight east and west on Edwards Street. Lincoln's home is only two blocks north of it.

And it seems to me Mason and Dixon's line runs around every country in the world, around France, Japan, Canada, or Mexico or any other sovereignty. It is the terrible line, that should be the line of love and good-will, and witty conversation, but may be the bloody line of misunderstanding. When Graham and I climbed into Alberta, Canada, from Glacier Park, Montana, we crossed a Canadian-American line almost obliterated. Every line should be that way. We must have no Gettysburg of the nations. I still thrill to Andrew Jackson's old toast at the famous banquet: "The Federal Union,— it must and shall be preserved." But I would alter it to: "The League of Nations, it must and shall be preserved." And in my fancy I see Old Jackson rising to propose that toast to the world. Something like this is the implication beneath all the political poems, and the implication beneath the prose work, *The Golden Book of Springfield.*

Come, let us be bold with our songs.

VACHEL LINDSAY.

October 15, 1922.

# SECTION I

# NIGHTINGALES

# THE CHINESE NIGHTINGALE

## A Song in Chinese Tapestries

"How, how," he said. "Friend Chang," I said,
"San Francisco sleeps as the dead—
Ended license, lust and play:
Why do you iron the night away?
Your big clock speaks with a deadly sound,
With a tick and a wail till dawn comes round.
While the monster shadows glower and creep,
What can be better for man than sleep?"

"I will tell you a secret," Chang replied;
"My breast with vision is satisfied,
And I see green trees and fluttering wings,
And my deathless bird from Shanghai sings."
Then he lit five firecrackers in a pan.
"Pop, pop," said the firecrackers, "cra-cra-crack."
He lit a joss stick long and black.
Then the proud gray joss in the corner stirred;
On his wrist appeared a gray small bird,
And this was the song of the gray small bird:
"Where is the princess, loved forever,
Who made Chang first of the kings of men?"

And the joss in the corner stirred again;
And the carved dog, curled in his arms, awoke,
Barked forth a smoke-cloud that whirled and broke.
It piled in a maze round the ironing-place,

27

And there on the snowy table wide
Stood a Chinese lady of high degree,
With a scornful, witching, tea-rose face. . . .
Yet she put away all form and pride,
And laid her glimmering veil aside
With a childlike smile for Chang and for me.

The walls fell back, night was aflower,
The table gleamed in a moonlit bower,
While Chang, with a countenance carved of **stone,**
Ironed and ironed, all alone.
And thus she sang to the busy man Chang:
"Have you forgotten . . .
Deep in the ages, long, long ago,
I was your sweetheart, there on the sand—
Storm-worn beach of the Chinese land?
We sold our grain in the peacock town—
Built on the edge of the sea-sands brown—
Built on the edge of the sea-sands brown. . . .

When all the world was drinking blood
From the skulls of men and bulls
And all the world had swords and clubs of stone,
We drank our tea in China beneath the sacred spice-trees,
And heard the curled waves of the harbor moan.
And this gray bird, in Love's first spring,
With a bright-bronze breast and a bronze-brown wing,
Captured the world with his carolling.
Do you remember, ages after,
At last the world we were born to own?
You were the heir of the yellow throne—
The world was the field of the Chinese man
And we were the pride of the Sons of Han?
We copied deep books and we carved in jade,
And wove blue silks in the mulberry shade. . . ."

28

# THE CHINESE NIGHTINGALE

"I remember, I remember
That Spring came on forever,
That Spring came on forever,"
Said the Chinese nightingale.

My heart was filled with marvel and dream,
Though I saw the western street-lamps gleam,
Though dawn was bringing the western day,
Though Chang was a laundryman ironing away. . . .
Mingled there with the streets and alleys,
The railroad-yard and the clock-tower bright,
Demon clouds crossed ancient valleys;
Across wide lotus-ponds of light
I marked a giant firefly's flight.

And the lady, rosy-red,
Flourished her fan, her shimmering fan,
Stretched her hand toward Chang, and said:
"Do you remember,
Ages after,
Our palace of heart-red stone?
Do you remember
The little doll-faced children
With their lanterns full of moon-fire,
That came from all the empire
Honoring the throne?—
The loveliest fête and carnival
Our world had ever known?
The sages sat about us
With their heads bowed in their beards,
With proper meditation on the sight.
Confucius was not born;
We lived in those great days
Confucius later said were lived aright. . . .
And this gray bird, on that day of spring,

With a bright-bronze breast, and a bronze-brown wing,
Captured the world with his carolling.
Late at night his tune was spent.
Peasants,
Sages,
Children,
Homeward went,
And then the bronze bird sang for you and me.
We walked alone.  Our hearts were high and free.
I had a silvery name, I had a silvery name,
I had a silvery name—do you remember
The name you cried beside the tumbling sea?"

Chang turned not to the lady slim—
He bent to his work, ironing away;
But she was arch, and knowing and glowing,
For the bird on his shoulder spoke for him.

"Darling . . . darling . . . darling . . . darling . . ."
Said the Chinese nightingale.

The great gray joss on the rustic shelf,
Rakish and shrewd, with his collar awry,
Sang impolitely, as though by himself,
Drowning with his bellowing the nightingale's cry:
"Back through a hundred, hundred years
Hear the waves as they climb the piers,
Hear the howl of the silver seas,
Hear the thunder.
Hear the gongs of holy China
How the waves and tunes combine
In a rhythmic clashing wonder,
Incantation old and fine:
    'Dragons, dragons, Chinese dragons,
    Red firecrackers, and green firecrackers
    And dragons, dragons, Chinese dragons, "

Then the lady, rosy-red,
Turned to her lover Chang and said:
"Dare you forget that turquoise dawn
When we stood in our mist-hung velvet lawn,
And worked a spell this great joss taught
Till a God of the Dragons was charmed and caught?
From the flag high over our palace home
He flew to our feet in rainbow-foam—
A king of beauty and tempest and thunder
Panting to tear our sorrows asunder.
A dragon of fair adventure and wonder.
We mounted the back of that royal slave
With thoughts of desire that were noble and grave.
We swam down the shore to the dragon-mountains,
We whirled to the peaks and the fiery fountains.
To our secret ivory house we were borne.
We looked down the wonderful wing-filled regions
Where the dragons darted in glimmering legions.
Right by my breast the nightingale sang;
The old rhymes rang in the sunlit mist
That we this hour regain—
Song-fire for the brain.
When my hands and my hair and my feet you kissed,
When you cried for your heart's new pain,
What was my name in the dragon-mist,
In the rings of rainbowed rain?"

"Sorrow and love, glory and love,"
Said the Chinese nightingale.
"Sorrow and love, glory and love,"
Said the Chinese nightingale.

And now the joss broke in with his song:
"Dying ember, bird of Chang,
Soul of Chang, do you remember?—

31

Ere you returned to the shining harbor
There were pirates by ten thousand
Descended on the town
In vessels mountain-high and red and brown,
Moon-ships that climbed the storms and cut the skies.
On their prows were painted terrible bright eyes.
But I was then a wizard and a scholar and a priest;
I stood upon the sand;
With lifted hand I looked upon them
And sunk their vessels with my wizard eyes,
And the stately lacquer-gate made safe again.
Deep, deep below the bay, the seaweed and the spray,
Embalmed in amber every pirate lies,
Embalmed in amber every pirate lies."

Then this did the noble lady say:
"Bird, do you dream of our home-coming day
When you flew like a courier on before
From the dragon-peak to our palace-door,
And we drove the steed in your singing path—
The ramping dragon of laughter and wrath:
And found our city all aglow,
And knighted this joss that decked it so?
There were golden fishes in the purple river
And silver fishes and rainbow fishes.
There were golden junks in the laughing river,
And silver junks and rainbow junks:
There were golden lilies by the bay and river,
And silver lilies and tiger-lilies,
And tinkling wind-bells in the gardens of the town
By the black-lacquer gate
Where walked in state
The kind king Chang
And his sweetheart mate. . . .
With his flag-born dragon

32

And his crown of pearl . . . and . . . jade,
And his nightingale reigning in the mulberry shade,
And sailors and soldiers on the sea-sands brown,
And priests who bowed them down to your song—
By the city called Han, the peacock town,
By the city called Han, the nightingale town,
The nightingale town."

Then sang the bird, so strangely gay,
Fluttering, fluttering, ghostly and gray,
A vague, unravelling, final tune,
Like a long unwinding silk cocoon;
Sang as though for the soul of him
Who ironed away in that bower dim:—
    "I have forgotten
    Your dragons great,
      Merry and mad and friendly and bold.
Dim is your proud lost palace-gate.
I vaguely know
There were heroes of old,
Troubles more than the heart could hold,
There were wolves in the woods
Yet lambs in the fold,
Nests in the top of the almond tree. . . .
The evergreen tree . . . and the mulberry tree . . .
Life and hurry and joy forgotten,
Years on years I but half-remember . . .
Man is a torch, then ashes soon,
May and June, then dead December,
Dead December, then again June.
Who shall end my dream's confusion?
Life is a loom, weaving illusion . . .
I remember, I remember
There were ghostly veils and laces . . .
In the shadowy bowery places . . .

With lovers' ardent faces
Bending to one another,
Speaking each his part.
They infinitely echo
In the red cave of my heart.
'Sweetheart, sweetheart, sweetheart,'
They said to one another.
They spoke, I think, of perils past.
They spoke, I think, of peace at last.
One thing I remember:
Spring came on forever,
Spring came on forever,"
Said the Chinese nightingale.


# SHANTUNG, OR THE EMPIRE OF CHINA IS CRUMBLING DOWN

## (Dedicated to William Rose Benét)

"Confucius appeared, according to Mencius, one of his most distinguished followers, at a crisis in the nation's history. 'The world,' he says, 'had fallen into decay, and right principles had disappeared. Perverse discourses and oppressive deeds were waxen rife. Ministers murdered their rulers, and sons their fathers. Confucius was frightened by what he saw,—and he undertook the work of reformation.'

"He was a native of the state of Lu, a part of the modern Shantung. . . . Lu had a great name among the other states of Chow . . . etc." Rev. James Legge, Professor of Chinese, University of Oxford.

I have found the poem Shantung an especial favorite with the audience when I have been called upon to recite for the staff of some public library.

34

# SHANTUNG

## I

*Now let the generations pass—*
*Like sand through Heaven's blue hour-glass.*

In old Shantung,
By the capital where poetry began,
Near the only printing presses known to man,
Young Confucius walks the shore
On a sorrowful day.
The town, all books, is tumbling down
Through the blue bay.
The bookworms writhe
From rusty musty walls.
They drown themselves like rabbits in the sea.
*Venomous foreigners harry mandarins*
With pitchfork, blunderbuss and snickersnee.

In the book-slums there is thunder;
Gunpowder, that sad wonder,
Intoxicates the knights and beggar-men.
The old grotesques of war begin again:
Rebels, devils, fairies are set free.

So . . .
Confucius hears a carol and a hum:
A picture sea-child whirs from off his fan
In one quick breath of peach-bloom fantasy.
Then, in an instant bows the reverent knee—
A full-grown sweetheart, chanting his renown.
And then she darts into the Yellow Sea,
Calling, calling:
"Sage with holy brow,
Say farewell to China now;
Live like the swine,
Leave off your scholar-gown!

35

This city of books is falling, falling,
The Empire of China is crumbling down."

## II

*Confucius, Confucius, how great was Confucius—*
*The sage of Shantung, and the master of Mencius?*

Alexander fights the East.
Just as the Indus turns him back
He hears of tempting lands beyond,
With sword-swept cities on the rack
With crowns outshining India's crown:
The Empire of China, crumbling down.
Later the Roman sibyls say:
"Egypt, Persia and Macedon,
Tyre and Carthage, passed away:
And the Empire of China is crumbling down.
Rome will never crumble down."

## III

*See how the generations pass—*
*Like sand through Heaven's blue hour-glass.*

Arthur waits on the British shore
One thankful day,
For Galahad sails back at last
To Camelot Bay.

The *pure* knight lands and tells the tale:
"Far in the east
A sea-girl led us to a king,
The king to a feast,

36

In a land where poppies bloom for miles,
Where books are made like bricks and tiles.
I taught that king to love your name—
Brother and Christian he became.

"His Town of Thunder-Powder keeps
A giant hound that never sleeps,
A crocodile that sits and weeps.

"His Town of Cheese the mouse affrights
With fire-winged cats that light the nights.
They glorify the land of rust;
Their sneeze is music in the dust.
(And deep and ancient is the dust.)

"All towns have one same miracle
With the Town of Silk, the capital—
Vast bookworms in the book-built walls.
Their creeping shakes the silver halls;
They look like cables, and they seem
Like writhing roots on trees of dream.
Their sticky cobwebs cross the street,
Catching scholars by the feet,
Who own the tribes, yet rule them not,
Bitten by bookworms till they rot.
Beggars and clowns rebel in might
Bitten by bookworms till they fight."

Arthur calls to his knights in rows:
"I will go if Merlin goes;
These rebels must be flayed and sliced
Let us cut their throats for Christ."
But Merlin whispers in his beard:
"China has witches to be feared."

Arthur stares at the sea-foam's rim
Amazed. The fan-girl beckons him!—
That slender and peculiar child
Mongolian and brown and wild.
His eyes grow wide, his senses drown,
She laughs in her wing, like the sleeve of a gown.
She lifts a key of crimson stone.
"The Great Gunpowder-town you own."
She lifts a key with chains and rings:
"I give the town where cats have wings."
She lifts a key as white as milk:
"This unlocks the Town of Silk"—
Throws forty keys at Arthur's feet:
"These unlock the land complete."

Then, frightened by suspicious knights,
And Merlin's eyes like altar-lights,
And the Christian towers of Arthur's town,
She spreads blue fins—she whirs away;
Fleeing far across the bay,
Wailing through the gorgeous day:
"My sick king begs
That you save his crown
And his learned chiefs from the worm and clown—
The Empire of China is crumbling down."

# IV

*Always the generations pass,*
*Like sand through Heaven's blue hour-glass!*

The time the King of Rome is born—
Napoleon's son, that eaglet thing—
Bonaparte finds beside his throne
One evening, laughing in her wing,

The Chinese sea-child; and she cries,
Breaking his heart with emerald eyes
And fairy-bred unearthly grace:
"Master, take your destined place—
Across white foam and water blue
The streets of China call to you:
The Empire of China is crumbling down."
Then he bends to kiss her mouth,
And gets but incense, dust and drouth.

Custodians, custodians!
Mongols and Manchurians!
Christians, wolves, Mohammedans!

In hard Berlin they cried: "O King,
China's way is a shameful thing!"

In Tokio they cry: "O King,
China's way is a shameful thing!"

And thus our song might call the roll
Of every land from pole to pole,
And every rumor known to time
Of China doddering—or sublime.

## V

*Slowly the generations pass—*
*Like sand through Heaven's blue hour-glass.*

So let us find tomorrow now:
Our towns are gone;
Our books have passed; ten thousand years
Have thundered on.

The Sphinx looks far across the world
In fury black:
She sees all western nations spent
Or on the rack.
Eastward she sees one land she knew
When from the stone
Priests of the sunrise carved her out
And left her lone.
She sees the shore Confucius walked
On his sorrowful day:
*Impudent foreigners rioting,*
In the ancient way;
Officials, futile as of old,
Have gowns more bright;
Bookworms are fiercer than of old,
Their skins more white;
Dust is deeper than of old,
More bats are flying;
More songs are written than of old—
More songs are dying.

Where Galahad found forty towns
Now fade and glare
Ten thousand towns with book-tiled roof
And garden-stair,
Where beggars' babies come like showers
Of classic words:
They rule the world—immortal brooks
And magic birds.

The lion Sphinx roars at the sun:
"I hate this nursing you have done!
The meek inherit the earth too long—
When will the world belong to the strong?"

She soars; she claws his patient face—
The girl-moon screams at the disgrace.
The sun's blood fills the western sky;
He hurries not, and will not die.

The baffled Sphinx, on granite wings,
Turns now to where young China sings.
One thousand of ten thousand towns
Go down before her silent wrath;
Yet even lion-gods may faint
And die upon their brilliant path.
She sees the Chinese children romp
In dust that she must breathe and eat.
Her tongue is reddened by its lye;
She craves its grit, its cold and heat.
The Dust of Ages holds a glint
Of fire from the foundation-stones,
Of spangles from the sun's bright face,
Of sapphires from earth's marrow-bones.
Mad-drunk with it, she ends her day—
Slips when a high sea-wall gives way,
Drowns in the cold Confucian sea
Where the whirring fan-girl first flew free.

*In the light of the maxims of Chesterfield, Mencius,*
*Wilson, Roosevelt, Tolstoy, Trotsky,*
*Franklin or Nietzsche, how great was Confucius?*

*"Laughing Asia"* brown and wild,
That lyric and immortal child,
His fan's gay daughter, crowned with sand,
Between the water and the land
Now cries on high in irony,
With a voice of night-wind alchemy:

"O cat, O Sphinx,
O stony-face,
The joke is on Egyptian pride,
The joke is on the human race:
"The meek inherit the earth too long—
When will the world belong to the strong?"
I am born from off the holy fan
Of the world's most patient gentleman.
So answer me,
O courteous sea!
O deathless sea!"

And thus will the answering Ocean call:
China will fall,
The Empire of China will crumble down,
When the Alps and the Andes crumble down;
When the sun and the moon have crumbled down,
The Empire of China will crumble down,
Crumble down."

## THE SPICE-TREE

This is the song
The spice-tree sings:
"Hunger and fire,
Hunger and fire,
Sky-born Beauty—
Spice of desire."
Under the spice-tree
Watch and wait,
Burning maidens
And lads that mate.

The spice-tree spreads
And its boughs come down

Shadowing village and farm and town.
And none can see
But the pure of heart
The great green leaves
And the boughs descending,
And hear the song that is never ending.

The deep roots whisper,
The branches say:—
"Love tomorrow,
And love today,
And till Heaven's day,
And till Heaven's day."

The moon is a bird's nest in its branches,
The moon is hung in its topmost spaces.
And there, tonight, two doves play house
While lovers watch with uplifted faces.
Two doves go home
To their nest, the moon.
It is woven of twigs of broken light,
With threads of scarlet and threads of gray
And a lining of down for silk delight.
To their Eden, the moon, fly home our doves,
Up through the boughs of the great spice-tree;—
And one is the kiss I took from you,
And one is the kiss you gave to me.


## I KNOW ALL THIS WHEN GIPSY FIDDLES CRY

Oh, gipsies, proud and stiff-necked and perverse,
Saying: "We tell the fortunes of the nations,
And revel in the deep palm of the world.

43

The head-line is the road we choose for trade.
The love-line is the lane wherein we camp.
The life-line is the road we wander on.
Mount Venus, Jupiter, and all the rest
Are finger-tips of ranges clasping round
And holding up the Romany's wide sky."
Oh, gipsies, proud and stiff-necked and perverse,
Saying: "We will swap horses till the doom,
And mend the pots and kettles of mankind,
And lend our sons to big-time vaudeville,
Or to the race-track, or the learned world.
But India's Brahma waits within their breasts.
They will return to us with gipsy grins,
And chatter Romany, and shake their curls
And hug the dirtiest babies in the camp.
They will return to the moving pillar of smoke,
The whitest toothed, the merriest laughers known,
The blackest haired of all the tribes of men.
What trap can hold such cats? The Romany
Has crossed such delicate palms with lead or gold,
Wheedling in sun and rain, through perilous years,
All coins now look alike. The palm is all.
Our greasy pack of cards is still the book
Most read of men. The heart's librarians,
We tell all lovers what they want to know.
So, out of the famed Chicago Library,
Out of the great Chicago orchestras,
Out of the skyscraper, the Fine Arts Building,
Our sons will come with fiddles and with loot,
Dressed, as of old, like turkey-cocks and zebras,
Like tiger-lilies and chameleons,
Go west with us to California,
Telling the fortunes of the bleeding world,
And kiss the sunset, ere their day is done."

Oh, gipsies, proud and stiff-necked and perverse
Picking the brains and pockets of mankind,
You will go westward for one-half hour yet.
You will turn eastward in a little while.
You will go back, as men turn to Kentucky,
Land of their fathers, dark and bloody ground.
When all the Jews go home to Syria,
When Chinese cooks go back to Canton, China,
When Japanese photographers return
With their black cameras to Tokio,
And Irish patriots to Donegal,
And Scotch accountants back to Edinburgh,
You will go back to India, whence you came.
When you have reached the borders of your quest,
Homesick at last, by many a devious way,
Winding the wonderlands circuitous,
By foot and horse will trace the long way back!
Fiddling for ocean liners, while the dance
Sweeps through the decks, your brown tribes all will go!
Those east-bound ships will hear your long farewell
On fiddle, piccolo, and flute and timbrel.
I know all this, when gipsy fiddles cry.

That hour of their homesickness, I myself
Will turn, will say farewell to Illinois,
To old Kentucky and Virginia,
And go with them to India, whence they came.
For they have heard a singing from the Ganges,
And cries of orioles,—from the temple caves,—
And Bengal's oldest, humblest villages.
They smell the supper smokes of Amritsar.
Green monkeys cry in Sanskrit to their souls
From lofty bamboo trees of hot Madras.
They think of towns to ease their feverish eyes,

And make them stand and meditate forever,
Domes of astonishment, to heal the mind.
I know all this, when gipsy fiddles cry.

What music will be blended with the wind
When gipsy fiddlers, nearing that old land,
Bring tunes from all the world to Brahma's house?
Passing the Indus, winding poisonous forests,
Blowing soft flutes at scandalous temple girls,
Filling the highways with their magpie loot,
What brass from my Chicago will they heap,
What gems from Walla Walla, Omaha,
Will they pile near the Bodhi Tree, and laugh?
They will dance near such temples as best suit them,
Though they will not quite enter, or adore,
Looking on roofs, as poets look on lilies,
Looking at towers, as boys at forest vines,
That leap to tree-tops through the dizzy air.
I know all this, when gipsy fiddles cry.

And with the gipsies there will be a king
And a thousand desperadoes just his style,
With all their rags dyed in the blood of roses,
Splashed with the blood of angels, and of demons.
And he will boss them with an awful voice.
And with a red whip he will beat his wife.
He will be wicked on that sacred shore,
And rattle cruel spurs against the rocks,
And shake Calcutta's walls with circus bugles.
He will kill Brahmins there, in Kali's name,
And please the thugs, and blood-drunk of the earth.
I know all this, when gipsy fiddles cry.

Oh, sweating thieves, and hard-boiled scalawags,
That still will boast your pride until the doom.

46

Smashing every caste rule of the world,
Reaching at last your Hindu goal to smash
The caste rules of old India, and shout:
"Down with the Brahmins, let the Romany reign."

When gipsy girls look deep within my hand
They always speak so tenderly and say
That I am one of those star-crossed to wed
A princess in a forest fairy-tale.
So there will be a tender gipsy princess,
My Juliet, shining through this clan.
And I would sing you of her beauty now.
And I will fight with knives the gipsy man
Who tries to steal her wild young heart away.
And I will kiss her in the waterfalls,
And at the rainbow's end, and in the incense
That curls about the feet of sleeping gods,
And sing with her in canebrakes and in rice fields
In Romany, eternal Romany.
We will sow secret herbs, and plant old roses,
And fumble through dark, snaky palaces,
Stable our ponies in the Taj Mahal,
And sleep outdoors ourselves.
In her strange fairy mill-wheel eyes will wait
All windings and unwindings of the highways,
From India, across America,—
All windings and unwindings of my fancy,
All windings and unwindings of all souls,
All windings and unwindings of the heavens.
I know all this, when gipsy fiddles cry.

We gipsies, proud and stiff-necked and perverse,
Standing upon the white Himalayas,
Will think of far divine Yosemite.
We will heal Hindu hermits there with oil

47

Brought from California's tall sequoias.
And we will be like gods that heap the thunders,
And start young redwood trees on Time's own mountains,
We will swap horses with the rising moon,
And mend that funny skillet called Orion,
Color the stars like San Francisco's street-lights,
And paint our sign and signature on high
In planets like a bed of crimson pansies;
While a million fiddles shake all listening hearts,
Crying good fortune to the Universe,
Whispering adventure to the Ganges waves,
And to the spirits, and all winds and gods.
Till mighty Brahma puts his golden palm
Within the gipsy king's great striped tent,
And asks his fortune told by that great love-line
That winds across his palm in splendid flame.

Only the hearthstone of old India
Will end the endless march of gipsy feet.
I will go back to India with them
When they go back to India whence they came.
I know all this, when gipsy fiddles cry.


# A RHYME FOR ALL ZIONISTS

## The Eyes of Queen Esther, and How They Conquered King Ahasuerus

"Esther had not showed her people nor her kindred."

### I

He harried lions up the peaks.
In blood and moss and snow they died.
He wore a cloak of lions' manes
To satisfy his curious pride.

48

Men saw it, trimmed with emerald bands,
Flash on the crested battle-tide.

Where Bagdad stands, he hunted kings,
Burned them alive, his soul to cool.
Yet in his veins god Ormazd wrought
To make a just man of a fool.
He spoke the rigid truth, and rode,
And drew the bow, by Persian rule.

## II

Ahasuerus in his prime
Was gracious and voluptuous.
He saw a pale face turn to him,
A gleam of Heaven's righteousness:
A girl with hair of David's gold
And Rachel's face of loveliness.

He dropped his sword, he bowed his head.
She led his steps to courtesy.
He took her for his white north star:
A wedding of true majesty.
Oh, what a war for gentleness
Was in her bridal fantasy!

Why did he fall by candlelight
And press his bull-heart to her feet?
He found them as the mountain-snow
Where lions died. Her hands were sweet
As ice upon a blood-burnt mouth,
As mead to reapers in the wheat.

The little nation in her soul
Bloomed in her girl's prophetic face.

She named it not, and yet he felt
One challenge: her eternal race.
This was the mystery of her step,
Her trembling body's sacred grace.

He stood, a priest, a Nazarite,
A rabbi reading by a tomb.
The hardy raider saw and feared
Her white knees in the palace gloom,
Her pouting breasts and locks well combed
Within the humming, reeling room.

Her name was *Meditation* there:
Fair opposite of bullock's brawn.
I sing her eyes that conquered him.
He bent before his little fawn,
Her dewy fern, her bitter weed,
Her secret forest's floor and lawn.

He gave his towers and towns to her.
She hated them, and turned not back.
Her eyes kept hunting through his soul
As one may seek through battle black
For one dear banner held on high,
For one bright bugle in the rack.

The scorn that loves the sexless stars:
Traditions passionless and bright:
The ten commands (to him unknown),
The pillar of the fire by night:—
Flashed from her alabaster crown
The while they kissed by candlelight.

The rarest psalms of David came
From her dropped veil (odd dreams to him).

## INCENSE

It prophesied, he knew not how,
Against his endless armies grim.
He saw his Shushan in the dust—
Far in the ages growing dim.

Then came a glance of steely blue,
Flash of her body's silver sword.
Her eyes of law and temple prayer
Broke him who spoiled the temple hoard.
The thief who fouled all little lands
Went mad before her, and adored.

The girl was Eve in Paradise,
Yet Judith, till her war was won.
All of the future tyrants fell
In this one king, ere night was done,
And Israel, captive then as now
Ruled with tomorrow's rising sun.

And in the logic of the skies
He who keeps Israel in his hand,
The God whose hope for joy on earth
The Gentile yet shall understand,
Through powers like Esther's steadfast eyes
Shall free each little tribe and land.

These verses were written for the Phi Beta Kappa Society
of Philadelphia and read at their meeting, December 8, 1917.


## INCENSE

Think not that incense-smoke has had its day.
My friends, the incense-time has but begun.
Creed upon creed, cult upon cult shall bloom,
Shrine after shrine grow gray beneath the sun.

And mountain-boulders in our aged West
Shall guard the graves of hermits truth-endowed:
And there the scholar from the Chinese hills
Shall do deep honor, with his wise head bowed.

And on our old, old plains some muddy stream,
Dark as the Ganges, shall, like that strange tide—
(Whispering mystery to half the earth)—
Gather the praying millions to its side,

And flow past halls with statues in white stone
To saints unborn today, whose lives of grace
Shall make one shining, universal church
Where all Faiths kneel, as brothers, in one place.

## A NET TO SNARE THE MOONLIGHT

*(What the Man of Faith Said)*

The dew, the rain and moonlight
All prove our Father's mind.
The dew, the rain and moonlight
Descend to bless mankind.

Come, let us see that all men
Have land to catch the rain,
Have grass to snare the spheres of dew,
And fields spread for the grain.

Yea, we would give to each poor man
Ripe wheat and poppies red,—
A peaceful place at evening
With the stars just overhead:

**THE OLD COURT HOUSE**
SPRINGFIELD, ILLINOIS

A net to snare the moonlight,
A sod spread to the sun,
A place of toil by daytime,
Of dreams when toil is done.


## ABRAHAM LINCOLN WALKS AT MIDNIGHT

### (In Springfield, Illinois)

It is portentous, and a thing of state
That here at midnight, in our little town
A mourning figure walks, and will not rest,
Near the old court-house pacing up and down,

Or by his homestead, or in shadowed yards
He lingers where his children used to play,
Or through the market, on the well-worn stones
He stalks until the dawn-stars burn away.

A bronzed, lank man! His suit of ancient black,
A famous high top-hat and plain worn shawl
Make him the quaint great figure that men love,
The prairie-lawyer, master of us all.

He cannot sleep upon his hillside now.
He is among us:—as in times before!
And we who toss and lie awake for long
Breathe deep, and start, to see him pass the door.

His head is bowed. He thinks on men and kings.
Yea, when the sick world cries, how can he sleep?
Too many peasants fight, they know not why,
Too many homesteads in black terror weep.

The sins of all the war-lords burn his heart.
He sees the dreadnaughts scouring every main.
He carries on his shawl-wrapped shoulders now
The bitterness, the folly and the pain.

He cannot rest until a spirit-dawn
Shall come;—the shining hope of Europe free:
The league of sober folk, the Workers' Earth,
Bringing long peace to Cornland, Alp and Sea.

It breaks his heart that kings must murder still,
That all his hours of travail here for men
Seem yet in vain.  And who will bring white peace
That he may sleep upon his hill again?


## NIAGARA

### I

Within the town of Buffalo
Are prosy men with leaden eyes.
Like ants they worry to and fro
(Important men, in Buffalo).
But only twenty miles away
A deathless glory is at play:
Niagara, Niagara.

The women buy their lace and cry:—
"O such a delicate design,"
And over ostrich feathers sigh,
By counters there, in Buffalo.
The children haunt the trinket shops,
They buy false-faces, hells, and tops,
Forgetting great Niagara.

# NIAGARA

Within the town of Buffalo
Are stores with garnets, sapphires, pearls,
Rubies, emeralds aglow,—
Opal chains in Buffalo,
Cherished symbols of success.
They value not your rainbow dress:—
Niagara, Niagara.

The shaggy meaning of her name
This Buffalo, this recreant town,
Sharps and lawyers prune and tame;
Few pioneers in Buffalo;
Except young lovers flushed and fleet
And winds hallooing down the street:
"Niagara, Niagara."

The journalists are sick of ink:
Boy prodigals are lost in wine,
By night where white and red lights blink,
The eyes of Death, in Buffalo.
And only twenty miles away
Are starlit rocks and healing spray:—
Niagara, Niagara.

Above the town a tiny bird,
A shining speck at sleepy dawn,
Forgets the ant-hill so absurd,
This self-important Buffalo.
Descending twenty miles away
He bathes his wings at break of day—
Niagara, Niagara.

## II

*What marching men of Buffalo*
*Flood the streets in rash crusade?*
*Fools-to-free-the-world, they go,*
*Primeval hearts from Buffalo.*
*Red cataracts of France today*
*Awake, three thousand miles away*
*An echo of Niagara,*
*The cataract Niagara.*

# MAE MARSH, MOTION PICTURE ACTRESS

(In "Man's Genesis," "The Wild Girl of the Sierras," "The
Wharf Rat," "A Girl of the Paris Streets," etc.)

## I

The arts are old, old as the stones
From which man carved the sphinx austere.
Deep are the days the old arts bring:
Ten thousand years of yesteryear.

## II

She is madonna in an art
As wild and young as her sweet eyes:
A frail dew flower from this hot lamp
That is today's divine surprise.

Despite raw lights and gloating mobs
She is not seared: a picture still:

EPITAPHS FOR TWO PLAYERS

Rare silk the fine director's hand
May weave for magic if he will.

When ancient films have crumbled like
Papyrus rolls of Egypt's day,
Let the dust speak: "Her pride was high,
All but the artist hid away:

"Kin to the myriad artist clan
Since time began, whose work is dear."
The deep new ages come with her,
Tomorrow's years of yesteryear.

## EPITAPHS FOR TWO PLAYERS

### I. Edwin Booth

(An old actor at the Players' Club told me that Edwin
Booth first impersonated Hamlet when a barnstormer in
California. There were few theatres but the hotels were pro-
vided with crude assembly rooms for strolling players.)

The youth played in the blear hotel.
The rafters gleamed with glories strange.
And winds of mourning Elsinore
Howling at chance and fate and change;
Voices of old Europe's dead
Disturbed the new-built cattle-shed,
The street, the high and solemn range.

The while the coyote barked afar
All shadowy was the battlement.
The ranch-boys huddled and grew pale,
Youths who had come on riot bent.

Forgot were pranks well-planned to sting.
Behold there rose a ghostly king,
And veils of smoking Hell were rent.

When Edwin Booth played Hamlet, then
The camp-drab's tears could not but flow.
Then Romance lived and breathed and burned.
She felt the frail queen-mother's woe,
Thrilled for Ophelia, fond and blind,
And Hamlet, cruel, yet so kind,
And moaned, his proud words hurt her so.

A haunted place, though new and harsh!
The Indian and the Chinaman
And Mexican were fain to learn
What had subdued the Saxon clan.
Why did they mumble, brood, and stare
When the court-players curtsied fair
And the Gonzago scene began?

And ah, the duel scene at last!
They cheered their prince with stamping feet.
A death-fight in a palace! Yea,
With velvet hangings incomplete,
A pasteboard throne, a pasteboard crown,
And yet a monarch tumbled down,
A brave lad fought in splendor meet.

Was it a palace or a barn?
Immortal as the gods he flamed.
There, in his last great hour of rage,
His foil avenged a mother shamed.
In duty stern, in purpose deep
He drove that king to his black sleep
And died, all godlike and untamed.

* * * * * * *

I was not born in that far day.
I hear the tale from heads grown white.
And then I walk that earlier street,
The mining camp at candlelight.
I meet him wrapped in musings fine
Upon some whispering silvery line
He yet resolves to speak aright.


## II. EPITAPH FOR JOHN BUNNY, MOTION-PICTURE COMEDIAN

(In which he is remembered in similitude, by reference to
Yorick, the king's jester, who died when Hamlet and
Ophelia were children)

Yorick is dead.  Boy Hamlet walks forlorn
Beneath the battlements of Elsinore.
Where are those oddities and capers now
That used to "set the table on a roar"?

And do his bauble-bells beyond the clouds
Ring out, and shake with mirth the planets bright?
No doubt he brings the blessed dead good cheer,
But silence broods on Elsinore tonight.

That little elf, Ophelia, eight years old,
Upon her battered doll's staunch bosom weeps.
("O best of men, that wove glad fairy-tales.")
With tear-burned face, at last the darling sleeps.

Hamlet himself could not give cheer or help,
Though firm and brave, with his boy-face controlled.
For every game they started out to play
Yorick invented, in the days of old.

The times are out of joint! O cursed spite!
The noble jester Yorick comes no more.
And Hamlet hides his tears in boyish pride
By some lone turret-stair of Elsinore.


## HAMLET

(Remembering how Walker Whiteside played Hamlet in Chatterton's Old Opera House, thirty years ago)

Horatio took me to the cliff
Upon the edge of things
And said: "Behold a cataract
Of the thrones of old dream kings."
And I saw the thrones falling
From the high stars to the deep:
Red thrones, green thrones,
To everlasting sleep.
I saw crowns falling
From the zenith to the pit:
Crowns of man's mighty moods
And whims of little wit.
And all the birds of Elsinore
Flew round Horatio's head
And crying said:—
"Though all the crowns go down,
Hamlet, Hamlet, will never lose his crown."

Oh, monarchs muddled, stabbed and lost,
Who have no more to say:
Gone with Caesar, with the Czar,
And the Kaiser on his way!

60

# HAMLET

But now I see a student-prince
More real than all such kings,
Hamlet, home from Wittenberg,
And every bird sings:—
"Though all the crowns go down,
Hamlet, Hamlet, will never lose his crown."

Some of the dreams we saw dethroned
Were merely hopes of mine:—
One that a child might love me,
And give one leaf for a sign;
One dream I had in babyhood
That my rag-doll was alive;
One that I had in boyhood
That a sparrow, caged, would thrive.
One that I had for years and years
That my church held no disgrace.
One that I had but yesterday:—
Faith in Wisdom's face.

Oh, royal crowns, falling fast
From the days of boy's delight
The frost-bright time when first I made
A giant snow-man white.
And the time of my first Christmas tree,
My first Thanksgiving Day,
My first loud Independence dawn
When the cannon blazed away. . . .
Oh, high fantastic hours
That died like dog and clown,
Into the awful pit
We saw their crowns go down,
But Hamlet, Hamlet, will never lose his crown.

As sages walk with sages
On the proud Socratic way,

Hamlet struts with players
Till the world's last day.
With seeming shameless strollers
He swaggers his black cloak,
With a prince's glittering eye.
He spoils the townsmen's joke.
As I watch him and attend him
He compels them to give room,
And makes Fifth Street our battlement
Against the shades of doom.
With poetry, authority,
With every known pride
Hamlet stands with drawn sword,
His Gypsies at his side.

And all the gardens of the town
Are but Ophelia's flowers,
And all the shades of Elsinore
Fly round our Springfield towers;
And Hamlet kneels by all the hearts
That truly bleed or bloom,
As saints do stations of the cross
To Christ"'s white tomb.
And all the birds keep singing
To my heart bowed down:
"Hamlet, Hamlet, will never lose his crown."

## SPRINGFIELD MAGICAL

In this, the City of my Discontent,
Sometimes there comes a whisper from the grass,
"Romance, Romance—is here.  No Hindu town
Is quite so strange.  No Citadel of Brass
By Sinbad found, held half such love and hate;

## HOW A LITTLE GIRL SANG

No picture-palace in a picture-book
Such webs of Friendship, Beauty, Greed and Fate!"

In this, the City of my Discontent,
Down from the sky, up from the smoking deep
Wild legends new and old burn round my bed
While trees and grass and men are wrapped in sleep.
Angels come down, with Christmas in their hearts,
Gentle, whimsical, laughing, heaven-sent;
And, for a day, fair Peace have given me
In this, the City of my Discontent!


## HOW A LITTLE GIRL SANG

(Written for Mary Tiffany)

Ah, she was music in herself,
A symphony of joyousness.
She sang, she sang from finger tips,
From every tremble of her dress.
I saw sweet haunting harmony,
An ecstasy, an ecstasy,
In that strange curling of her lips,
That happy curling of her lips.
And quivering with melody
Those eyes I saw, that tossing head.

And so I saw what music was,
Tho' still accursed with ears of lead.

## HOW A LITTLE GIRL DANCED

(Dedicated to Lucy Bates)

(Being a reminiscence of certain private theatricals)
Oh, cabaret dancer, *I* know a dancer,
Whose eyes have not looked on the feasts that are vain.
*I* know a dancer, *I* know a dancer,
Whose soul has no bond with the beasts of the plain:
Judith the dancer, Judith the dancer,
With foot like the snow, and with step like the rain.

Oh, thrice-painted dancer, vaudeville dancer,
Sad in your spangles, with soul all astrain,
*I* know a dancer, *I* know a dancer,
Whose laughter and weeping are spiritual gain,
A pure-hearted, high-hearted maiden evangel,
With strength the dark cynical earth to disdain.

Flowers of bright Broadway, you of the chorus,
Who sing in the hope of forgetting your pain:
I turn to a sister of Sainted Cecilia,
A white bird escaping the earth's tangled skein:—
The music of God is her innermost brooding,
The whispering angels her footsteps sustain.

Oh, proud Russian dancer: praise for your dancing.
No clean human passion my rhyme would arraign.
You dance for Apollo with noble devotion,
A high cleansing revel to make the heart sane.
But Judith the dancer prays to a spirit
More white than Apollo and all of his train.

I know a dancer who finds the true Godhead,
Who bends o'er a brazier in Heaven's clear plain.

FOR ALL WHO EVER SENT LACE VALENTINES

I know a dancer, I know a dancer,
Who lifts us toward peace, from this earth that is vain:
Judith the dancer, Judith the dancer,
With foot like the snow, and with step like the rain.

## FOR ALL WHO EVER SENT LACE VALENTINES

The little-boy lover
And little-girl lover
Met the first time
At the house of a friend.
And great the respect
Of the little-boy lover.
The awe and the fear of her
Stayed to the end.

The little girl chattered,
Incessantly chattered,
Hardly would look
When he tried to be nice.
But deeply she trembled
The little girl lover,
Eaten with flame
While she tried to be ice.

The lion of loving,
The terrible lion,
Woke in the two
Long before they could wed.
The world said: "Child hearts
You must keep till the summer.
It is not allowed
That your hearts should be red."

If only a wizard,
A kindly gray wizard,
Had built them a house
In a cave underground.
With an emerald door,
And honey to eat!
But it seemed that no wizard
Was waiting around,
But it seemed that no wizard
Was waiting around.
The rarest of notions,
The rarest of passions
And hopes here below!
Many a child,
His young heart too timid
Has fled from his princess
No other to know.

I have seen them with faces
Like books out of Heaven,
With messages there
The harsh world should read,
The lions and roses and lilies of love,
Its tender, mystic, tyrannical need.

Were I god of the village
My servants should mate them.
Were I priest of the church
I would set them apart.
If the wide state were mine
It should live for such darlings,
And hedge with all shelter
The child-wedded heart.

# THE MOON'S THE NORTH WIND'S COOKY

## (*What the Little Girl Said*)

The Moon's the North Wind's cooky.
He bites it, day by day,
Until there's but a rim of scraps
That crumble all away.

The South Wind is a baker.
He kneads clouds in his den,
And bakes a crisp new moon *that . . . greedy*
*North . . . Wind . . . eats . . . again!*

# THE LITTLE TURTLE

## (A Recitation for Martha Wakefield, Three Years Old)

There was a little turtle.
He lived in a box.
He swam in a puddle.
He climbed on the rocks.

He snapped at a mosquito.
He snapped at a flea.
He snapped at a minnow.
And he snapped at me.

He caught the mosquito.
He caught the flea.
He caught the minnow.
But he didn't catch me.

# YET GENTLE WILL THE GRIFFIN BE

## (*What Grandpa Told the Children*)

The moon? It is a griffin's egg,
Hatching to-morrow night.
And how the little boys will watch
With shouting and delight
To see him break the shell and stretch
And creep across the sky.
The boys will laugh. The little girls,
I fear, may hide and cry.
Yet gentle will the griffin be,
Most decorous and fat,
And walk up to the Milky Way
And lap it like a' cat.


# THE SUN SAYS HIS PRAYERS

"The sun says his prayers," said the fairy,
Or else he would wither and die.
"The sun says his prayers," said the fairy,
"For strength to climb up through the sky.
He leans on invisible angels,
And Faith is his prop and his rod.
The sky is his crystal cathedral.
And dawn is his altar to God."


# THE SHIELD OF FAITH

The full moon is the Shield of Faith:
    As long as it shall rise,

68

## THE LEADEN-EYED

I know that Mystery comes again,
  That Wonder never dies.

I know that Shadow has its place,
  That Noon is not our goal,
That Heaven has non-official hours
  To soothe and mend the soul;

That witchcraft can be angel-craft
  And wizard deeds sublime;
That utmost darkness bears a flower,
  Though long the budding-time.


## LOVE AND LAW

True Love is founded in rocks of Remembrance
In stones of Forbearance and mortar of Pain.
The workman lays wearily granite on granite,
And bleeds for his castle 'mid sunshine and rain.

Love is not velvet, not all of it velvet,
Not all of it banners, not gold-leaf alone.
'Tis stern as the ages and old as Religion.
With Patience its watchword, and Law for its throne.


## THE LEADEN-EYED

Let not young souls be smothered out before
  They do quaint deeds and fully flaunt their pride.
It is the world's one crime its babes grow dull,
  Its poor are ox-like, limp and leaden-eyed.

Not that they starve, but starve so dreamlessly,
Not that they sow, but that they seldom reap,
Not that they serve, but have no gods to serve,
Not that they die but that they die like sheep.


## THE TRAVELLER-HEART

(To a Man who maintained that the Mausoleum is the
Stateliest Possible Manner of Interment)

I would be one with the dark, dark earth:—
Follow the plow with a yokel tread.
I would be part of the Indian corn,
Walking the rows with the plumes o'erhead.

I would be one with the lavish earth,
Eating the bee-stung apples red:
Walking where lambs walk on the hills;
By oak-grove paths to the pools be led.

I would be one with the dark-bright night
When sparkling skies and the lightning wed—
Walking on with the vicious wind
By roads whence even the dogs have fled.

I would be one with the sacred earth
On to the end, till I sleep with the dead.
Terror shall put no spears through me.
Peace shall jewel my shroud instead.

I shall be one with all pit-black things
Finding their lowering threat unsaid:
Stars for my pillow there in the gloom,—
Oak-roots arching about my head!

Stars, like daisies, shall rise through the earth,
Acorns fall round my breast that bled.
Children shall weave there a flowery chain,
Squirrels on acorn-hearts be fed:—

Fruit of the traveller-heart of me,
Fruit of my harvest-songs long sped:
Sweet with the life of my sunburned days,
When the sheaves were ripe, and the apples red.

## A GOSPEL OF BEAUTY

*I recited these three poems more than any others in my
mendicant preaching tour through the West. Taken as a
triad, they hold in solution my theory of American civilization.*

### I. THE PROUD FARMER

#### (In memory of E. S. Frazee, Rush County, Indiana)

Into the acres of the newborn state
He poured his strength, and plowed his ancient name,
And, when the traders followed him, he stood
Towering above their furtive souls and tame.

That brow without a stain, that fearless eye
Oft left the passing stranger wondering
To find such knighthood in the sprawling land,
To see a democrat well-nigh a king.

He lived with liberal hand, with guests from far,
With talk and joke and fellowship to spare,—
Watching the wide world's life from sun to sun,
Lining his walls with books from everywhere.

71

He read by night, he built his world by day.
The farm and house of God to him were one.
For forty years he preached and plowed and wrought—
A statesman in the fields, who bent to none.

His plowmen-neighbors were as lords to him.
His was an ironside, democratic pride.
He served a rigid Christ, but served him well—
And, for a lifetime, saved the countryside.

Here lie the dead, who gave the church their best
Under his fiery preaching of the word.
They sleep with him beneath the ragged grass . . .
The village withers, by his voice unstirred.

And tho' his tribe be scattered to the wind
From the Atlantic to the China Sea,
Yet do they think of that bright lamp he burned
Of family worth and proud integrity.

And many a sturdy grandchild hears his name
In reverence spoken, till he feels akin
To all the lion-eyed who build the world—
And lion-dreams begin to burn within.


## II. THE ILLINOIS VILLAGE

O you who lose the art of hope,
Whose temples seem to shrine a lie,
Whose sidewalks are but stones of fear,
Who weep that Liberty must die,
Turn to the little prairie towns,
Your higher hope shall yet begin.
On every side awaits you there
Some gate where glory enters in.

Yet when I see the flocks of girls,
Watching the Sunday train go thro'
(As tho' the whole wide world went by)
With eyes that long to travel too,
I sigh, despite my soul made glad
By cloudy dresses and brown hair,
Sigh for the sweet life wrenched and torn
By thundering commerce, fierce and bare.
Nymphs of the wheat these girls should be:
Kings of the grove, their lovers, strong.
Why are they not inspired, aflame?
This beauty calls for valiant song—
For men to carve these fairy-forms
And faces in a fountain-frieze;
Dancers that own immortal hours;
Painters that work upon their knees;
Maids, lovers, friends, so deep in life,
So deep in love and poet's deeds,
The railroad is a thing disowned,
The city but a field of weeds.

Who can pass a village church
By night in these clean prairie lands
Without a touch of Spirit-power?
So white and fixed and cool it stands—
A thing from some strange fairy-town,
A pious amaranthine flower,
Unsullied by the winds, as pure
As jade or marble, wrought this hour:—
Rural in form, foursquare and plain,
And yet our sister, the new moon,
Makes it a praying wizard's dream.
The trees that watch at dusty noon
Breaking its sharpest lines, veil not
The whiteness it reflects from God,

Flashing like Spring on many an eye,
Making clean flesh, that once was clod.

Who can pass a district school
Without the hope that there may wait
Some baby-heart the books shall flame
With zeal to make his playmates great,
To make the whole wide village gleam
A strangely carved celestial gem,
Eternal in its beauty-light,
The Artist's town of Bethlehem!

### III. ON THE BUILDING OF SPRINGFIELD

Let not our town be large, remembering
That little Athens was the Muses' home,
That Oxford rules the heart of London still,
That Florence gave the Renaissance to Rome.

Record it for the grandson of your son—
A city is not builded in a day:
Our little town cannot complete her soul
Till countless generations pass away.

Now let each child be joined as to a church
To her perpetual hopes, each man ordained:
Let every street be made a reverent aisle
Where Music grows and Beauty is unchained.

Let Science and Machinery and Trade
Be slaves of her, and make her all in all,
Building against our blatant, restless time
An unseen, skilful, medieval wall.

74

## ON THE BUILDING OF SPRINGFIELD

Let every citizen be rich toward God.
Let Christ the beggar, teach divinity.
Let no man rule who holds his money dear.
Let this, our city, be our luxury.

We should build parks that students from afar
Would choose to starve in, rather than go home,
Fair little squares, with Phidian ornament,
Food for the spirit, milk and honeycomb.

Songs shall be sung by us in that good day,
Songs we have written, blood within the rhyme
Beating, as when Old England still was glad,—
The purple, rich Elizabethan time.

.   .   .   .   .   .   .   .   .   .

Say, is my prophecy too fair and far?
I only know, unless her faith be high,
The soul of this, our Nineveh, is doomed,
Our little Babylon will surely die.

Some city on the breast of Illinois
No wiser and no better at the start
By faith shall rise redeemed, by faith shall rise
Bearing the western glory in her heart.

The genius of the Maple, Elm and Oak,
The secret hidden in each grain of corn,
The glory that the prairie angels sing
At night when sons of Life and Love are born,

Born but to struggle, squalid and alone,
Broken and wandering in their early years.
When will they make our dusty streets their goal,
Within our attics hide their sacred tears?

When will they start our vulgar blood athrill
With living language, words that set us free?
When will they make a path of beauty clear
Between our riches and our liberty?

We must have many Lincoln-hearted men.
A city is not builded in a day.
And they must do their work, and come and go,
While countless generations pass away.


## THE FLUTE OF THE LONELY

(To the tune of "Gaily the Troubadour")

Faintly the ne'er-do-well
Breathed through his flute:
All the tired neighbor-folk,
Hearing, were mute.
In their neat doorways sat,
Labors all done,
Helpless, relaxed, o'er-wrought,
Evening begun.

None of them there beguiled
Work-thoughts away,
Like to this reckless, wild
Loafer by day.
(Weeds in his flowers upgrown!
Fences awry!
Rubbish and bottles heaped!
Yard like a sty!)

There in his lonely door,
Leering and lean,

76

Staggering, liquor-stained,
Outlawed, obscene——
Played he his moonlight thought,
Mastered his flute.
All the tired neighbor-folk,
Hearing, were mute.
None but he, in that block,
Knew such a tune.
All loved the strain, and all
*Looked at the moon!*


## THE BRONCHO THAT WOULD NOT BE BROKEN

A little colt—broncho, loaned to the farm
To be broken in time without fury or harm,
Yet black crows flew past you, shouting alarm,
Calling "Beware," with lugubrious singing . . .
The butterflies there in the bush were romancing,
The smell of the grass caught your soul in a trance,
So why be a-fearing the spurs and the traces,
O broncho that would not be broken of dancing?

You were born with the pride of the lords great and olden
Who danced, through the ages, in corridors golden.
In all the wide farm-place the person most human.
You spoke out so plainly with squealing and capering,
With whinnying, snorting contorting and prancing,
As you dodged your pursuers, looking askance,
With Greek-footed figures, and Parthenon paces,
O broncho that would not be broken of dancing.

The grasshoppers cheered. "Keep whirling," they said.
The insolent sparrows called from the shed

77

"If men will not laugh, make them wish they were dead."
But arch were your thoughts, all malice displacing,
Though the horse-killers came, with snake-whips advancing.
You bantered and cantered away your last chance.
And they scourged you, with Hell in their speech and their
    faces,
O broncho that would not be broken of dancing.

"Nobody cares for you," rattled the crows,
As you dragged the whole reaper, next day, down the rows.
The three mules held back, yet you danced on your toes.
You pulled like a racer, and kept the mules chasing.
You tangled the harness with bright eyes side-glancing,
While the drunk driver bled you—a pole for a lance—
And the giant mules bit at you—keeping their places.
O broncho that would not be broken of dancing.

In that last afternoon your boyish heart broke.
The hot wind came down like a sledge-hammer stroke.
The blood-sucking flies to a rare feast awoke.
And they searched out your wounds, your death-warrant
    tracing.
And the merciful men, their religion enhancing,
Stopped the red reaper, to give you a chance.
Then you died on the prairie, and scorned all disgraces,
O broncho that would not be broken of dancing.

SOUVENIR OF GREAT BEND, KANSAS.


## THE GHOST OF THE BUFFALOES

Last night at black midnight I woke with a cry,
The windows were shaking, there was thunder on high,
The floor was atremble, the door was ajar,
White fires, crimson fires, shone from afar.

78

# THE GHOST OF THE BUFFALOES

I rushed to the dooryard.   The city was gone.
My home was a hut without orchard or lawn.
It was mud-smear and logs near a whispering stream,
Nothing else built by man could I see in my dream . . .
Then . . .
Ghost-kings came headlong, row upon row,
Gods of the Indians, torches aglow.

They mounted the bear and the elk and the deer,
And eagles gigantic, aged and sere,
They rode long-horn cattle, they cried "A-la-la."
They lifted the knife, the bow, and the spear,
They lifted ghost-torches from dead fires below,
The midnight made grand with the cry "A-la-la."
The midnight made grand with a red-god charge,
A red-god show,
A red-god show,
"A-la-la, a-la-la, a-la-la, a-la-la."

With bodies like bronze, and terrible eyes
Came the rank and the file, with catamount cries,
Gibbering, yipping, with hollow-skull clacks,
Riding white bronchos with skeleton backs,
Scalp-hunters, beaded and spangled and bad,
Naked and lustful and foaming and mad,
Flashing primeval demoniac scorn,
Blood-thirst and pomp amid darkness reborn,
Power and glory that sleep in the grass
While the winds and the snows and the great rains pass.
They crossed the gray river, thousands abreast,
They rode in infinite lines to the west,
Tide upon tide of strange fury and foam,
Spirits and wraiths, the blue was their home,
The sky was their goal where the star-flags were furled,
And on past those far golden splendors they whirled.

They burned to dim meteors, lost in the deep.
And I turned in dazed wonder, thinking of sleep.

And the wind crept by
Alone, unkempt, unsatisfied,
The wind cried and cried—
Muttered of massacres long past,
Buffaloes in shambles vast . . .
An owl said: "Hark, what is a-wing?"
I heard a cricket carolling,
I heard a cricket carolling,
I heard a cricket carolling.

Then . . .
Snuffing the lightning that crashed from on high
Rose royal old buffaloes, row upon row.
The lords of the prairie came galloping by.
And I cried in my heart "A-la-la, a-la-la,
A red-god show,
A red-god show,
A-la-la, a-la-la, a-la-la, a-la-la."

Buffaloes, buffaloes, thousands abreast,
A scourge and amazement, they swept to the west.
With black bobbing noses, with red rolling tongues,
Coughing forth steam from their leather-wrapped lungs,
Cows with their calves, bulls big and vain,
Goring the laggards, shaking the mane,
Stamping flint feet, flashing moon eyes.
Pompous and owlish, shaggy and wise.
Like sea-cliffs and caves resounded their ranks
With shoulders like waves, and undulant flanks.
Tide upon tide of strange fury and foam,
Spirits and wraiths, the blue was their home,
The sky was their goal where the star-flags are furled,
And on past those far golden splendors they whirled.

## THE GHOST OF THE BUFFALOES

They burned to dim meteors, lost in the deep,
And I turned in dazed wonder, thinking of sleep.

I heard a cricket's cymbals play,
A scarecrow lightly flapped his rags,
And a pan that hung by his shoulder rang,
Rattled and thumped in a listless way,
And now the wind in the chimney sang,
The wind in the chimney,
The wind in the chimney,
The wind in the chimney,
  Seemed to say:—
"Dream, boy, dream,
If you anywise can.
To dream is the work
Of beast or man.
Life is the west-going dream-storms' breath,
Life is a dream, the sigh of the skies,
The breath of the stars, that nod on their pillows
With their golden hair mussed over their eyes."
The locust played on his musical wing,
Sang to his mate of love's delight.
I heard the whippoorwill's soft fret.
I heard a cricket carolling,
I heard a cricket carolling,
I heard a cricket say: "Good-night, good-night,
Good-night, good-night, . . . good-night."

  .    .    .    .    .    .    .    .    .

## IN PRAISE OF JOHNNY APPLESEED *

### (Born 1775; died 1847)

### I. OVER THE APPALACHIAN BARRICADE

In the days of President Washington,
The glory of the nations,
Dust and ashes,
Snow and sleet,
And hay and oats and wheat,
Blew west,
Crossed the Appalachians,

*To be read
like old leaves
on the elm
tree of Time,
Sifting soft
winds with
sentence and
rhyme.*

Found the glades of rotting leaves, the soft deer-pastures,
The farms of the far-off future
In the forest.
Colts jumped the fence,
Snorting, ramping, snapping, sniffing,
With gastronomic calculations,
Crossed the Appalachians,
The east walls of our citadel,
And turned to gold-horned unicorns,
Feasting in the dim, volunteer farms of the forest.
Stripedest, kickingest kittens escaped,
Caterwauling "Yankee Doodle Dandy."
Renounced their poor relations,
Crossed the Appalachians,
And turned to tiny tigers
In the humorous forest.
Chickens escaped
From farmyard congregations,

* The best account of John Chapman's career, under the name
"Johnny Appleseed," is to be found in *Harper's Monthly Magazine*,
November, 1871.

# IN PRAISE OF JOHNNY APPLESEED

Crossed the Appalachians,
And turned to amber trumpets
On the ramparts of our Hoosiers' nest and citadel,
Millennial heralds
Of the foggy mazy forest.
Pigs broke loose, scrambled west,
Scorned their loathsome stations,
Crossed the Appalachians,
Turned to roaming, foaming wild boars
Of the forest.
The smallest, blindest puppies toddled west
While their eyes were coming open,
And, with misty observations,
Crossed the Appalachians,
Barked, barked, barked
At the glow-worms and the marsh lights and the lightning
    bugs,
And turned to ravening wolves
Of the forest.
Crazy parrots and canaries flew west,
Drunk on May-time revelations,
Crossed the Appalachians,
And turned to delirious, flower-dressed fairies
Of the lazy forest.
Haughtiest swans and peacocks swept west,
And, despite soft derivations,
Crossed the Appalachians,
And turned to blazing warrior souls
Of the forest,
Singing the ways
Of the Ancient of Days.
And the "Old Continentals
In their ragged regimentals,"
With bard's imaginations,
Crossed the Appalachians.

And
A boy
Blew west,
And with prayers and incantations,
And with "Yankee Doodle Dandy,"
Crossed the Appalachians,
And was "young John Chapman,"
Then
"Johnny Appleseed, Johnny Appleseed,"
Chief of the fastnesses, dappled and vast,
In a pack on his back,
In a deer-hide sack,
The beautiful orchards of the past,
The ghosts of all the forests and the groves—
In that pack on his back,
In that talisman sack,
To-morrow's peaches, pears, and cherries,
To-morrow's grapes and red raspberries,
Seeds and tree-souls, precious things,
Feathered with microscopic wings,
All the outdoors the child heart knows,
And the apple, green, red, and white,
Sun of his day and his night—
The apple allied to the thorn,
Child of the rose.
Porches untrod of forest houses
All before him, all day long,
"Yankee Doodle" his marching song;
And the evening breeze
Joined his psalms of praise
As he sang the ways
Of the Ancient of Days.
Leaving behind august Virginia,
Proud Massachusetts, and proud Maine,
Planting the trees that would march and train

# IN PRAISE OF JOHNNY APPLESEED

On, in his name to the great Pacific,
Like Birnam wood to Dunsinane,
Johnny Appleseed swept on,
Every shackle gone,
Loving every sloshy brake,
Loving every skunk and snake,
Loving every leathery weed,
Johnny Appleseed, Johnny Appleseed,
Master and ruler of the unicorn-ramping forest,
The tiger-mewing forest,
The rooster-trumpeting, boar-foaming, wolf-ravening forest,
The spirit-haunted, fairy-enchanted forest,
Stupendous and endless,
Searching its perilous ways
In the name of the Ancient of Days.


## II. THE INDIANS WORSHIP HIM, BUT HE HURRIES ON

Painted kings in the midst of the clearing
Heard him asking his friends the eagles
To guard each planted seed and seedling.
Then he was a god, to the red man's dreaming;
Then the chiefs brought treasures grotesque and fair,—
Magical trinkets and pipes and guns,
Beads and furs from their medicine-lair,—
Stuck holy feathers in his hair.
Hailed him with austere delight.
The orchard god was their guest through the night.

While the late snow blew from bleak Lake Erie,
Scourging rock and river and reed,
All night long they made great medicine
For Jonathan Chapman,
Johnny Appleseed,

Johnny Appleseed;
And as though his heart were a wind-blown wheat-sheaf,
As though his heart were a new built nest,
As though their heaven house were his breast,
In swept the snowbirds singing glory.
And I hear his bird heart beat its story,
Hear yet how the ghost of the forest shivers,
Hear yet the cry of the gray, old orchards,
Dim and decaying by the rivers,
And the timid wings of the bird-ghosts beating,
And the ghosts of the tom-toms beating, beating.

But he left their wigwams and their love.
By the hour of dawn he was proud and stark,
Kissed the Indian babes with a sigh,
Went forth to live on roots and bark,
Sleep in the trees, while the years howled by.
Calling the catamounts by name,
And buffalo bulls no hand could tame.
Slaying never a living creature,
Joining the birds in every game,
With the gorgeous turkey gobblers mocking,
With the lean-necked eagles boxing and shouting;
Sticking their feathers in his hair,—
Turkey feathers,
Eagle feathers,
Trading hearts with all beasts and weathers
He swept on, winged and wonder-crested,
Bare-armed, barefooted, and bare-breasted.
The maples, shedding their spinning seeds,
Called to his appleseeds in the ground,
Vast chestnut-trees, with their butterfly na-
    tions,
Called to his seeds without a sound.

*While you read, hear the hoof-beats of deer in the snow. And see, by their track, bleeding footprints we know.*

*While you read, see conventions of deer go by. The bucks toss their*

86

And the chipmunk turned a "summerset." *horns, the*
And the foxes danced the Virginia reel; *fuzzy fawns*
Hawthorne and crab-thorn bent, rain-wet, *fly.*
And dropped their flowers in his night-black hair;
And the soft fawns stopped for his perorations;
And his black eyes shone through the forest-gleam,
And he plunged young hands into new-turned earth,
And prayed dear orchard boughs into birth;
And he ran with the rabbit and slept with the stream.
And he ran with the rabbit and slept with the stream,
And he ran with the rabbit and slept with the stream.
And so for us he made great medicine,
And so for us he made great medicine,
And so for us he made great medicine.
In the days of President Washington.


### III. JOHNNY APPLESEED'S OLD AGE

Long, long after,
When settlers put up beam and rafter,
They asked of the birds: "Who gave this fruit?
Who watched this fence till the seeds took root?
Who gave these boughs?" They asked the
    sky,
And there was no reply. *To be read*
But the robin might have said, *like faint*
    *hoof-beats*
"To the farthest West he has followed the sun, *of fawns*
His life and his empire just begun." *long gone*
Self-scourged, like a monk, with a throne for *From re-*
    wages, *spectable*
    *pasture, and*
Stripped, like the iron-souled Hindu sages, *park and*
Draped like a statue, in strings like a scare- *lawn,*
    crow, *And heart-*

His helmet-hat an old tin pan,
But worn in the love of the heart of man,
More sane than the helm of Tamerlane!
Hairy Ainu, wild man of Borneo, Robinson
    Crusoe—Johnny Appleseed!
And the robin might have said,
"Sowing, he goes to the far, new West,
With the apple, the sun of his burning
    breast—
The apple allied to the thorn,
Child of the rose."

*beats of
fawns that
are coming
again
When the
forest, once
more, is the
master of
men.*

Washington buried in Virginia,
Jackson buried in Tennessee,
Young Lincoln, brooding in Illinois,
And Johnny Appleseed, priestly and free,
Knotted and gnarled, past seventy years,
Still planted on in the woods alone.
Ohio and young Indiana—
These were his wide altar-stone,
Where still he burnt out flesh and bone.
Twenty days ahead of the Indian, twenty years ahead of the
    white man,
At last the Indian overtook him, at last the Indian hurried
    past him;
At last the white man overtook him, at last the white man
    hurried past him;
At last his own trees overtook him, at last his own trees
    hurried past him.
Many cats were tame again,
Many ponies tame again,
Many pigs were tame again,
Many canaries tame again;
And the real frontier was his sunburnt breast.

# IN PRAISE OF JOHNNY APPLESEED

From the fiery core of that apple, the earth,
Sprang apple-amaranths divine.
Love's orchards climbed to the heavens of the West,
And snowed the earthly sod with flowers.
Farm hands from the terraces of the blest
Danced on the mists with their ladies fine;
And Johnny Appleseed laughed with his dreams,
And swam once more the ice-cold streams.
And the doves of the spirit swept through the hours,
With doom-calls, love-calls, death-calls, dream-calls;
And Johnny Appleseed, all that year,
Lifted his hands to the farm-filled sky,
To the apple-harvesters busy on high;
And so once more his youth began,
And so for us he made great medicine—
Johnny Appleseed, medicine-man.
Then
The sun was their turned-up broken barrel,
Out of which their juicy apples rolled,
Down the repeated terraces,
Thumping across the gold,
An angel in each apple that touched the forest mold,
A ballot-box in each apple,
A state capital in each apple,
Great high schools, great colleges,
All America in each apple,
Each red, rich, round, and bouncing moon
That touched the forest mold.
Like scrolls and rolled-up flags of silk,
He saw the fruits unfold,
And all our expectations in one wild-flower written dream.
Confusion, and death-sweetness, and a thicket of crab-thorns!
Heart of a hundred midnights, heart of the merciful morns.
Heaven's boughs bent down with their alchemy.

Perfumed airs, and thoughts of wonder.
And the dew on the grass and his own cold tears
Were one in brooding mystery,
Though death's loud thunder came upon him,
Though death's loud thunder struck him down—
The boughs and the proud thoughts swept through the thun-
    der,
Till he saw our wide nation, each State a flower,
Each petal a park for holy feet,
With wild fawns merry on every street,
With wild fawns merry on every street,
The vista of ten thousand years, flower-lighted and complete.

Hear the lazy weeds murmuring, bays and rivers whispering,
From Michigan to Texas, California to Maine;
Listen to the eagles screaming, calling,
"Johnny Appleseed, Johnny Appleseed,"
There by the doors of old Fort Wayne.

In the four-poster bed Johnny Appleseed built,
Autumn rains were the curtains, autumn leaves were the
    quilt.
He laid him down sweetly, and slept through the night,
Like a stone washed white,
There by the doors of old Fort Wayne.


## THE STATUE OF OLD ANDREW JACKSON

When the statue of Andrew Jackson before the White
House in Washington is removed, America is doomed. The
nobler days of America's innocence, in which it was set up,
always have a special tang for those who are tasty. But this
is not all. It is only the America that has the courage of
her complete past that can hold up her head in the world of
the artists, priests and sages. It is for us to put the iron

dog and deer back upon the lawn, the John Rogers group back into the parlor, and get new inspiration from these and from Andrew Jackson ramping in bronze replica in New Orleans, Nashville and Washington, and add to them a sense of humor, till it becomes a sense of beauty that will resist the merely dulcet and affettuoso.

Please read Lorado Taft's *History of American Sculpture,* pages 123-127, with these matters in mind. I quote a few bits:

". . . The maker of the first equestrian statue in the history of American sculpture: Clark Mills. . . . Never having seen General Jackson or an equestrian statue, he felt himself incompetent . . . the incident, however, made an impression on his mind, and he reflected sufficiently to produce a design which was the very one subsequently executed. . . . Congress appropriated the old cannon captured by General Jackson. . . . Having no notion, nor even suspicion of a dignified sculptural treatment of a theme, the clever carpenter felt, nevertheless, the need of a feature. . . . He built a colossal horse, adroitly balanced on the hind legs, and America gazed with bated breath. Nobody knows or cares whether the rider looks like Jackson or not.

"The extraordinary pose of the horse absorbs all attention, all admiration. There may be some subconscious feeling of respect for a rider who holds on so well. . . ."

(Written while America was in the midst of the war with Germany, August, 1918.)


Andrew Jackson was eight feet tall.
His arm was a hickory limb and a maul.
His sword was so long he dragged it on the ground.
Every friend was an equal. Every foe was a hound.

Andrew Jackson was a Democrat,
Defying kings in his old cocked hat.

His vast steed rocked like a hobby-horse.
But he sat straight up.  He held his course.

He licked the British at Noo Orleans;
Beat them out of their elegant jeans.
He piled the cotton-bales twenty feet high,
And he snorted "freedom," and it flashed from his eye.

And the American Eagle swooped through the air,
And cheered when he heard the Jackson swear:—
"By the Eternal, let them come.
Sound Yankee Doodle.  Let the bullets hum."

And his wild men, straight from the woods, fought on
Till the British fops were dead and gone.

And now old Andrew Jackson fights
To set the sad big world to rights.
He joins the British and the French.
He cheers up the Italian trench.
He's making Democrats of these,
And freedom's sons of Japanese.
His hobby horse will gallop on
Till all the infernal Huns are gone.

Yes,
Yes,
Yes!
By the Eternal!
Old Andrew Jackson!

## JOHN L. SULLIVAN, THE STRONG BOY OF BOSTON

(Inscribed to Louis Untermeyer and Robert Frost)

When I was nine years old, in 1889,
I sent my love a lacy Valentine.
Suffering boys were dressed like Fauntleroys,
While Judge and Puck in giant humor vied.
The Gibson Girl came shining like a bride
To spoil the cult of Tennyson's Elaine.
Louisa Alcott was my gentle guide. . . .
Then . . .
I heard a battle trumpet sound.
Nigh New Orleans
Upon an emerald plain
John L. Sullivan
The strong boy
Of Boston
Fought seventy-five red rounds with Jake Kilrain.

In simple sheltered 1889
Nick Carter I would piously deride.
Over the Elsie Books I moped and sighed.
St. Nicholas Magazine was all my pride,
While coarser boys on cellar doors would slide.
The grown-ups bought refinement by the pound.
Rogers groups had not been told to hide.
E. P. Roe had just begun to wane.
Howells was rising, surely to attain!
The nation for a jamboree was gowned.—
Her hundredth year of roaring freedom crowned.
The British Lion ran and hid from Blaine
The razzle-dazzle hip-hurrah from Maine.
The mocking bird was singing in the lane. . . .
Yet . . .

*"East side, west side, all around the town*
*The tots sang: 'Ring a rosie—'*
*'London Bridge is falling down.' "*
And . . .
John L. Sullivan
The strong boy
Of Boston
Broke every single rib of Jake Kilrain.

*To be sung.*
*Let the*
*audience join*
*in softly on*
*this tune,*
*wherever it*
*appears.*

In dear provincial 1889,
Barnum's bears and tigers could astound.
Ingersoll was called a most vile hound,
And named with Satan, Judas, Thomas Paine!
Robert Elsmere riled the pious brain.
Phillips Brooks for heresy was fried.
Boston Brahmins patronized Mark Twain.
The baseball rules were changed.   That was a gain.
Pop Anson was our darling, pet and pride.
Native sons in Irish votes were drowned.
Tammany once more escaped its chain.
Once more each raw saloon was raising Cain.
The mocking bird was singing in the lane. . . .
Yet . . .
"East side, west side, all around the town
The tots sang: 'Ring a rosie'
'London Bridge is falling down.' "
And . . .
John L. Sullivan
The strong boy
Of Boston
Finished the ring career of Jake Kilrain.

In mystic, ancient 1889,
Wilson with pure learning was allied.
Roosevelt gave forth a chirping sound.
Stanley found old Emin and his train.

94

Stout explorers sought the pole in vain.
To dream of flying proved a man insane.
The newly rich were bathing in champagne.
Van Bibber Davis, at a single bound
Displayed himself, and simpering glory found.
John J. Ingalls, like a lonely crane
Swore and swore, and stalked the Kansas plain.
The Cronin murder was the ages' stain.
Johnstown was flooded, and the whole world cried.
We heard not of Louvain nor of Lorraine,
Or a million heroes for their freedom slain.
Of Armageddon and the world's birth-pain—
The League of Nations, the new world allied,
With Wilson, crucified, then justified.
We *thought* the world would loaf and sprawl and mosey.
The gods of Yap and Swat were sweetly dozy.
We *thought* the far-off gods of Chow had died.
The mocking bird was singing in the lane. . . .
Yet . . .
"East side, west side, all around the town
The tots sang: 'Ring a rosie'
'London Bridge is Falling Down.' "
And . . .
John L. Sullivan knocked out Jake Kilrain.


## THE EAGLE THAT IS FORGOTTEN

### (John P. Altgeld. Born December 30, 1847; died March 12, 1902)

Sleep softly . . . eagle forgotten . . . under the stone.
Time has its way with you there, and the clay has its own.

"We have buried him now," thought your foes, and in secret
rejoiced.
They made a brave show of their mourning, their hatred
unvoiced.

They had snarled at you, barked at you, foamed at you day
    after day.
Now you were ended. They praised you, . . . and laid you
    away.

The others that mourned you in silence and terror and truth,
The widow bereft of her crust, and the boy without youth,
The mocked and the scorned and the wounded, the lame
    and the poor
'That should have remembered forever, . . . remember no
    more.

Where are those lovers of yours, on what name do they call
The lost, that in armies wept over your funeral pall?
They call on the names of a hundred high-valiant ones,
A hundred white eagles have risen the sons of your sons,
The zeal in their wings is a zeal that your dreaming began
The valor that wore out your soul in the service of man.

Sleep softly, . . . eagle forgotten, . . . under the stone,
Time has its way with you there and the clay has its own.
Sleep on, O brave-hearted, O wise man, that kindled the
    flame—
To live in mankind is far more than to live in a name,
To live in mankind, far, far more . . . than to live in a
    name.


## BRYAN, BRYAN, BRYAN, BRYAN

### THE CAMPAIGN OF EIGHTEEN NINETY-SIX, AS VIEWED AT THE TIME BY A SIXTEEN-YEAR-OLD, ETC.

### I

In a nation of one hundred fine, mob-hearted, lynching,
    relenting, repenting millions,

# BRYAN, BRYAN, BRYAN, BRYAN

There are plenty of sweeping, swinging, stinging, gorgeous
    things to shout about,
And knock your old blue devils out.

I brag and chant of Bryan, Bryan, Bryan,
Candidate for president who sketched a silver Zion,
The one American Poet who could sing outdoors,
He brought in tides of wonder, of unprecedented splendor,
Wild roses from the plains, that made hearts tender,
All the funny circus silks
Of politics unfurled,
Bartlett pears of romance that were honey at the cores,
And torchlights down the street, to the end of the world.

There were truths eternal in the gab and tittle-tattle.
There were real heads broken in the fustian and the rattle.
There were real lines drawn:
Not the silver and the gold,
But Nebraska's cry went eastward against the dour and old,
The mean and cold.

It was eighteen ninety-six, and I was just sixteen
And Altgeld ruled in Springfield, Illinois,
When there came from the sunset Nebraska's shout of joy:
In a coat like a deacon, in a black Stetson hat
He scourged the elephant plutocrats
With barbed wire from the Platte.
The scales dropped from their mighty eyes.
They saw that summer's noon
A tribe of wonders coming
To a marching tune.

Oh, the longhorns from Texas,
The jay hawks from Kansas,
The plop-eyed bungaroo and giant giassicus,
The varmint, chipmunk, bugaboo,

The horned-toad, prairie-dog and ballyhoo,
From all the newborn states arow,
Bidding the eagles of the west fly on,
Bidding the eagles of the west fly on.
The fawn, prodactyl and thing-a-ma-jig,
The rakaboor, the hellangone,
The whangdoodle, batfowl and pig,
The coyote, wild-cat and grizzly in a glow,
In a miracle of health and speed, the whole breed abreast,
They leaped the Mississippi, blue border of the West,
From the Gulf to Canada, two thousand miles long:—
Against the towns of Tubal Cain,
Ah,—sharp was their song.
Against the ways of Tubal Cain, too cunning for the young,
The longhorn calf, the buffalo and wampus gave tongue,.

These creatures were defending things Mark Hanna never
    dreamed:
The moods of airy childhood that in desert dews gleamed,
The gossamers and whimsies,
The monkeyshines and didoes
Rank and strange
Of the canyons and the range,
The ultimate fantastics
Of the far western slope,
And of prairie schooner children
Born beneath the stars,
Beneath falling snows,
Of the babies born at midnight
In the sod huts of lost hope,
With no physician there,
Except a Kansas prayer,
With the Indian raid a howling through the air.

And all these in their helpless days
By the dour East oppressed,

Mean paternalism
Making their mistakes for them,
Crucifying half the West,
Till the whole Atlantic coast
Seemed a giant spiders' nest.

And these children and their sons
At last rode through the cactus,
A cliff of mighty cowboys
On the lope,
With gun and rope.
And all the way to frightened Maine the old East heard
  them call,
And saw our Bryan by a mile lead the wall
Of men and whirling flowers and beasts,
The bard and the prophet of them all.
Prairie avenger, mountain lion,
Bryan, Bryan, Bryan, Bryan,
Gigantic troubadour, speaking like a siege gun,
Smashing Plymouth Rock with his boulders from the West,
And just a hundred miles behind, tornadoes piled across the
  sky,
Blotting out sun and moon,
A sign on high.

Headlong, dazed and blinking in the weird green light,
The scalawags made moan,
Afraid to fight.

## II

When Bryan came to Springfield, and Altgeld gave him
  greeting,
Rochester was deserted, Divernon was deserted,
Mechanicsburg, Riverton, Chickenbristle, Cotton Hill,

Empty: for all Sangamon drove to the meeting—
In silver-decked racing cart,
Buggy, buckboard, carryall,
Carriage, phaeton, whatever would haul,
And silver-decked farm-wagons gritted, banged and rolled,
With the new tale of Bryan by the iron tires told.


The State House loomed afar,
A speck, a hive, a football,
A captive balloon!
And the town was all one spreading wing of bunting, plumes,
    and sunshine,
Every rag and flag, and Bryan picture sold,
When the rigs in many a dusty line
Jammed our streets at noon,
And joined the wild parade against the power of gold.


We roamed, we boys from High School,
With mankind,
While Springfield gleamed,
Silk-lined.
Oh, Tom Dines, and Art Fitzgerald,
And the gangs that they could get!
I can hear them yelling yet.
Helping the incantation,
Defying aristocracy,
With every bridle gone,
Ridding the world of the low down mean,
Bidding the eagles of the West fly on,
Bidding the eagles of the West fly on,
We were bully, wild and woolly,
Never yet curried below the knees.
We saw flowers in the air,
Fair as the Pleiades, bright as Orion,
—Hopes of all mankind,

100

Made rare, resistless, thrice refined.
Oh, we bucks from every Springfield ward!
Colts of democracy—
Yet time-winds out of Chaos from the star-fields of the Lord.

The long parade rolled on. I stood by my best girl.
She was a cool young citizen, with wise and laughing eyes.
With my necktie by my ear, I was stepping on my dear,
But she kept like a pattern, without a shaken curl.

She wore in her hair a brave prairie rose.
Her gold chums cut her, for that was not the pose.
No Gibson Girl would wear it in that fresh way.
But we were fairy Democrats, and this was our day.

The earth rocked like the ocean, the sidewalk was a deck.
The houses for the moment were lost in the wide wreck.
And the bands played strange and stranger music as they
    trailed along.
Against the ways of Tubal Cain,
Ah, sharp was their song!
The demons in the bricks, the demons in the grass,
The demons in the bank-vaults peered out to see us pass,
And the angels in the trees, the angels in the grass,
The angels in the flags, peered out to see us pass.
And the sidewalk was our chariot, and the flowers bloomed
    higher,
And the street turned to silver and the grass turned to fire,
And then it was but grass, and the town was there again,
A place for women and men.


III

Then we stood where we could see
Every band,

And the speaker's stand.
And Bryan took the platform.
And he was introduced.
And he lifted his hand
And cast a new spell.
Progressive silence fell
In Springfield,
In Illinois,
Around the world.
Then we heard these glacial boulders across the prairie rolled:
*"The people have a right to make their own mistakes. . . .*
*You shall not crucify mankind*
*Upon a cross of gold."*

And everybody heard him—
In the streets and State House yard.
And everybody heard him
In Springfield,
In Illinois,
Around and around and around the world,
That danced upon its axis
And like a darling broncho whirled.

## IV

July, August, suspense.
Wall Street lost to sense.
August, September, October,
More suspense,
And the whole East down like a wind-smashed fence.

Then Hanna to the rescue,
Hanna of Ohio,
Rallying the roller-tops,

Rallying the bucket-shops.
Threatening drouth and death,
Promising manna,
Rallying the trusts against the bawling flannelmouth;
Invading misers' cellars,
Tin-cans, socks,
Melting down the rocks,
Pouring out the long green to a million workers,
Spondulix by the mountain-load, to stop each new tornado,
And beat the cheapskate, blatherskite,
Populistic, anarchistic,
Deacon—desperado.

## V

Election night at midnight:
Boy Bryan's defeat.
Defeat of western silver.
Defeat of the wheat.
Victory of letterfiles
And plutocrats in miles
With dollar signs upon their coats,
Diamond watchchains on their vests
And spats on their feet.
Victory of custodians,
Plymouth Rock,
And all that inbred landlord stock.
Victory of the neat.
Defeat of the aspen groves of Colorado valleys,
The blue bells of the Rockies,
And blue bonnets of old Texas,
By the Pittsburg alleys.
Defeat of alfalfa and the Mariposa lily.
Defeat of the Pacific and the long Mississippi.
Defeat of the young by the old and silly.

103

Defeat of tornadoes by the poison vats supreme.
Defeat of my boyhood, defeat of my dream.

## VI

Where is McKinley, that respectable McKinley,
The man without an angle or a tangle,
Who soothed down the city man and soothed down the farmer,
The German, the Irish, the Southerner, the Northerner,
Who climbed every greasy pole, and slipped through every
      crack;
Who soothed down the gambling hall, the bar-room, the
      church,
The devil vote, the angel vote, the neutral vote,
The desperately wicked, and their victims on the rack,
The gold vote, the silver vote, the brass vote, the lead vote,
Every vote? . . .

Where is McKinley, Mark Hanna's McKinley,
His slave, his echo, his suit of clothes?
Gone to join the shadows, with the pomps of that time,
And the flame of that summer's prairie rose.

Where is Cleveland whom the Democratic platform
Read from the party in a glorious hour,
Gone to join the shadows with pitchfork Tillman,
And sledge-hammer Altgeld who wrecked his power.

Where is Hanna, bulldog Hanna.
Low-browed Hanna, who said: "Stand pat"?
Gone to his place with old Pierpont Morgan.
Gone somewhere . . . with lean rat Platt.

Where is Roosevelt, the young dude cowboy,
Who hated Bryan, then aped his way?

Gone to join the shadows with mighty Cromwell
And tall King Saul, till the Judgment day.

Where is Altgeld, brave as the truth,
Whose name the few still say with tears?
Gone to join the ironies with Old John Brown,
Whose fame rings loud for a thousand years.

Where is that boy, that Heaven-born Bryan,
That Homer Bryan, who sang from the West?
Gone to join the shadows with Altgeld the Eagle,
Where the kings and the slaves and the troubadours rest.

**Written at the Guanella Ranch, Empire, Colorado, August, 1919.**

## OUR MOTHER POCAHONTAS

(NOTE:—Pocahontas is buried at Gravesend, England.)

"Pocahontas' body, lovely as a poplar, sweet as a red haw
in November or a pawpaw in May—did she wonder? does
she remember—in the dust—in the cool tombs?"

CARL SANDBURG.

### I

Powhatan was conqueror,
Powhatan was emperor.
He was akin to wolf and bee,
Brother of the hickory tree.
Son of the red lightning stroke
And the lightning-shivered oak.
His panther-grace bloomed in the maid
Who laughed among the winds and played

In excellence of savage pride,
Wooing the forest, open-eyed,
In the springtime,
In Virginia,
Our Mother, Pocahontas.
Her skin was rosy copper-red.
And high she held her beauteous head.
Her step was like a rustling leaf:
Her heart a nest, untouched of grief.
She dreamed of sons like Powhatan,
And through her blood the lightning ran.
Love-cries with the birds she sung,
Birdlike
In the grape-vine swung.
The Forest, arching low and wide
Gloried in its Indian bride.
Rolfe, that dim adventurer,
Had not come a courtier.
John Rolfe is not our ancestor.
We rise from out the soul of her
Held in native wonderland,
While the sun's rays kissed her hand,
In the springtime,
In Virginia,
Our Mother, Pocahontas.


II


She heard the forest talking,
And from her grave came walking,
Across the sea came walking,
And traced the paths of Daniel Boone,
Then westward chased the painted moon.
She passed with wild young feet
On to Kansas wheat,

On to the miners' west,
The echoing cañons' guest,
Then the Pacific sand,
Waking,
Thrilling,
The midnight land. . . .

On Adams Street and Jefferson—
Flames coming up from the ground!
On Jackson Street and Washington—
Flames coming up from the ground!
And why, until the dawning sun
Are flames coming up from the ground?
Because, through drowsy Springfield sped
This redskin queen, with feathered head,
With winds and stars, that pay her court
And leaping beasts, that make her sport;
Because, gray Europe's rags august
She tramples in the dust;
Because we are her fields of corn;
Because our fires are all reborn
From her bosom's deathless embers,
Flaming
As she remembers
The springtime
And Virginia,
Our Mother, Pocahontas.

## III

We here renounce our Saxon blood.
Tomorrow's hopes, an April flood
Come roaring in. The newest race
Is born of her resilient grace.

We here renounce our Teuton pride:
Our Norse and Slavic boasts have died:
Italian dreams are swept away,
And Celtic feuds are lost today. . . .
She sings of lilacs, maples, wheat,
Her own soil sings beneath her feet,
Of springtime
And Virginia,
Our Mother, Pocahontas.

# SECTION II

# ORATIONS, COLLEGE WAR-CRIES, AND OLYMPIC GAMES

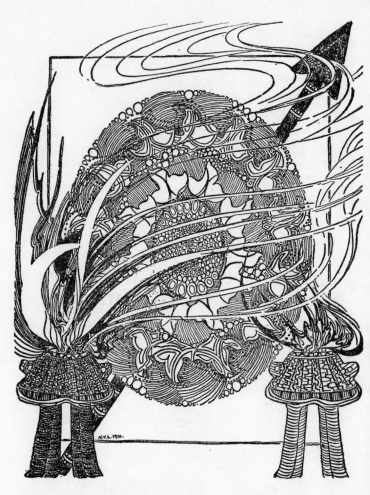

THE SHIELD OF LUCIFER

# LUCIFER

In the following narrative, Lucifer is not Satan, King of Evil, who in the beginning led the rebels from Heaven, establishing the underworld.

Lucifer is here taken as a character appearing much later, the first singing creature weary of established ways in music, moved with the lust of wandering. He finds the open road between the stars too lonely. He wanders to the kingdom of of Satan, there to sing a song that so moves demons and angels that he is, at its climax, momentary emperor of Hell and Heaven, and the flame kindled of the tears of the demons devastates the golden streets.

Therefore it is best for the established order of things that this wanderer shall be cursed with eternal silence and death. But since then there has been music in every temptation, in every demon voice.

Along with a set of verses called "The Heroes of Time," and another "The Tree of Laughing Bells," I exchanged "The Last Song of Lucifer" for a night's lodging in New Jersey, Pennsylvania and Ohio, as narrated in *A Handy Guide for Beggars*.

The fourteenth chapter of Isaiah contains these words on Lucifer:

"Thy pomp is brought down to the grave, and the noise of thy viols: the worm is spread under thee and the worms cover thee.

"How art thou fallen from heaven, O Lucifer, son of the morning! How art thou cut down to the ground, which didst weaken the nations!

111

"For thou hast said in thine heart, I will ascend into heaven, I will exalt my throne above the stars of God. . . .

"All the kings of the nations, even all of them, lie in glory, every one in his own house.

"But thou art cast out of thy grave like an abominable branch, and as the raiment of those that are slain, thrust through with a sword, that go down to the stones of the pit; as a carcas trodden under feet.

"Thou shalt not be joined with them in burial, because thou hast destroyed thy land."

## THE LAST SONG OF LUCIFER

### (To Be Read Like a Meditation)

When Lucifer was undefiled,
When Lucifer was young,
When only angel-music
Fell from his glorious tongue,
Dreaming in his innocence
Beneath God's golden trees
By genius pure his fancy fell—
By sweet divine disease—
To a wilderness of sorrows dim
Beneath the ether seas.
That father of radiant harmony,
Of music transcendently bright—
Truest to art since Heaven began,
Wrapped in royal, melodious light—
That beautiful light-bearer, lofty and loyal
Dreamed bitter dreams of enigma and night.

But soon the singer woke and stood
And tuned his harp to sing anew

*Lucifer dreams of his fate and then forgets the dream.*

112

# THE LAST SONG OF LUCIFER

And scorned the dreams (as well he should)
For only to the evil crew
Are dreams of dread and evil true,
Remembered well, or understood.

But when a million years were done
And a million, million years beside,
He broke his harp-strings one by one;
He sighed, aweary of rich things,
He spread his pallid, heavy wings
And flew to find the deathless stains,
The wounds that come with wanderings.

*The dream is
fulfilled.*

He chose the solemn paths of Hell,
He sang for that dumb land too well,
Defying their disdain
Till he was cursed and slain.
Ah—he shall never dream again—
Mourn, for he shall not dream again—
But the demons dream in pain,
Of wandering in the night,
And singing in the night,
Singing till they reign.
Oh, hallowed are the demons,
A-dreaming songs again,
And holy to my heart the ancient music-art,
That echo of a memory in demon-haunted men,
That hope of music, sweet hope, vain,
That sets the world a-seeking—
A passion pure, a subtle pain
Too dear for song or speaking.
Oh, who would not with the demons be,
For the fullness of their memory
Of that dayspring song,
Of that holy thing

*He will never
dream again,
but the de-
mons dream
of wandering
and singing,
and doing all
things just as
he did in his
day.*

*Music is holy,
even in the in-
fernal world.*

*If Lucifer's
song could be
completely re-
membered,
one would be
willing to pay*

113

That Lucifer alone could sing, *the great*
That Hell and Earth so hopelessly *price.*
And gloriously are seeking!

.    .    .    .    .

.    .    .    .    .

Now FOLLOWS
WHAT EVERY
DEMON SAYS IN
HIS HEART, RE-
MEMBERING
THAT TIME

Oh, Lucifer, great Lucifer,
Oh, fallen, ancient Lucifer,
Master lost, of the angel choir—
Silent, suffering Lucifer:                   *How the sing-*
Once your alchemies of Hell                  *er made his*
Wrought your chains to a magic lyre          *lyre.*
All strung with threads of purple fire,
Till the hell-hounds moaned from your bitter spell—
The sweetest song since the demons fell—
Haunting song of the heart's desire.

Oh, Lucifer, great Lucifer,                  *How the song*
You who have sung in vain,                    *began.*
Ecstasy of sweet regret,
Ecstasy of pain,
Strain that the angels can never forget,
Haunting the children of punishment yet,
Bowing them, bringing their tears in the darkness;
Oh, the night-caves of Chaos are breathing it yet!
The last that your bosom may ever deliver,
Oh, musical master of æons and æons. . . .
Nor devils nor dragons may ever forget,
Though the walls of our prison should crumble and shiver,
And the death-dews of Chaos our armor should wet,
For the song of the infamous Lucifer
Was an anthem of glorious scorning
And courage, and horrible pain—
Was the song of a Son of the Morning,
A song that was sung in vain.

114

## THE LAST SONG OF LUCIFER

Oh, singing was only in Heaven
Ere Lucifer's melody came,
But when Lucifer's harp-strings grew loud in their sighing,
When he called up the dragons by name—
The song was the sorrow of sorrows,
The song was the Hope of Despair,
Or the smile of a warrior falling—
A prayer and a curse and a prayer—
Or a soul going down through the shadows and calling,
Or the laughter of Night in his lair;
The song was the fear of ten thousand tomorrows—
On the racks of grief and of pain—
The herald of silences, dreadful, unending,
When the last little echo should listen in vain. . . .

It was memory, memory,
Visions of glory,—
Memory, memory,
Visions of fight.
The pride of the onset,
The banners that fluttered,
The wails of the battle-pierced angels of light.
Song of the times of the Nether Empire
The age when our desperate band
Heaped our redoubts with the horrible fire
On the fringes of Holier Land—
Conquering always, conquering never,
Building a throne of sand—
When Satan still wielded that glorious scepter—
The sword of his glorious hand.

*How the song made the demons dream they were still fighting for Satan.*

Then rang the martial music
Sung by the hosts of God
In the first of the shameful years of fear
When we bit the purple sod:

He sang that shameful battle-story—
He twanged each threaded torture-flame;
Wherever his leprous fingers came
They drew from the strings a groan of glory:

Then we dreamed at last,
Then we lost the past,
We dreamed we were angels in battle-array:
We tore our hearts with God's battle-yell
And the sound crashed up from the smoky fen
And the battle sweat stood forth
On the awful brows of our fighting men:
And the magical singer, grim and wild,
Swept his harp again, and smiled,
And the harp-strings lifted our cries that day
Till the thundering charge reached the City on High—
God's charge, that he thought
Had passed for aye.
When our last fond hope went down to die.

*How the song
enchanted
them till they
were in fancy
the good war-
riors of God,
and they
shouted their
enemy's bat-
tle-cry.*

Oh, throbbing, sweet enthralling spell!
Madly, madly, oh, my heart—
Heart of anguish, heart of Hell—
Beat the music through your night—
Pierced the strain that the wanderer
Wrought with fingers white;
For last he sang—of the morning—
The song of the Sons of the Morning—
The fire of the star-souled Lucifer
Before he had known a stain;
That song which came when the suns were
        young
And the Dayspring knew his place—
That joy, full born, that unknown tongue,
That shouting chant of the Sons of God
When first they saw Jehovah's face.

*How, at the
climax of the
song Lucifer
almost re-
stored the
first day of
creation, when
the Universe
was happy
and sinless.*

*How the tears
of the dis-
tracted de-
mons became*

116

And the Wanderer laughed, then sang it at last
Till it leaped as a flame to the forest on high
And the tears of the demons were fire in the
    sky.

*a heaven-*
*climbing*
*flame.*

And just for a breath he conquered and reigned,
For one quick pulse of time he stood;
By flame was crowned where God had been
Himself the Word sublime—
Himself the Most High Love unstained,
The Great, Good King of the Stars and Years—
Crowned, enthroned, by a leaping flame—
The fire of our love-born tears.

*How Lucifer*
*seemed to*
*make himself*
*God.*

And the angels bowed down, for his glory was
    vast—
Loving their conqueror, weeping aghast—
While we sobbed, for a moment repenting the
    past,
And the mock-hope came, that eats and stings,
The hope for innocent dawns above,
The joy of it beat in our ears like wings,
Our iron cheeks seared with the tears of love—
Was it not enough,
Was it not enough
That our cheeks were seared with the tears of
    Love?

*How the an-*
*gels were con-*
*quered by the*
*sound of his*
*music from*
*afar, and the*
*Demons were*
*torn with love.*

So we cursed the harping of Lucifer
The lyre was lost from his leper hands
And the hell-hounds tore his living heart.
And the angels cursed great Lucifer
For his purple flame consumed their lands
Till golden ways were desert sands;
They hurled him down, afar, apart.

*Demons and*
*angels curse*
*the singer.*

117

Beneath where the Gulfs of Silence end, *The Punish-*
Where never sighs nor songs descend, *ment.*
Never a hell-flare in his eyes
Alone, alone, afar he lies. . . . .
Fearfully alone, beyond immortal ken
He is further down in the deep of pain
Than is Hell from the grief of men;
And his memories of music
Are rare as desert-rain.

Ended forever the ecstasy
And song too sweet for scorning—
The song that was still in vain;
And the shout of the battle-charge of God—
Ended forever the Song of the Morning—
The Song that was sung in vain.


## THE KALLYOPE YELL

(To be given in the peculiar whispered manner of the University of Kansas "Jay-Hawk Yell")

### J

Proud men
Eternally
Go about,
Slander me,
Call me the "Calliope,"
Sizz. . . .
Fizz. . . .

### II

I am the Gutter Dream,
Tune-maker, born of steam,

Tooting joy, tooting hope.
I am the Kallyope,
Car called the Kallyope.
Willy willy willy wah HOO!
See the flags: snow-white tent,
See the bear and elephant,
See the monkey jump the rope,
Listen to the Kallyope, Kallyope, Kallyope!
Soul of the rhinoceros
And the hippopotamus
(Listen to the lion roar!)
Jaguar, cockatoot,
Loons, owls,
Hoot, Hoot.
Listen to the lion roar,
Listen to the lion roar,
Listen to the lion R-O-A-R!
Hear the leopard cry for gore,
Willy willy willy wah HOO!
Hail the bloody Indian band,
Hail, all hail the popcorn stand,
Hail to Barnum's picture there,
People's idol everywhere,
Whoop, whoop, whoop, WHOOP!
Music of the mob am I,
Circus day's tremendous cry:—
I am the Kallyope, Kallyope, Kallyope!
Hoot toot, hoot toot, hoot toot, hoot toot,
Willy willy willy wah HOO!
Sizz, fizz. . . .


### III

Born of mobs, born of steam,
Listen to my golden dream,

Listen to my golden dream,
Listen to my G-O-L-D-E-N D-R-E-A-M!
Whoop whoop whoop whoop WHOOP!
I will blow the proud folk low,
Humanize the dour and slow,
I will shake the proud folk down,
(Listen to the lion roar!)
Popcorn crowds shall rule the town—
Willy willy willy wah HOO!
Steam shall work melodiously,
Brotherhood increase.
You'll see the world and all it holds
For fifty cents apiece.
Willy willy willy wah HOO!
Every day a circus day.

*What?*

Well, *almost* every day.
Nevermore the sweater's den,
Nevermore the prison pen.
Gone the war on land and sea
That aforetime troubled men.
Nations all in amity,
Happy in their plumes arrayed
In the long bright street parade.
Bands a-playing every day.

*What?*

Well, *almost* every day.
I am the Kallyope, Kallyope, Kallyope!
Willy willy willy wah HOO!
Hoot, toot, hoot, toot,
Whoop whoop whoop whoop,

Willy willy willy wah HOO!
Sizz, fizz. . . .

## IV

Every soul
Resident
In the earth's one circus tent!
Every man a trapeze king
Then a pleased spectator there.
On the benches! In the ring!
While the neighbors gawk and stare
And the cheering rolls along.
Almost every day a race
When the merry starting gong
Rings, each chariot on the line,
Every driver fit and fine
With a steel-spring Roman grace.
Almost every day a dream,
Almost every day a dream.
Every girl,
Maid or wife,
Wild with music,
Eyes agleam
With that marvel called desire:
Actress, princess, fit for life,
Armed with honor like a knife,
Jumping thro' the hoops of fire.
(Listen to the lion roar!)
Making all the children shout
Clowns shall tumble all about,
Painted high and full of song
While the cheering rolls along,
Tho' they scream,

121

Tho' they rage,
Every beast in his cage,
Every beast in his den,
That aforetime troubled men.


## V


I am the Kallyope, Kallyope, Kallyope,
Tooting hope, tooting hope, tooting hope, toot-
     ing hope;
Shaking window-pane and door
With a crashing cosmic tune,
With the war-cry of the spheres,
Rhythm of the roar of noon,
Rhythm of Niagara's roar,
Voicing planet, star and moon,
SHRIEKING of the better years.
Prophet-singers will arise,
Prophets coming after me,
Sing my song in softer guise
With more delicate surprise;
I am but the pioneer
Voice of the Democracy;
I am the gutter dream,
I am the golden dream,
Singing science, singing steam.
I will blow the proud folk down,
(Listen to the lion roar!)
I am the Kallyope, Kallyope, Kallyope,
Tooting hope, tooting hope, tooting hope, toot-
     ing hope,
Willy willy willy wah HOO!
Hoot, toot, hoot toot, hoot toot, hoot toot,

Whoop whoop, whoop whoop,
Whoop whoop, whoop whoop,
Willy willy willy wah HOO!
Sizz. . . .
Fizz. . . .

## GENERAL WILLIAM BOOTH
## ENTERS INTO HEAVEN

(To be sung to the tune of "The Blood of the Lamb" with
indicated instrument)

### I

*(Bass drum beaten loudly.)*
Booth led boldly with his big bass drum—
(Are you washed in the blood of the Lamb?)
The Saints smiled gravely and they said: "He's come."
(Are you washed in the blood of the Lamb?)
Walking lepers followed, rank on rank,
Lurching bravos from the ditches dank,
Drabs from the alleyways and drug fiends pale—
Minds still passion-ridden, soul-powers frail:—
Vermin-eaten saints with moldy breath,
Unwashed legions with the ways of Death—
(Are you washed in the blood of the Lamb?)

*(Banjos.)*
Every slum had sent its half-a-score
The round world over. (Booth had groaned for more.)
Every banner that the wide world flies
Bloomed with glory and transcendent dyes.

123

Big-voiced lasses made their banjos bang,
Tranced, fanatical they shrieked and sang:—
"Are you washed in the blood of the Lamb?"
Hallelujah! It was queer to see
Bull-necked convicts with that land make free.
Loons with trumpets blowed a blare, blare, blare
On, on upward thro' the golden air!
(Are you washed in the blood of the Lamb?)

## II

(*Bass drum slower and softer.*)
Booth died blind and still by faith he trod,
Eyes still dazzled by the ways of God.
Booth led boldly, and he looked the chief
Eagle countenance in sharp relief,
Beard a-flying, air of high command
Unabated in that holy land.

(*Sweet flute music.*)
Jesus came from out the court-house door,
Stretched his hands above the passing poor.
Booth saw not, but led his queer ones there
Round and round the mighty court-house square.
Then, in an instant all that blear review
Marched on spotless, clad in raiment new.
The lame were straightened, withered limbs uncurled
And blind eyes opened on a new, sweet world.

(*Bass drum louder.*)
Drabs and vixens in a flash made whole!
Gone was the weasel-head, the snout, the jowl!
Sages and sibyls now, and athletes clean,
Rulers of empires, and of forests green!

124

*(Grand chorus of all instruments. Tambourines to the foreground.)*
The hosts were sandalled, and their wings were fire!
(Are you washed in the blood of the Lamb?)
But their noise played havoc with the angel-choir.
(Are you washed in the blood of the Lamb?)
Oh, shout Salvation! It was good to see
Kings and Princes by the Lamb set free.
The banjos rattled and the tambourines
Jing-jing-jingled in the hands of Queens.

*(Reverently sung, no instruments.)*
And when Booth halted by the curb for prayer
He saw his Master thro' the flag-filled air.
Christ came gently with a robe and crown
For Booth the soldier, while the throng knelt down.
He saw King Jesus. They were face to face,
And he knelt a-weeping in that holy place.
Are you washed in the blood of the Lamb?

## THE KING OF YELLOW BUTTERFLIES

### (A Poem Game)

The King of Yellow Butterflies,
The King of Yellow Butterflies,
The King of Yellow Butterflies,
Now orders forth his men.
He says "The time is almost here
When violets bloom again."
Adown the road the fickle rout
Goes flashing proud and bold,
Adown the road the fickle rout
Goes flashing proud and bold,
Adown the road the fickle rout

Goes flashing proud and bold,
They shiver by the shallow pools,
They shiver by the shallow pools,
They shiver by the shallow pools,
And whimper of the cold.
They drink and drink. A frail pretense!
They love to pose and preen.
Each pool is but a looking glass,
Where their sweet wings are seen.
Each pool is but a looking glass,
Where their sweet wings are seen.
Each pool is but a looking glass,
Where their sweet wings are seen.
Gentlemen adventurers! Gypsies every whit!
They live on what they steal. Their wings
By briars are frayed a bit.
Their loves are light. They have no house.
And if it rains today,
They'll climb into your cattle-shed,
They'll climb into your cattle-shed,
They'll climb into your cattle-shed,
And hide them in the hay,
And hide them in the hay,
And hide them in the hay,
And hide them in the hay.

## THE POTATOES' DANCE

### (A Poem Game)

### I

"Down cellar," said the cricket,
"Down cellar," said the cricket,

"Down cellar," said the cricket,
"I saw a ball last night,
In honor of a lady,
In honor of a lady,
In honor of a lady,
Whose wings were pearly white.
The breath of bitter weather,
The breath of bitter weather,
The breath of bitter weather,
Had smashed the cellar pane.
We entertained a drift of leaves,
We entertained a drift of leaves,
We entertained a drift of leaves,
And then of snow and rain.
But we were dressed for winter,
But we were dressed for winter,
But we were dressed for winter,
And loved to hear it blow
In honor of the lady,
In honor of the lady,
In honor of the lady,
Who makes potatoes grow,
Our guest the Irish lady,
The tiny Irish lady,
The airy Irish lady,
Who makes potatoes grow.


II


"Potatoes were the waiters,
Potatoes were the waiters,
Potatoes were the waiters,
Potatoes were the band,
Potatoes were the dancers

127

Kicking up the sand,
Kicking up the sand,
Kicking up the sand,
Potatoes were the dancers
Kicking up the sand.
Their legs were old burnt matches,
Their legs were old burnt matches,
Their legs were old burnt matches,
Their arms were just the same.
They jigged and whirled and scrambled,
Jigged and whirled and scrambled,
Jigged and whirled and scrambled,
In honor of the dame,
The noble Irish lady
Who makes potatoes dance,
The witty Irish lady,
The saucy Irish lady,
The laughing Irish lady
Who makes potatoes prance.

## III

"There was just one sweet potato.
He was golden brown and slim.
The lady loved his dancing,
The lady loved his dancing,
The lady loved his dancing,
She danced all night with him,
She danced all night with him.
Alas, he wasn't Irish.
So when she flew away,
They threw him in the coal-bin,
And there he is today,
Where they cannot hear his sighs

128

And his weeping for the lady,
The glorious Irish lady,
The beauteous Irish lady,
Who
Gives
Potatoes
Eyes."

## ALADDIN AND THE JINN

"Bring me soft song," said Aladdin.
"This tailor-shop sings not at all.
Chant me a word of the twilight,
Of roses that mourn in the fall.
Bring me a song like hashish
That will comfort the stale and the sad,
For I would be mending my spirit,
Forgetting these days that are bad,
Forgetting companions too shallow,
Their quarrels and arguments thin,
Forgetting the shouting Muezzin:"
"I AM YOUR SLAVE," said the Jinn.

"Bring me old wines," said Aladdin.
"I have been a starved pauper too long.
Serve them in vessels of jade and of shell,
Serve them with fruit and with song:—
Wines of pre-Adamite Sultans
Digged from beneath the black seas:—
New-gathered dew from the heavens
Dripped down from Heaven's sweet trees,
Cups from the angels' pale tables
That will make me both handsome and wise,

For I have beheld her, the princess,
Firelight and starlight her eyes.
Pauper I am, I would woo her.
And—let me drink wine, to begin,
Though the Koran expressly forbids it."
"I AM YOUR SLAVE," said the Jinn.

"Plan me a dome," said Aladdin,
"That is drawn like the dawn of the MOON,
When the sphere seems to rest on the mountains,
Half-hidden, yet full-risen soon.
Build me a dome," said Aladdin,
"That shall cause all young lovers to sigh,
The fullness of life and of beauty,
Peace beyond peace to the eye—
A palace of foam and of opal,
Pure moonlight without and within,
Where I may enthrone my sweet lady."
"I AM YOUR SLAVE," said the Jinn.

## THE MASTER OF THE DANCE

(A chant to which it is intended a group of children shall
dance and improvise pantomime led by their dancing-
teacher)

### I

A master deep-eyed
Ere his manhood was ripe,
He sang like a thrush,
He could play any pipe.
So dull in the school
That he scarcely could spell,

He read but a bit,
And he figured not well.
A barefooted fool,
Shod only with grace;
Long hair streaming down
Round a wind-hardened face;
He smiled like a girl,
Or like clear winter skies,
A virginal light
Making stars of his eyes.
In swiftness and poise,
A proud child of the deer,
A white fawn he was,
Yet a fawn without fear.
No youth thought him vain,
Or made mock of his hair,
Or laughed when his ways
Were most curiously fair.
A mastiff at fight,
He could strike to the earth
The envious one
Who would challenge his worth.
However we bowed
To the schoolmaster mild,
Our spirits went out
To the fawn-footed child.
His beckoning led
Our troop to the brush.
We found nothing there
But a wind and a hush.
He sat by a stone
And he looked on the ground,
As if in the weeds
There was something profound.
His pipe seemed to neigh,

131

Then to bleat like a sheep,
Then sound like a stream
Or a waterfall deep.
It whispered strange tales,
Human words it spoke not.
Told fair things to come,
And our marvellous lot
If now with fawn-steps
Unshod we advanced
To the midst of the grove
And in reverence danced.
We obeyed as he piped
Soft grass to young feet,
Was a medicine mighty,
A remedy meet.
Our thin blood awoke,
It grew dizzy and wild,
Though scarcely a word
Moved the lips of a child.
Our dance gave allegiance,
It set us apart,
We tripped a strange measure,
Uplifted of heart.

## II

We thought to be proud
Of our fawn everywhere.
We could hardly see how
Simple books were a care.
No rule of the school
This strange student could tame.
He was banished one day,
While we quivered with shame.

He piped back our love
On a moon-silvered night,
Enticed us once more
To the place of delight.
A greeting he sang
And it made our blood beat,
It tramped upon custom
And mocked at defeat.
He builded a fire
And we tripped in a ring,
The embers our books
And the fawn our good king.
And now we approached
All the mysteries rare
That shadowed his eyelids
And blew through his hair.
That spell now was peace
The deep strength of the trees,
The children of nature
We clambered her knees.
Our breath and our moods
Were in tune with her own,
Tremendous her presence,
Eternal her throne.
The ostracized child
Our white foreheads kissed,
Our bodies and souls
Became lighter than mist.
Sweet dresses like snow
Our small lady-loves wore,
Like moonlight the thoughts
That our bosoms upbore.
Like a lily the touch
Of each cold little hand.
The loves of the stars
We could now understand.

O quivering air!
O the crystalline night!
O pauses of awe
And the faces swan-white!
O ferns in the dusk!
O forest-shrined hour!
O earth that sent upward
The thrill and the power,
To lift us like leaves,
A delirious whirl,
The masterful boy
And the delicate girl!
What child that strange night-time
Can ever forget?
His fealty due
And his infinite debt
To the folly divine,
To the exquisite rule
Of the perilous master,
The fawn-footed fool?


## III

Now soldiers we seem,
And night brings a new thing,
A terrible ire,
As of thunder a-wing.
A warrior power,
That old chivalry stirred,
When knights took up arms,
As the maidens gave word.
THE END OF OUR WAR,
WILL BE GLORY UNTOLD.
WHEN THE TOWN LIKE A GREAT
BUDDING ROSE SHALL UNFOLD!

A DIRGE FOR A RIGHTEOUS KITTEN

*Near, nearer that war,*
*And that ecstasy comes,*
*We hear the trees beating*
*Invisible drums.*
*The fields of the night*
*Are starlit above,*
*Our girls are white torches*
*Of conquest and love.*
*No nerve without will,*
*And no breast without breath*
*We whirl with the planets*
*That never know death!*


## A DIRGE FOR A RIGHTEOUS KITTEN

(To be intoned, all but the two italicized lines, which are
to be spoken in a snappy, matter-of-fact way)

Ding-dong, ding-dong, ding-dong.
Here lies a kitten good, who kept
A kitten's proper place.
He stole no pantry eatables,
Nor scratched the baby's face.
*He let the alley-cats alone.*
He had no yowling vice.
His shirt was always laundried well,
He freed the house of mice.
Until his death he had not caused
His little mistress tears,
He wore his ribbon prettily,
*He washed behind his ears.*
Ding-dong, ding-dong, ding-dong.

## THE LAME BOY AND THE FAIRY

(To the rythm of Chopin's Berceuse)

A lame boy
Met a fairy
In a meadow
Where the bells grow.

And the fairy
Kissed him gaily.

And the fairy
Gave him friendship,
Gave him healing,
Gave him wings.

"All the fashions
I will give you.
You will fly, dear,
All the long year.

"Wings of springtime,
Wings of summer,
Wings of autumn,
Wings of winter!

"Here is
A dress for springtime."
And she gave him
A dress of grasses,
Orchard blossoms,
Wild-flowers found in
Mountain passes,

136

*Shoes of song and*
*Wings of rhyme.*

"Here is
A dress for summer."
And she gave him
A hat of sunflowers,
A suit of poppies,
Clover, daisies,
All from wheat-sheaves
In harvest time;
*Shoes of song and*
*Wings of rhyme.*

"Here is
A dress for autumn."
And she gave him
A suit of red haw,
Hickory, apple,
Elder, pawpaw,
Maple, hazel,
Elm and grape leaves,
And blue
And white
Cloaks of smoke,
And veils of sunlight,
From the Indian summer prime!
*Shoes of song and*
*Wings of rhyme.*

"Here is
A dress for winter."
And she gave him
A polar bear suit,
And he heard the

Christmas horns toot,
And she gave him
Green festoons and
Red balloons and
All the sweet cakes
And the snowflakes
Of Christmas time,
*Shoes of song and*
*Wings of rhyme.*

And the fairy
Kept him laughing,
Led him dancing,
Kept him climbing
On the hilltops
Toward the moon.

"We shall see silver ships.
We shall see singing ships,
Valleys of spray today,
Mountains of foam.
We have been long away,
Far from our wonderland.
Here come the ships of love
Taking us home.

"Who are our captains bold?
They are the saints of old.
One is Saint Christopher.
He takes your hand.
He leads the cloudy fleet.
He gives us bread and meat.
His is our ship till
We reach our dear land.

138

## THE BLACKSMITH'S SERENADE

"Where is our house to be?
Far in the ether sea.
There where the North Star
Is moored in the deep.
Sleepy old comets nod
There on the silver sod.
Sleepy young fairy flowers
Laugh in their sleep.

"A hundred years
And
A day,
There we will fly
And play
*I-spy* and *cross-tag.*
And meet on the highway,
And call to the game
Little Red Riding Hood,
Goldilocks, Santa Claus,
Every beloved
And heart-shaking name."

And the lame child
And the fairy
Journeyed far, far
To the North Star.


## THE BLACKSMITH'S SERENADE

(A pantomime and farce, to be acted by My Lady on one
side of a shutter while the singer chants on the other, to an
iron guitar)

John Littlehouse the redhead was a large ruddy man
Quite proud to be a blacksmith, and he loved Polly Ann,
    Polly Ann.
Straightway to her window with his iron guitar he came
Breathing like a blacksmith—his wonderful heart's flame.
Though not very bashful and not very bold
He had reached the plain conclusion his passion must be told.
And so he sang: "Awake, awake,"—this hip-hoo-ray-ious
    man.
"Do you like me, do you love me, Polly Ann, Polly Ann?
The rooster on my coalshed crows at break of day.
It makes a person happy to hear his roundelay.
The fido in my woodshed barks at fall of night.
He makes one feel so safe and snug. He barks exactly right.
I swear to do my stylish best and purchase all I can
Of the flummeries, flunkeries and mummeries of man.
And I will carry in the coal and the water from the spring
And I will sweep the porches if you will cook and sing.
No doubt your Pa sleeps like a rock. Of course Ma is awake
But dares not say she hears me, for gentle custom's sake.
Your sleeping father knows I am a decent honest man.
Will you wake him, Polly Ann,
And if he dares deny it I will thrash him, lash bash mash
Hash him, Polly Ann.
Hum hum hum, fee fie fo fum—
And my brawn should wed your beauty.
Do you hear me, Polly Ann, Polly Ann?"

Polly had not heard of him before, but heard him now.
She blushed behind the shutters like a pippin on the bough.
She was not overfluttered, she was not overbold.
She was glad a lad was living with a passion to be told.
But she spoke up to her mother: "Oh, what an awful man:—"
This merry merry quite contrary tricky trixy, Polly Ann,
    Polly Ann.

The neighbors put their heads out of the windows. They
      said:—
"What sort of turtle dove is this that seems to wake the
      dead?"
Yes, in their nighties whispered this question to the night.
They did not dare to shout it. It wouldn't be right.
And so, I say, they whispered:—"Does she hear this awful
      man,
Polly Ann, Polly Ann?"

John Littlehouse the redhead sang on of his desires:
"Steel makes the wires of lyres, makes the frames of terrible
      towers
And circus chariots' tires.
Believe me, dear, a blacksmith man can feel.
I will bind you, if I can to my ribs with hoops of steel.
Do you hear me, Polly Ann, Polly Ann?"

And then his tune was silence, for he was not a fool.
He let his voice rest, his iron guitar cool.
And thus he let the wind sing, the stars sing and the grass
      sing,
The prankishness of love sing, the girl's tingling feet sing,
Her trembling sweet hands sing, her mirror in the dark sing,
Her grace in the dark sing, her pillow in the dark sing,
The savage in her blood sing, her starved little heart sing,
Silently sing.

"Yes, I hear you, Mister Man,"
To herself said Polly Ann, Polly Ann.

He shouted one great loud *"Good night,"* and laughed,
And skipped home.
And every star was winking in the wide wicked dome.

And early in the morning, sweet Polly stole away.
And though the town went crazy, she is his wife today.


## THE FAIRY BRIDAL HYMN

(This is the hymn to Eleanor, daughter of Mab and a
golden drone, sung by the locust choir when the fairy child
marries her God, the yellow rose.)

> This is a song to the white-armed one
> Cold in the breast as the frost-wrapped Spring,
> Whose feet are slow on the hills of life,
> Whose round mouth rules by whispering.
>
> This is a song to the white-armed one
> Whose breast shall burn as a Summer field,
> Whose wings shall rise to the doors of gold,
> Whose poppy lips to the God shall yield.
>
> This is a song to the white-armed one
> When the closing rose shall bind her fast,
> And a song of the song their blood shall sing,
> When the Rose-God drinks her soul at last.


## A DOLL'S "ARABIAN NIGHTS"

(A Rhymed Scenario for Mae Marsh, when she acts in the
new many-colored films)

> I dreamed the play was real.
> I walked into the screen.

## A DOLL'S "ARABIAN NIGHTS"

Like Alice through the looking-glass,
I found a curious scene.
The black stones took on flame.
The shadows shone with eyes.
The colors poured and changed
In a Hell's debauch of dyes,
In a street with incense thick,
In a court of witch-bazaars,
With flambeaux by the stalls
Whose splutter hid the stars.
Camels stalked in line.
Courtezans tripped by
Dressed in silks and gems,
Copper diadems,
All the wealth they had.


*Oh quivering lights,*
*Arabian Nights!*
*Bagdad,*
*Bagdad!*

*This refrain*
*to be elabo-*
*rately articu-*
*lated and the*
*instrumental*
*music then*
*made to match*
*it precisely.*

You were a guarded girl
In a palanquin of gold.
I was buying figs:
All my hands could hold.
You slipped a note to me.
Your eyes made me your slave.
"Twelve paces back," you wrote.
No other word gave.
The delicate dove house swayed
Close-veiled, a snare most sweet.
"Joy," said the silver bells
On the palanquin-bearers' feet.

143

Then by a mosque, a dervish
Yelled and whirled like mad.

*Oh quivering lights,*
*Arabian Nights!*
*Bagdad,*
*Bagdad!*

I reached a dim, still court.
I saw you there afar,
Beckoning from the roof,
Veiled, a cloud-wrapped star.
And your black slave said: "Proud boy,
Do you dare everything
With your young arm and bright steel?
Then climb. You are her king."
And I heard a hiss of knives
In the doorway dark and bad.

*Oh quivering lights,*
*Arabian Nights!*
*Bagdad,*
*Bagdad!*

The stairway climbed and climbed.
It spoke. It shouted lies.
I reached a tar-black room,
A panther's belly gloom,
Filled with howls and sighs.
I found the roof. Twelve kings
Rose up to stab me there.
But I sent them to their graves.
My singing shook the air.
My scimitar seemed more

144

# A DOLL'S "ARABIAN NIGHTS"

Than any steel could be,
A whirling wheel, a pack
Of death-hounds guarding me.
And then you came like May.
You bound my torn breast well
With your discarded veil.
And flowery silence fell.
While Mohammed spread his wings
In the stars, you bent me back,
With a quick kiss touched my mouth,
And my heart was on the rack.
Oh dreadful, deathless love!
Oh kiss of Islam fire.
And your flashing hands were more
Than all a thief's desire.

I woke by twelve dead curs
On bloody, stony ground.
And the gray watch muttered
    "shame"
As he tottered on his round.
You had written on my sword:—
"Goodby, O iron arm.
I love you much too well
To do you further harm.
And as my pledge and sign
You are in crimson clad."

*The morning after is always noted in the Arabian Nights.*

*Oh quivering lights,*
*Arabian Nights!*
*Bagdad,*
*Bagdad!*

. . . . . .
. . . . . .

145

The rocs scream in the air.
The ghouls my pathway clear.
For I have drunk the soul
Of the dazzling maid they fear.
The long handclasp you gave
Still shakes upon my hands.
O, daughter of a Jinn
I plot in Islam lands,
Haunting purple streets,
Hissing, snarling, bold,

A robber never jailed,
A beggar never cold.
I shall be sultan yet
In this old crimson clad.

*Oh quivering lights,*
*Arabian Nights!*
*Bagdad,*
*Bagdad!*


## TWO OLD CROWS

Two old crows sat on a fence rail.
Two old crows sat on a fence rail,
Thinking of effect and cause,
Of weeds and flowers,
And nature's laws.
One of them muttered, one of them stuttered,
One of them stuttered, one of them muttered.
Each of them thought far more than he uttered.
One crow asked the other crow a riddle.
One crow asked the other crow a riddle:

## THE DRUNKARD'S FUNERAL

The muttering crow
Asked the stuttering crow,
"Why does a bee have a sword to his fiddle?
Why does a bee have a sword to his fiddle?"
"Bee-cause," said the other crow,
"Bee-cause,
B B B B B B B B B B B B B B B-cause."
Just then a bee flew close to their rail:—
"Buzzzzzzzzzzzzzzzzzz     zzzzzzzz     zzzzzzzzzzzzzzz
ZZZZZZZ."
And those two black crows
Turned pale,
And away those crows did sail.
Why?
B B B B B B B B B B B B B B B-cause.
B B B B B B B B B B B B B B B-cause.
"Buzzzzzzzzzzzzzzzzzz     zzzzzzzzzz     zzzzzzzzzzzzzz
ZZZZZZZ."

## THE DRUNKARD'S FUNERAL

"Yes," said the sister with the little pinched face,
The busy little sister with the funny little tract:—
"This is the climax, the grand fifth act.
There rides the proud, at the finish of his race.
There goes the hearse, the mourners cry,
The respectable hearse goes slowly by.
The wife of the dead has money in her purse,
The children are in health, so it might have been worse.
The fellow in the coffin led a life most foul.
A fierce defender of the red bartender,
At the church he would rail,
At the preacher he would howl.

He planted every deviltry to see it grow.
He wasted half his income on the lewd and the low.
He would trade engender for the red bar-tender,
He would homage render to the red bar-tender,
And in ultimate surrender to the red bar-tender,
He died of the tremens, as crazy as a loon,
And his friends were glad, when the end came soon.
There goes the hearse, the mourners cry,
The respectable hearse goes slowly by.
And now, good friends, since you see how it ends,
Let each nation-mender flay the red bar-tender,—
Abhor
The transgression
Of the red bar-tender,—
Ruin
The profession
Of the red bar-tender:
Force him into business where his work does good.
Let him learn how to plough, let him learn to chop wood,
Let him learn how to plough, let him learn to chop wood.


"The moral,
The conclusion,
The verdict now you know:—
'The saloon must go,
The saloon must go,
The saloon,
The saloon,
The saloon,
Must go.' "
"You are right, little sister," I said to myself,
"You are right, good sister," I said.
"Though you wear a mussy bonnet
On your little gray head,
You are right, little sister," I said.

# THE SEA SERPENT CHANTEY

## I

There's a snake on the western wave
And his crest is red.
He is long as a city street,
And he eats the dead.
There's a hole in the bottom of the sea
Where the snake goes down.
And he waits in the bottom of the sea
For the men that drown.

    Chorus:—
  This is the voice of the sand
  (The sailors understand)
  "There is far more sea than sand,
  There is far more sea than land.
    Yo . . . ho, yo . . . ho."

*Let the audience join in the chorus.*

## II

He waits by the door of his cave
While the ages moan.
He cracks the ribs of the ships
With his teeth of stone.
In his gizzard deep and long
Much treasure lies.
Oh, the pearls and the Spanish gold. . . .
And the idols' eyes. . . .
Oh, the totem poles . . . the skulls . . .
The altars cold . . .
The wedding rings, the dice . . .
The buoy bells old.

    Chorus:—This is the voice, etc.

## III

Dive, mermaids, with sharp swords
And cut him through,
And bring us the idols' eyes
And the red gold too.
Lower the grappling hooks
Good pirate men
And drag him up by the tongue
From his deep wet den.
We will sail to the end of the world,      *Repeat as a*
We will nail his hide                       *second chorus*
To the mainmast of the moon                 *many times.*
In the evening tide.

## IV

Or will you let him live,
The deep-sea thing,
With the wrecks of all the world
In a black wide ring
By the hole in the bottom of the sea
Where the snake goes down,
Where he waits in the bottom of the sea
For the men that drown?
      Chorus:—This is the voice, etc.

## KANSAS

Oh, I have walked in Kansas
Through many a harvest field,

And piled the sheaves of glory there
And down the wild rows reeled:

Each sheaf a little yellow sun,
A heap of hot-rayed gold;
Each binder like Creation's hand
To mould suns, as of old.

Straight overhead the orb of noon
Beat down with brimstone breath:
The desert wind from south and west
Was blistering flame and death.

Yet it was gay in Kansas,
A-fighting that strong sun;
And I and many a fellow-tramp
Defied that wind and won.

And we felt free in Kansas
From any sort of fear,
For thirty thousand tramps like us
There harvest every year.

She stretches arms for them to come,
She roars for helpers then,
And so it is in Kansas
That tramps, one month, are men.

We sang in burning Kansas
The songs of Sabbath-school,
The "Day Star" flashing in the East,
The "Vale of Eden" cool.

We sang in splendid Kansas
"The flag that set us free"—

That march of fifty thousand men
With Sherman to the sea.

We feasted high in Kansas
And had much milk and meat.
The tables groaned to give us power
Wherewith to save the wheat.

Our beds were sweet alfalfa hay
Within the barn-loft wide.
The loft doors opened out upon
The endless wheat-field tide.

I loved to watch the windmills spin
And watch that big moon rise.
I dreamed and dreamed with lids half-shut,
The moonlight in my eyes.

For all men dream in Kansas
By noonday and by night,
By sunrise yellow, red and wild
And moonrise wild and white.

The wind would drive the glittering clouds,
The cottonwoods would croon,
And past the sheaves and through the leaves
Came whispers from the moon.


# THE SANTA-FÉ TRAIL   (A HUMORESQUE)

(I asked the old negro: "What is that bird that sings so
well?"  He answered: "That is the Rachel-Jane."  "Hasn't
it another name—lark, or thrush, or the like?"  "No.  Jus'
Rachel-Jane.")

# THE SANTA-FÉ TRAIL (A HUMORESQUE)

## I. In Which a Racing Auto Comes from the East

This is the order of the music of the morning:—

First, from the far East comes but a crooning.

The crooning turns to a sunrise singing.

Hark to the *calm*-horn, *balm*-horn, *psalm*-horn.

Hark to the *faint*-horn, *quaint*-horn, *saint*-horn . . . .

*To be sung delicately, to an improvised tune.*

Hark to the *pace*-horn, *chase*-horn, *race*-horn.

And the holy veil of the dawn has gone.

Swiftly the brazen car comes on.

It burns in the East as the sunrise burns.

I see great flashes where the far trail turns.

Its eyes are lamps like the eyes of dragons.

It drinks gasoline from big red flagons.

Butting through the delicate mists of the morning,

It comes like lightning, goes past roaring.

It will hail all the windmills, taunting, ringing,

Dodge the cyclones,

Count the milestones,

On through the ranges the prairie-dog tills—

Scooting past the cattle on the thousand hills. . . .

*To be sung or read with great speed.*

Ho for the tear-horn, scare-horn, dare-horn,

Ho for the *gay*-horn, *bark*-horn, *bay*-horn.

*Ho for Kansas, land that restores us*

*When houses choke us, and great books bore us!*

*To be read or sung in a rolling bass, with some deliberation.*

153

*Sunrise Kansas, harvesters' Kansas,*
*A million men have found you before us.*
*A million men have found you before us.*

## II. In Which Many Autos Pass Westward

I want live things in their pride to remain.      *In an even,*
I will not kill one grasshopper vain              *deliberate,*
Though he eats a hole in my shirt like a          *narrative*
    door.                     *manner.*
I let him out, give him one chance more.
Perhaps, while he gnaws my hat in his whim,
Grasshopper lyrics occur to him.

I am a tramp by the long trail's border,
Given to squalor, rags and disorder.
I nap and amble and yawn and look,
Write fool-thoughts in my grubby book,
Recite to the children, explore at my ease,
Work when I work, beg when I please,
Give crank-drawings, that make folks stare
To the half-grown boys in the sunset glare,
And get me a place to sleep in the hay
At the end of a live-and-let-live day.

I find in the stubble of the new-cut weeds
A whisper and a feasting, all one needs:
The whisper of the strawberries, white and
    red
Here where the new-cut weeds lie dead.

But I would not walk all alone till I die
Without some life-drunk horns going by.
And up round this apple-earth they come
Blasting the whispers of the morning
    dumb:—

# THE SANTA-FÉ TRAIL (A HUMORESQUE)

Cars in a plain realistic row.
And fair dreams fade
When the raw horns blow.

On each snapping pennant
A big black name:—
The careering city
Whence each car came.
They tour from Memphis, Atlanta, Savannah,
Tallahassee and Texarkana.
They tour from St. Louis, Columbus, *Like a train-*
    Manistee, *caller in a*
    *Union Depot.*
They tour from Peoria, Davenport, Kan-
    kakee.
Cars from Concord, Niagara, Boston,
Cars from Topeka, Emporia, and Austin.
Cars from Chicago, Hannibal, Cairo.
Cars from Alton, Oswego, Toledo.
Cars from Buffalo, Kokomo, Delphi,
Cars from Lodi, Carmi, Loami.
Ho for Kansas, land that restores us
When houses choke us, and great books bore us!
While I watch the highroad
And look at the sky,
While I watch the clouds in amazing grandeur
Roll their legions without rain
Over the blistering Kansas plain—
While I sit by the milestone
And watch the sky,
The United States
Goes by.

Listen to the iron-horns, ripping, racking. *To be given*
Listen to the quack-horns, slack and clack- *very harshly,*
    ing. *with a*
*snapping ex-*
Way down the road, trilling like a toad, *plosiveness.*

155

Here comes the *dice*-horn, here comes the
    *vice*-horn,
Here comes the *snarl*-horn, *brawl*-horn, *lewd*-
    horn,
Followed by the *prude*-horn, bleak and
    squeaking :—
(Some of them from Kansas, some of them
    from Kansas.)
Here comes the *hod*-horn, *plod*-horn, *sod*-
    horn,
Nevermore-to-*roam*-horn, *loam*-horn, *home*-
    horn.
(Some of them from Kansas, some of them
    from Kansas.)

    Far away the Rachel-Jane *To be read or*
    Not defeated by the horns *sung, well-nigh*
    Sings amid a hedge of thorns:— *in a whisper.*
    "Love and life,
    Eternal youth—
    Sweet, sweet, sweet, sweet,
    Dew and glory,
    Love and truth,
    Sweet, sweet, sweet, sweet."

WHILE SMOKE-BLACK FREIGHTS ON THE *Louder and*
    DOUBLE-TRACKED RAILROAD, *louder, faster*
DRIVEN AS THOUGH BY THE FOUL FIEND'S *and faster.*
    OX-GOAD,
SCREAMING TO THE WEST COAST, SCREAM-
    ING TO THE EAST,
CARRY OFF A HARVEST, BRING BACK A
    FEAST,
AND HARVESTING MACHINERY AND HARNESS
    FOR THE BEAST,

# THE SANTA-FÉ TRAIL (A HUMORESQUE)

THE HAND-CARS WHIZ, AND RATTLE ON THE
    RAILS,
THE SUNLIGHT FLASHES ON THE TIN
    DINNER-PAILS.

And then, in an instant, ye modern men,     *In a rolling*
Behold the procession once again,     *bass, with*
The United States goes by!     *increasing*
    *deliberation.*
Listen to the iron-horns, ripping, racking,
Listen to the *wise*-horn, desperate-to-*advise*     *With a snap-*
    horn,     *ping explosive-*
Listen to the *fast*-horn, *kill*-horn, *blast*-     *ness.*
    horn. . . .

      Far away the Rachel-Jane     *To be sung or*
      Not defeated by the horns     *read well-nigh*
      Sings amid a hedge of thorns:—     *in a whisper.*
      Love and life,
      Eternal youth,
      Sweet, sweet, sweet, sweet,
      Dew and glory,
      Love and truth.
      Sweet, sweet, sweet, sweet.

The mufflers open on a score of cars     *To be brawled*
With wonderful thunder,     *in the begin-*
CRACK, CRACK, CRACK,     *ning with a*
CRACK-CRACK, CRACK-CRACK,     *snapping*
CRACK, CRACK, CRACK,     *explosiveness.*
Listen to the gold-horn . . .     *ending in a*
Old-horn . . .     *languorous*
Cold horn . . .     *chant.*
And all of the tunes, till the night comes
    down
On hay-stack, and ant-hill, and wind-bitten
    town.

Then far in the west, as in the beginning,
Dim in the distance, sweet in retreating,
Hark to the faint-horn, quaint-horn, saint-
        horn,
Hark to the calm-horn, balm-horn, psalm-
        horn. . . .

*To be sung to
exactly the
same whis-
pered tune as
the first five
lines.*

They are hunting the goals that they under-
        stand:—
San-Francisco and the brown sea-sand.
My goal is the mystery the beggars win.
I am caught in the web the night-winds
        spin.
The edge of the wheat-ridge speaks to me.
I talk with the leaves of the mulberry tree.
And now I hear, as I sit all alone
In the dusk, by another big Santa-Fé stone,
The souls of the tall corn gathering round
And the gay little souls of the grass in the
        ground.
Listen to the tale the cottonwood tells.
Listen to the windmills, singing o'er the
        wells.
Listen to the whistling flutes without price
Of myriad prophets out of paradise.
Harken to the wonder
That the night-air carries. . . .
Listen . . . to . . . the . . . whisper . . .
Of . . . the . . . prairie . . . fairies

*This section
beginning
sonorously,
ending in a
languorous
whisper.*

        Singing o'er the fairy plain:—
        "Sweet, sweet, sweet, sweet.
        Love and glory,
        Stars and rain,
        Sweet, sweet, sweet, sweet. . . ."

*To the same
whispered tune
as the Rachel-
Jane song—
but very
slowly.*

158

# DANIEL

### (Inscribed to Isadora Bennett Reed)

Darius the Mede was a king and a wonder.    *Beginning*
His eye was proud, and his voice was thun-    *with a strain*
    der.    *of "Dixie."*
He kept bad lions in a monstrous den.
He fed up the lions on Christian men.

Daniel was the chief hired man of the land.    *With a touch*
He stirred up the music in the palace band.    *of "Alexan-*
He whitewashed the cellar.   He shovelled    *der's Ragtime*
    in the coal.    *Band."*
And Daniel kept a-praying:—"Lord save my soul."
Daniel kept a-praying:—"Lord save my soul."
Daniel kept a-praying:—"Lord save my soul."

Daniel was the butler, swagger and swell.
He ran up stairs.   He answered the bell.
And *he* would let in whoever came a-calling:—
Saints so holy, scamps so appalling.
"Old man Ahab leaves his card.
Elisha and the bears are a-waiting in the yard.
Here comes Pharaoh and his snakes a-calling.
Here comes Cain and his wife a-calling.
Shadrach, Meshach and Abednego for tea.
Here comes Jonah and the whale,
And the *Sea!*
Here comes St. Peter and his fishing pole.
Here comes Judas and his silver a-calling.
Here comes old Beelzebub a-calling."
And Daniel kept a-praying:—"Lord save my soul."
Daniel kept a-praying:—"Lord save my soul."
Daniel kept a-praying:—"Lord save my soul."

His sweetheart and his mother were Christian and meek.
They washed and ironed for Darius every week.
One Thursday he met them at the door:—
Paid them as usual, but acted sore.


He said:—"Your Daniel is a dead little pigeon.
He's a good hard worker, but he talks religion."
And he showed them Daniel in the lions' cage.
Daniel standing quietly, the lions in a rage.
His good old mother cried:—
"Lord save him."
And Daniel's tender sweetheart cried:—
"Lord save him."


And she was a golden lily in the dew.   *This to be*
And she was as sweet as an apple on the tree,   *repeated*
  *three times,*
And she was as fine as a melon in the corn-field, *very softly*
Gliding and lovely as a ship on the sea,   *and slowly.*
Gliding and lovely as a ship on the sea.


And she prayed to the Lord:—
"Send Gabriel. Send Gabriel."


King Darius said to the lions:—
"Bite Daniel. Bite Daniel.
Bite him. Bite him. Bite him!"


Thus roared the lions:—   *Here the au-*
"We want Daniel, Daniel, Daniel,   *dience roars*
  *with the*
We want Daniel, Daniel, Daniel."   *leader.*


And Daniel did not frown,
Daniel did not cry.

160

He kept on looking at the sky.
And the Lord said to Gabriel:—
"Go chain the lions down,
Go chain the lions down.
Go chain the lions down.
Go chain the lions down."

*The audience sings this with the leader, to the old negro tune.*

And *Gabriel* chained the lions,
And *Gabriel* chained the lions,
And *Gabriel* chained the lions,
And Daniel got out of the den,
And Daniel got out of the den,
And Daniel got out of the den.
And Darius said:—"You're a Christian child,"
Darius said:—"You're a Christian child,"
Darius said:—"You're a Christian child,"
And gave him his job again,
And gave him his job again,
And gave him his job again.


# THE BOOKER WASHINGTON TRILOGY

(A Memorial to Booker T. Washington)

## I. SIMON LEGREE—A NEGRO SERMON

(To be read in your own variety of negro dialect.)

Legree's big house was white and green.
His cotton-fields were the best to be seen.
He had strong horses and opulent cattle,
And bloodhounds bold, with chains that would rattle.
His garret was full of curious things:
Books of magic, bags of gold,

161

And rabbits' feet on long twine strings.
*But he went down to the Devil.*

Legree he sported a brass-buttoned coat,
A snake-skin necktie, a blood-red shirt.
Legree he had a beard like a goat,
And a thick hairy neck, and eyes like dirt.
His puffed-out cheeks were fish-belly white,
He had great long teeth, and an appetite.
He ate raw meat, 'most every meal,
And rolled his eyes till the cat would squeal.

His fist was an enormous size
To mash poor niggers that told him lies:
He was surely a witch-man in disguise.
*But he went down to the Devil.*

He wore hip-boots, and would wade all day
To capture his slaves that had fled away.
*But he went down to the Devil.*

He beat poor Uncle Tom to death
Who prayed for Legree with his last breath.
Then Uncle Tom to Eva flew,
To the high sanctoriums bright and new;
And Simon Legree stared up beneath,
And cracked his heels, and ground his teeth:
*And went down to the Devil.*

He crossed the yard in the storm and gloom;
He went into his grand front room.
He said, "I killed him, and I don't care."
He kicked a hound, he gave a swear;
He tightened his belt, he took a lamp,
Went down cellar to the webs and damp.

There in the middle of the mouldy floor
He heaved up a slab, he found a door—
*And went down to the Devil.*

His lamp blew out, but his eyes burned bright.
Simon Legree stepped down all night—
*Down, down to the Devil.*
Simon Legree he reached the place,
He saw one half of the human race,
He saw the Devil on a wide green throne,
Gnawing the meat from a big ham-bone,
And he said to Mister Devil:

"I see that you have much to eat—
A red ham-bone is surely sweet.
I see that you have lion's feet;
I see your frame is fat and fine,
I see you drink your poison wine—
Blood and burning turpentine."

And the Devil said to Simon Legree:
"I like your style, so wicked and free.
Come sit and share my throne with me,
And let us bark and revel."
And there they sit and gnash their teeth,
And each one wears a hop-vine wreath.
They are matching pennies and shooting craps,
They are playing poker and taking naps.
And old Legree is fat and fine:
He eats the fire, he drinks the wine—
Blood and burning turpentine—
*Down, down with the Devil;*
*Down, down with the Devil;*
*Down, down with the Devil.*

## II. John Brown

(To be sung by a leader and chorus, the leader singing
the body of the poem, while the chorus interrupts with the
question)

>I've been to Palestine.
>>*What did you see in Palestine?*
>I saw the ark of Noah—
>It was made of pitch and pine.
>I saw old Father Noah
>Asleep beneath his vine.
>I saw Shem, Ham and Japhet
>Standing in a line.
>I saw the tower of Babel
>In the gorgeous sunrise shine—
>By a weeping willow tree
>Beside the Dead Sea.

>I've been to Palestine.
>>*What did you see in Palestine?*
>I saw abominations
>And Gadarene swine.
>I saw the sinful Canaanites
>Upon the shewbread dine,
>And spoil the temple vessels
>And drink the temple wine.
>I saw Lot's wife, a pillar of salt
>Standing in the brine—
>By a weeping willow tree
>Beside the Dead Sea.

I've been to Palestine.
> *What did you see in Palestine?*
Cedars on Mount Lebanon,
Gold in Ophir's mine,
And a wicked generation
Seeking for a sign,
And Baal's howling worshippers
Their god with leaves entwine.
And . . .
I saw the war-horse ramping
And shake his forelock fine—
By a weeping willow tree
Beside the Dead Sea.

I've been to Palestine.
> *What did you see in Palestine?*
Old John Brown.
Old John Brown.
I saw his gracious wife
Dressed in a homespun gown.
I saw his seven sons
Before his feet bow down.
And he marched with his seven sons,
His wagons and goods and guns,
To his campfire by the sea,
By the waves of Galilee.

I've been to Palestine.
> *What did you see in Palestine?*
I saw the harp and psalt'ry
Played for Old John Brown.
I heard the ram's horn blow,
Blow for Old John Brown.
I saw the Bulls of Bashan—
They cheered for Old John Brown.

165

I saw the big Behemoth—
He cheered for Old John Brown.
I saw the big Leviathan—
He cheered for Old John Brown.
I saw the Angel Gabriel
Great power to him assign.
I saw him fight the Canaanites
And set God's Israel free.
I saw him when the war was done
In his rustic chair recline—
By his campfire by the sea
By the waves of Galilee.

I've been to Palestine.
    *What did you see in Palestine?*
Old John Brown.
Old John Brown.
And there he sits
To judge the world.
His hunting-dogs
At his feet are curled.
His eyes half-closed,
But John Brown sees
The ends of the earth,
The Day of Doom.
And his shot-gun lies
Across his knees—
Old John Brown,
Old John Brown.

## III. KING SOLOMON AND THE QUEEN OF SHEBA

### (A Poem Game)

"And when the Queen of Sheba heard of the fame of Solomon, . . . she came to prove him with hard questions."

MEN'S LEADER: The Queen of Sheba came to see King Solomon.

*The men's leader rises as he sees the Queen unveiling and approaching a position that gives her half of the stage.*

I am King Solomon,
I am King Solomon,
I am King Solomon.

*He bows three times.*

WOMEN'S LEADER: I am the Queen,
I am the Queen,
I am the Queen.

*She bows three times.*

BOTH LEADERS: We will be king and queen,
Reigning on mountains green,
Happy and free
For ten thousand years.

*They stand together stretching their hands over the land.*

BOTH LEADERS: King Solomon he had four hundred oxen.

CONGREGATION: We were the oxen.

*They stagger forward as though carrying a yoke together.*

167

BOTH LEADERS:  You shall feel goads no more.

Walk dreadful roads no more,
Free from your loads
For ten thousand years.

*Here King and Queen pause at the footlights. They walk backward, throwing off the yoke and rejoicing.*

BOTH LEADERS:  King Solomon he had four hundred sweethearts.

*The men's leader goes forward, the women's leader dances round him.*

CONGREGATION:  We were the sweethearts.

*Here he pauses at the footlights.*

BOTH LEADERS:  You shall dance round again,
You shall dance round again,
Cymbals s h a l l sound again,
Cymbals s h a l l sound again,
Wildflowers be found
For ten thousand years,
Wildflowers be found
For ten thousand years.

*He walks backward. Both clap their hands to the measure.*

*The Queen appears to gather wildflowers.*

BOTH LEADERS:  And every sweetheart had f o u r hundred swans.

*He continues to command the congregation, the woman to dance. He goes forward to the footlights.*

CONGREGATION:  We were the swans.

168

| | | |
|---|---|---|
| BOTH LEADERS: | You shall spread wings again, | *The King walks backward.* |
| | You shall spread wings again, | |
| | Fly in soft rings again, | *Here a special dance, by the Queen: swans flying in circles.* |
| | Fly in soft rings again, | |
| | Swim by cool springs | |
| | For ten thousand years, | |
| | Swim by cool springs | |
| | For ten thousand years. | |
| | | |
| MEN'S LEADER: | King Solomon, | *The refrain "King Solomon may be intoned by the men's leader whenever it is needed to enable the women's leader to get to her starting point. They bow to each other — then give a pantomime indicating a great rose garden.* |
| | King Solomon. | |
| | | |
| WOMEN'S LEADER: | The Queen of Sheba asked him like a lady, | |
| | Bowing most politely: | |
| | "What makes the roses bloom | |
| | Over the mossy tomb, | |
| | Driving away the gloom | |
| | Ten thousand years?" | |
| | | |
| MEN'S LEADER: | King Solomon made answer to the lady, | *They bow and confer. The Queen reserved, but taking cognizance. The King wooing with ornate gestures of respect, and* |
| | Bowing most politely: | |
| | "They b l o om forever thinking o f y o u r beauty, | |
| | Your step so queenly and your eyes so lovely. | |
| | These keep the roses fair, | |

189

Young and without a *courtly anima-*
care, *tion.*
Making so sweet the air,
Ten thousand years."

BOTH LEADERS:   King Solomon he had *The two, with*
four hundred sons. *a manner al-*
*most a cake*
*walk, go for-*
*ward.*

CONGREGATION:   We were the sons. *On this line,*
*King and*
*Queen pause*
*before the foot-*
*lights.*

BOTH LEADERS:   Crowned by the throngs *Pantomime of*
again, *crowning the*
You shall make songs *audience.*
again, *On this line*
Singing along *they walk*
For ten thousand years. *backward,*
*playing great*
*imaginary*
*harps.*

BOTH LEADERS:   He gave each son four *They go for-*
h u n d r e d prancing *ward in a pony*
ponies. *gallop, then*
*stand pawing.*

CONGREGATION:   We were the ponies.

BOTH LEADERS:   You shall eat hay again, *They nod, and*
In forests play again, *walk backward.*
Rampage and neigh *A pony dance*
For ten thousand years. *by both, in*
*circles.*

MEN'S LEADER:   King Solomon he asked
the Queen of Sheba,

170

Bowing most politely: *They bow to*
"What makes the oak- *each other,*
tree grow *standing so*
Hardy in sun and snow, *that each one*
Never by wind brought *commands half*
low *of the stage.*
Ten thousand years?"

WOMEN'S LEADER: The Queen of Sheba an-
swered like a lady,
Bowing most politely: *They bow to*
"It blooms forever think- *each other,*
ing of your wisdom, *again, with*
Your brave heart and the *pantomime*
way you rule your *indicating a*
kingdom. *forest.*
These keep the oak se-
cure,
Weaving its leafy lure,
Dreaming by fountains
pure
Ten thousand years."

BOTH LEADERS: The Queen of Sheba had *They go to the*
four hundred sailors. *footlights with*
*a sailors' lurch*
*and hitch.*

CONGREGATION: We were the sailors. *The King and*
*Queen pause.*

BOTH LEADERS: You shall bring spice and
ore
Over the ocean's floor, *They walk*
Shipmates once more, *backward with*
For ten thousand years. *slow long-*
*armed gestures*
*indicating the*
WOMEN'S LEADER: The Queen of Sheba *entire horizon*
asked him like a lady, *line.*

171

Bowing most politely:
"Why is the sea so deep,
What secret does it keep
While tides a-roaring leap
Ten thousand years?"

*They bow to each other, the Queen indicating the depths of the sea.*

MEN'S LEADER:

King Solomon made answer to the lady,
Bowing most politely:
"My love for you is like the stormy ocean—
Too deep to understand,
Bending to your command,
Bringing your ships to land
Ten thousand years."
King Solomon,
King Solomon.

*They bow to each other, then confer; the Queen reserved, but taking cognizance, the King wooing with ornate gestures of respect and courtly admiration.*

BOTH LEADERS:

King Solomon he had four hundred chieftains.

*They go to the footlights with the greatest possible strut.*

CONGREGATION:

We were the chieftains.

BOTH LEADERS:

You shall be proud again,
Dazzle the crowd again,
Laughing aloud
For ten thousand years.

*They stand proudly with arms folded. They walk backward haughtily, laughing on the last lines. From here on the whole production to be much more solemn, elevated, religious.*

172

BOTH LEADERS: King Solomon he had four hundred shepherds.

*The leaders go forward to the footlights carrying imaginary torches.*

CONGREGATION: We were the shepherds.

*The man and woman pause at the footlights.*

BOTH LEADERS: You shall have torches bright,
Watching the folds by night,
Guarding the lambs aright,
Ten thousand years.

*They wander over the stage as though looking for lost lambs, with torches held high.*

MEN'S LEADER: King Solomon he asked the Queen of Sheba,
Bowing most politely:
"Why are the stars so high,
There in the velvet sky,
Rolling in rivers by,
Ten thousand years?"

*The King kneels, and indicates the entire sky with one long slow gesture.*

WOMEN'S LEADER: The Queen of Sheba answered like a lady,
Bowing most politely:
"They're singing of your kingdom to the angels,
They guide your chariot with their lamps and candles,
Therefore they burn so far—
So you can drive your car

*The Queen kneels opposite the King, and gives the same gesture as she answers.*

173

Up where the prophets
are,
Ten thousand years."

MEN'S LEADER:    King Solomon,
King Solomon.

BOTH LEADERS:    King Solomon he kept
the Sabbath holy.
And spoke with tongues    *The two stand,*
in prophet words so    *commanding*
mighty    *the audience.*
We stamped and whirled    *The man and*
and wept and shouted:    *woman stamp*
    *and whirl with*
    *great noise and*
CONGREGATION    *solemnity.*
RISES AND JOINS
IN THE SONG:    . . . . "Glory."
We were his people.

BOTH LEADERS:    You shall be wild and    *On these two*
gay,    *lines, man and*
Green trees shall deck    *woman stamp*
your way,    *and whirl*
    *again, gravely,*
    *magnificently.*
Sunday be every day,    *On these two*
Ten thousand years.    *lines they*
    *kneel, com-*
    *manding the*
    *audience.*
King Solomon,    *Now they rise*
King Solomon.    *and bow to*
    *each other and*
    *the audience,*
    *maintaining a*
    *certain inten-*
    *tion of bene-*
    *diction.*

174

# HOW SAMSON BORE AWAY THE GATES OF GAZA

## A Negro Sermon

Once, in a night as black as ink,
She drove him out when he would not drink.
Round the house there were men in wait
Asleep in rows by the Gaza gate.
But the Holy Spirit was in this man.
Like a gentle wind he crept and ran.
("It is midnight," said the big town clock.)

He lifted the gates up, post and lock.
The hole in the wall was high and wide
When he bore away old Gaza's pride
Into the deep of the night:—
The bold Jack Johnson Israelite,—
Samson—
The Judge,
The Nazarite.

The air was black, like the smoke of a dragon.
Samson's heart was as big as a wagon.
He sang like a shining golden fountain.
He sweated up to the top of the mountain.
He threw down the gates with a noise like judgment.
And the quails all ran with the big arousement.

But he wept—"I must not love tough queens,
And spend on them my hard earned means.
I told that girl I would drink no more.
Therefore she drove me from her door.
Oh sorrow!
Sorrow!

I cannot hide.
Oh Lord look down from your chariot side.
You made me Judge, and I am not wise.
I am weak as a sheep for all my size."


*Let Samson*
*Be coming*
*Into your mind.*


The moon shone out, the stars were gay.
He saw the foxes run and play.
He rent his garments, he rolled around
In deep repentance on the ground.


Then he felt a honey in his soul.
Grace abounding made him whole.
Then he saw the Lord in a chariot blue.
The gorgeous stallions whinnied and flew.
The iron wheels hummed an old hymn-tune
And crunched in thunder over the moon.
And Samson shouted to the sky:
"My Lord, my Lord is riding high."


Like a steed, he pawed the gates with his hoof.
He rattled the gates like rocks on the roof,
And danced in the night
On the mountain-top,
Danced in the deep of the night:
The Judge, the holy Nazarite,
Whom ropes and chains could never bind.


*Let Samson*
*Be coming*
*Into your mind.*

# WHEN PETER JACKSON PREACHED IN OLD CHURCH

Whirling his arms, like a top he sped.
His long black hair flew round his head
Like an outstretched net of silky cord,
Like a wheel of the chariot of the Lord.

*Let Samson*
*Be coming*
*Into your mind.*

Samson saw the sun anew.
He left the gates in the grass and dew.
He went to a county-seat a-nigh.
Found a harlot proud and high:
Philistine that no man could tame—
Delilah was her lady-name.
Oh sorrow,
Sorrow,
She was too wise.
She cut off his hair,
She put out his eyes.

*Let Samson*
*Be coming*
*Into your mind.*

# WHEN PETER JACKSON PREACHED IN THE OLD CHURCH

(To be sung to the tune of the old negro spiritual "Every time I feel the spirit moving in my heart I'll pray")

Peter Jackson was a-preaching
And the house was still as snow.
He whispered of repentance

And the lights were dim and low
And were almost out
When he gave the first shout:
"Arise, arise,
Cry out your eyes."
And we mourned all our terrible sins away.
Clean, clean away.
Then we marched around, around,
And sang with a wonderful sound :—
"Every time I feel the spirit moving in my heart I'll pray.
Every time I feel the spirit moving in my heart I'll pray."
And we fell by the altar
And fell by the aisle,
And found our Savior
In just a little while,
We all found Jesus at the break of the day,
We all found Jesus at the break of the day.
Blessed Jesus,
Blessed Jesus.

## THE CONGO

### A Study of the Negro Race

(Being a memorial to Ray Eldred, a Disciple missionary
of the Congo River)

#### I. Their Basic Savagery

Fat black bucks in a wine-barrel room,
Barrel-house kings, with feet unstable,
Sagged and reeled and pounded on the *A deep rolling*
    table, *bass.*
Pounded on the table,
Beat an empty barrel with the handle of
    a broom,

178

## THE CONGO

Hard as they were able,
Boom, boom, Boom,
With a silk umbrella and the handle of a
    broom,
Boomlay, boomlay, boomlay, Boom.
Then I had religion, Then I had a vision.
I could not turn from their revel in derision.
Then I saw the Congo, creeping through
    the black,
Cutting through the forest with a
    golden track.

*More deliberate.*
*Solemnly*
*chanted.*

Then along that riverbank
A thousand miles
Tattooed cannibals danced in files;
Then I heard the boom of the blood-lust
    song
And a thigh-bone beating on a tin-pan gong.
And "Blood" screamed the whistles and the
    fifes of the warriors,
"Blood" screamed the skull-faced, lean witch-
    doctors,

*A rapidly*
*piling climax*
*of speed and*
*racket.*

"Whirl ye the deadly voo-doo rattle,
Harry the uplands,
Steal all the cattle,
Rattle-rattle, rattle-rattle,
Bing.
Boomlay, boomlay, boomlay, Boom,"
A roaring, epic, rag-time tune
From the mouth of the Congo
To the Mountains of the Moon.

*With a philo-*
*sophic pause.*

Death is an Elephant,
Torch-eyed and horrible,
Foam-flanked and terrible.
Boom, steal the pygmies,
Boom, kill the Arabs,

*Shrilly and*
*with a heavily*
*accented metre.*

179

Boom, kill the white men,
Hoo, Hoo, Hoo.
Listen to the yell of Leopold's ghost     *Like the wind*
Burning in Hell for his hand-maimed host.    *in the chimney.*
Hear how the demons chuckle and yell
Cutting his hands off, down in Hell.
Listen to the creepy proclamation,
Blown through the lairs of the forest-nation,
Blown past the white-ants' hill of clay,
Blown past the marsh where the butterflies
     play:—
"Be careful what you do,
Or Mumbo-Jumbo, God of the Congo,     *All the "o"*
And all of the other                  *sounds very*
Gods of the Congo,                   *golden. Heavy*
                                     *accents very*
Mumbo-Jumbo will hoo-doo you,     *heavy. Light*
Mumbo-Jumbo will hoo-doo you,     *accents very*
Mumbo-Jumbo will hoo-doo you."      *light. Last line*
                                     *whispered.*

## II. THEIR IRREPRESSIBLE HIGH SPIRITS

Wild crap-shooters with a whoop and a call    *Rather shrill*
Danced the juba in their gambling hall     *and high.*
And laughed fit to kill, and shook the town,
And guyed the policemen and laughed them
     down
With a boomlay, boomlay, boomlay, Boom.
THEN I SAW THE CONGO, CREEPING THROUGH    *Read exactly as*
     THE BLACK,                                  *in first section.*
CUTTING THROUGH THE FOREST WITH A
     GOLDEN TRACK.
A negro fairyland swung into view,      *Lay emphasis*
A minstrel river                       *on the delicate*
Where dreams come true.          *ideas. Keep as*
The ebony palace soared on high      *light-footed as*
                                     *possible.*

Through the blossoming trees to the evening
    sky.
The inlaid porches and casements shone
With gold and ivory and elephant-bone.
And the black crowd laughed till their
    sides were sore
At the baboon butler in the agate door,
And the well-known tunes of the parrot band
That trilled on the bushes of that magic land.

A troupe of skull-faced witch-men came      *With*
Through the agate doorway in suits of flame, *pomposity.*
Yea, long-tailed coats with a gold-leaf crust
And hats that were covered with diamond-
    dust.
And the crowd in the court gave a whoop
    and a call
And danced the juba from wall to wall.
But the witch-men suddenly stilled the      *With a great*
    throng                                  *deliberation*
With a stern cold glare, and a stern old    *and ghostliness.*
    song:—
"Mumbo-Jumbo will hoo-doo you." . . .
Just then from the doorway, as fat as shotes, *With over-*
Came the cake-walk princes in their long red *whelming as-*
    coats,                                   *surance, good*
Canes with a brilliant lacquer shine,        *cheer, and*
And tall silk hats that were red as wine.    *pomp.*
And they pranced with their butterfly part-
    ners there,                              *With growing*
Coal-black maidens with pearls in their hair, *speed and*
Knee-skirts trimmed with the jassamine      *sharply marked*
    sweet,                                   *dance-rhythm.*
And bells on their ankles and little black-
    feet.

181

And the couples railed at the chant and the
    frown
Of the witch-men lean, and laughed them
    down.
(Oh, rare was the revel, and well worth while
That made those glowering witch-men smile.)

The cake-walk royalty then began
To walk for a cake that was tall as a man
To the tune of "Boomlay, boomlay, Boom,"
While the witch-men laughed, with a sinister
    air,
And sang with the scalawags prancing
    there:—
"Walk with care, walk with care,
Or Mumbo-Jumbo, God of the Congo,
And all of the other Gods of the Congo,
Mumbo-Jumbo will hoo-doo you.
Beware, beware, walk with care,
Boomlay, boomlay, boomlay, boom.
Boomlay, boomlay, boomlay, boom.
Boomlay, boomlay, bocmlay, boom.
Boomlay, boomlay, boomlay,
Boom."
(Oh, rare was the revel, and well worth while
That made those glowering witch-men smile.)

*With a touch of negro dialect, and as rapidly as possible toward the end.*

*Slow philosophic calm.*

## III. The Hope of Their Religion

A good old negro in the slums of the town
Preached at a sister for her velvet gown.
Howled at a brother for his low-down ways,
His prowling, guzzling, sneak-thief days.
Beat on the Bible till he wore it out
Starting the jubilee revival shout.

*Heavy bass. With a literal imitation of camp-meeting racket, and trance.*

# THE CONGO

And some had visions, as they stood on chairs,
And sang of Jacob, and the golden stairs,
And they all repented, a thousand strong
From their stupor and savagery and sin and
      wrong
And slammed with their hymn books till they
      shook the room
With "glory, glory, glory,"
And "Boom, boom, BOOM."

THEN I SAW THE CONGO, CREEPING THROUGH
    THE BLACK,
CUTTING THROUGH THE JUNGLE WITH A
    GOLDEN TRACK.

*Exactly as in the first section. Begin with terror and power, end with joy.*

And the gray sky opened like a new-rent
    veil
And showed the Apostles with their coats of
    mail.
In bright white steele they were seated
    round
And their fire-eyes watched where the Congo
    wound.
And the twelve Apostles, from their thrones
    on high
Thrilled all the forest with their heavenly
    cry:—
"Mumbo-Jumbo will die in the jungle;
Never again will he hoo-doo you,
Never again will he hoo-doo you."

*Sung to the tune of "Hark, ten thousand harps and voices."*

Then along that river, a thousand miles
The vine-snared trees fell down in files.
Pioneer angels cleared the way
For a Congo paradise, for babes at play,
For sacred capitals, for temples clean.
Gone were the skull-faced witch-men lean.

*With growing deliberation and joy.*

There, where the wild ghost-gods had wailed
A million boats of the angels sailed
With oars of silver, and prows of blue
And silken pennants that the sun shone
    through.
'Twas a land transfigured, 'twas a new
    creation.
Oh, a singing wind swept the negro nation
And on through the backwoods clearing
    flew:—

*In a rather high key—as delicately as possible.*

"Mumbo-Jumbo is dead in the jungle.
Never again will he hoo-doo you.
Never again will he hoo-doo you.

*To the tune of "Hark, ten thousand harps and voices."*

Redeemed were the forests, the beasts and
    the men,
And only the vulture dared again
By the far, lone mountains of the moon
To cry, in the silence, the Congo tune:—
Mumbo-Jumbo will hoo-doo you,
"Mumbo-Jumbo will hoo-doo you.
Mumbo . . . Jumbo . . . will . . . hoo-doo . . .
    you."

*Dying down into a penetrating, terrified whisper.*

This poem, particularly the third section, was suggested by an allusion in a sermon by my pastor, F. W. Burnham, to the heroic life and death of Ray Eldred. Eldred was a missionary of the Disciples of Christ who perished while swimming a treacherous branch of the Congo. See *A Master Builder on the Congo*, by Andrew F. Henesey, published by Fleming H. Revell.

184

# SECTION III

# LITANY OF THE HEROES

*Being a chant about many men, good and bad, who have led and misled mankind, from the earliest times until now.*

# LITANY OF THE HEROES

## (Inscribed to George Mather Richards)

Would that young Amenophis Fourth returned
Prince Hamlet and the Poet Keats in one,
He mocked at fraud, even his own crown,
He loved all classic beauty in the town,
He rode abroad to build his lotus tomb,
Praising one god, and that one god, the sun.
The idol-worshippers chipped out his name
From wall and obelisk, to end his fame.

*Egypt
and
Israel in
History.*

Still let that brave, flower-loving King of Time
Be throned in your deep hearts, to raise for you
The hopes the prince and his mother Thi, well knew,
Filling these barren days with Mystery,
With Life, and Death, and Immortality,
The devouring ages, the triumphant Sun.
God keep us brooding on eternal things,
God make us wizard-kings.

Then let us raise that Egypt-nurtured youth,
Son of a Hebrew, with the dauntless scorn
And hate for bleating gods Egyptian-born,
Showing with signs to stubborn Mizraim
"God is one God, the God of Abraham,"
He who in the beginning *made* the Sun.
God send us Moses from his hidden grave,
God help us to be brave.

187

*The Soul of China in History.*

Would we were scholars of Confucius' time
Watching the feudal China crumbling down,
Frightening our master, shaking many a crown,
Until he makes more firm the father sages,
Restoring custom from the earliest ages
With prudent sayings, golden as the sun.
Lord, show us safe, august, established ways,
Fill us with yesterdays.

*The Soul of India in History.*

Would that by Hindu magic we became
Dark monks of jewelled India long ago,
Sitting at Prince Siddartha's feet to know
The foolishness of gold and love and station,
The gospel of the Great Renunciation,
The ragged cloak, the staff, the rain and sun,
The beggar's life, with far Nirvana gleaming:
Lord, make us Buddhas, dreaming.

*The Classic Spirit.*

Would that the joy of living came to-day,
Even as sculptured on Athena's shrine
In sunny conclave of serene design,
Maidens and men, procession flute and feast,
By Phidias, the ivory-hearted priest
Of beauty absolute, whose eyes the sun
Showed goodlier forms than our desires can guess
And more of happiness.

Would I might waken in you Alexander,
Murdering the nations wickedly,
Flooding his time with blood remorselessly,
Sowing new Empires, where the Athenian light,
Knowledge and music, slay the Asian night,
And men behold Apollo in the sun.
God make us splendid, though by grievous wrong.
God make us fierce and strong.

# LITANY OF THE HEROES

Would I might rouse the Cæsar in you all
(That which men hail as king, and bow them down),
Till you are crowned, or you refuse the crown.
Would I might wake the valor and the pride,
The eagle soul with which he soared and died,
Entering grandly then the fearful grave.
God help us build the world, like master-men,
God help us to be brave.

*Great Art and Letters in History.* Behold the Pharisees, proud, rich, and damned,
Boasting themselves in lost Jerusalem,
Gathered a weeping woman to condemn,
Then watching curiously, without a sound
The God of Mercy, writing on the ground.
How looked his sunburned face beneath the sun
Flushed with his Father's mighty angel-wine?
God make us all divine.

Would I might free St. Paul, singing in chains
In your deep hearts.  New heavenly love shall fight
And slay the subtle gods of Greek delight
And dreadful Roman gods, and light the world
With words of flame, till those false powers are hurled
Burning to ashes in the avenging grave.
"St. Paul" our battle-cry, and faith our shield,
God help us to be brave.

Yea, give the world no peace, till all men kneel,
Seeking with tears the grace of Christ our God.
Make us like Augustine beneath Thy rod.
Give us no other joy but Thy repentance,
Thunder our just, hereditary sentence
Till shame and fear of Hell blot out the sun.
Christ help us hold Thy blood-redemption dear.
Christ, give us holy fear.

*The
Secular
Spirit
in
History.*

Nay, let us have the marble peace of Rome,
Recorded in the Code Justinian,
Till Pagan Justice shelters man from man.
Fanatics snarl like mongrel dogs; the code
Will build each custom like a Roman Road,
Direct as daylight, clear-eyed as the sun.
God grant all crazy world-disturbers cease.
God give us honest peace.

*The
World-
Spirit of
Islam.*

Would that on horses swifter than desire
We rode behind Mohammed 'round the zones
With swords unceasing, sowing fields of bones,
Till New America, ancient Mizraim,
Cry: "Allah is the God of Abraham."
God make our host relentless as the sun,
Each soul your spear, your banner and your slave,
God help us to be brave.

*The
Medieval
Spirit
in
History.*

Would I might wake St. Francis in you all,
Brother of birds and trees, God's Troubadour,
Blinded with weeping for the sad and poor;
Our wealth undone, all strict Franciscan men,
Come, let us chant the canticle again
Of mother earth and the enduring sun.
God make each soul the lonely leper's slave;
God make us saints, and brave.

Would we were lean and grim, and shaken with hate
Like Dante, fugitive, o'er-wrought with cares,
And climbing bitterly the stranger's stairs,
Yet Love, Love, Love, divining: finding still
Beyond dark Hell the penitential hill,
And blessed Beatrice beyond the grave.
Jehovah lead us through the wilderness:
God make our wandering brave.

Would that we had the fortunes of Columbus.
Sailing his caravels a trackless way,
He found a Universe—he sought Cathay.
God give such dawns as when, his venture o'er,
The Sailor looked upon San Salvador.
God lead us past the setting of the sun
To wizard islands, of august surprise;
God make our blunders wise.

Would that such hills and cities round us sang,
Such vistas of the actual earth and man
As kindled Titian when his life began;
Would that this latter Greek could put his gold,
Wisdom and splendor in our brushes bold
Till Greece and Venice, children of the sun,
Become our everyday, and we aspire
To colors fairer far, and glories higher.

Would I might wake in you the whirlwind soul
Of Michelangelo, who hewed the stone
And Night and Day revealed, whose arm alone
Could draw the face of God, the titan high
Whose genius smote like lightning from the sky—
And shall he mold like dead leaves in the grave?
Nay, he is in us! Let us dare and dare.
God help us to be brave.

Would that in body and spirit Shakespeare came
Visible emperor of the deeds of Time,
With Justice still the genius of his rhyme,
Giving each man his due, each passion grace,
Impartial as the rain from Heaven's face
Or sunshine from the Heaven-enthroned sun.
Sweet Swan of Avon, come to us again.
Teach us to write, and writing, to be men.

191

Would we were blind with Milton, and we sang
With him of uttermost Heaven in a new song,
That men might see again the angel-throng,
And newborn hopes, true to this age, would rise,
Pictures to make men weep for paradise,
All glorious things beyond the defeated grave.
God smite us blind, and give us bolder wings;
God help us to be brave.

*The
Napoleonic
Ideal
in
History.*

Would that the cold adventurous Corsican
Woke with new hope of glory, strong from sleep,
Instructed how to conquer and to keep
More justly, having dreamed awhile, yea crowned
With shining flowers, God-given; while the sound
Of singing continents, following the sun,
Calls freeborn men to guard Napoleon's throne
Who makes the eternal hopes of man his own.

*The Eye
of
Science
in History.*

Would that the dry hot wind called Science came,
Forerunner of a higher mystic day,
Though vile machine-made commerce clear the way—
Though nature losing shame should lose her veil,
And ghosts of buried angel-warriors wail
The fall of Heaven, and the relentless Sun
Smile on, as Abraham's God forever dies—
Lord, give us Darwin's eyes!

*The
American
Spirit in
History.*

Would I might rouse the Lincoln in you all,
That which is gendered in the wilderness
From lonely prairies and God's tenderness.
Imperial soul, star of a weedy stream,
Born where the ghosts of buffaloes still gleam,
Whose spirit hoof-beats storm above his grave,
Above that breast of earth and prairie-fire—
Fire that freed the slave.

192

# LITANY OF THE HEROES

Then let us seek out shining Emerson
Teacher of Whitman, and better priest of man,
The self-reliant granite American.
Give us his Heaven-sent right to strike and spare,
Give us the wools and hair-shirts prophets wear,
Then Adam's freedom in the Eden-sun.
God help us make each state an Eden-flower,
And blaze long trails to power.

These were the spacious days of Roosevelt.
Would that among you chiefs like him arose
To win the wrath of our united foes,
To chain King Mammon in the donjon-keep,
To rouse our godly citizens that sleep
Till, as one soul, we shout up to the sun
The battle-yell of freedom and the right—
"Lord, let good men unite."

Nay, I would have you lonely and despised.
Statesmen whom only statesmen understand,
Artists whom only artists can command,
Sages whom all but sages scorn, whose fame
Dies down in lies, in synonyms for shame
With the best populace beneath the sun.
God give us tasks that martyrs can revere,
Still too much hated to be whispered here.

*he
onclusion
nd the
ltimate
nd Final
eroes of
his Song:
Vilson and
ocrates.*

Yea, I would have you like stern Woodrow Wilson
Drinking his cup, as such proud men have done
Since Amenophis Fourth addressed the sun.
Staking his last strength and his final fight
That cost him all, to set the old world right.
The League of Nations course is yet to run.
The Idol-worshippers would end its fame,
And cut from every wall its builder's name.

193

Would we might drink, with knowledge high and kind,
The hemlock cup of Socrates the king,
Knowing right well we know not anything,
With full life done, bowing before the law,
Binding young thinkers' hearts with loyal awe,
And fealty fixed as the ever-enduring sun—
God let us live, seeking the highest light,
God help us die aright.

Nay, I would have you grand, and still forgotten,
Hid like the stars at noon, as he who set
The Egyptian magic of man's alphabet;
Or that Egyptian, first to dream in pain
That dauntless souls cannot by death be slain—
Conquering for all men then, the fearful grave.
God keep us hid, yet vaster far than death.
God help us to be brave.

# SECTION IV

## VERSES OF AN ESPECIALLY INSCRIPTIONAL CHARACTER

*Being songs of my art-student days, written for my drawings. Most of the drawings are the property of citizens of Springfield, Illinois*

## THE QUEEN OF BUBBLES

### (Written for a picture)

*The Youth speaks:—*
  "Why do you seek the sun
  In your bubble-crown ascending?
  Your chariot will melt to mist.
  Your crown will have an ending."

*The Goddess replies:—*
  "Nay, sun is but a bubble,
  Earth is a whiff of foam—
  To my caves on the coast of Thule
  Each night I call them home.
  Thence Faiths blow forth to angels
  And loves blow forth to men—
  They break and turn to nothing
  And I make them whole again.
  On the crested waves of chaos
  I ride them back reborn:
  New stars I bring at evening
  For those that burst at morn;
  My soul is the wind of Thule
  And evening is the sign—
  The sun is but a bubble,
  A fragile child of mine."

## GHOSTS IN LOVE

"Tell me, where do ghosts in love
Find their bridal veils?"

"If you and I were ghosts in love
We'd climb the cliffs of Mystery,
Above the Sea that Wails,
I'd trim your gray and streaming hair
With veils of Fantasy
From the tree of Memory.
'Tis there the ghosts that fall in love
Find their bridal veils."

## COLD SUNBEAMS

The Question:
"Tell me, where do fairy queens
Find their bridal veils?"

The Answer:
"If you were now a fairy queen
Then I, your faithless page and bold
Would win the realm by winning you.
Your veil would be transparent gold
White magic spiders wove for you
At cold gray dawn, from sunbeams cold
While robins sang amid the dew."

## SWEETHEARTS OF THE YEAR

### *Sweetheart Spring*

Our Sweetheart, Spring, came softly,
Her gliding hands were fire,
Her lilac breath upon our cheeks
Consumed us with desire.

By her our God began to build,
Began to sow and till.
He laid foundations in our loves
For every good and ill.
We asked Him not for blessing,
We asked Him not for pain—
Still, to the just and unjust
He sent His fire and rain.

### *Sweetheart Summer*

We prayed not, yet she came to us,
The silken, shining one,
On Jacob's noble ladder
Descended from the sun.
She reached our town of Every Day,
Our dry and dusty sod—
We prayed not, yet she brought to us
The misty wine of God.

### *Sweetheart Autumn*

The woods were black and crimson,
The frost-bit flowers were dead,

199

But Sweetheart Indian Summer came
With love-winds round her head.
While fruits God-given and splendid
Belonged to her domain:
Baskets of corn in perfect ear
And grapes with purple stain,
The treacherous winds persuaded her
Spring Love was in the wood
Altho' the end of love was hers—
Fruition, Motherhood.

### Sweetheart Winter

We had done naught of service
To win our Maker's praise.
Yet Sweetheart Winter came to us
To gild our waning days.
Down Jacob's winding ladder
She came from Sunshine Town,
Bearing the sparkling mornings
And clouds of silver-brown;
Bearing the seeds of Springtime.
Upon her snowy seas
Bearing the fairy star-flowers
For baby Christmas trees.

## SWEET BRIARS OF THE STAIRWAYS

We are happy all the time
Even when we fight:
Sweet briars of the stairways,
Gay fairies of the grime;
*We, who are playing to-night.*

200

"Our feet are in the gutters,
Our eyes are sore with dust,
But still our eyes are bright.
The wide street roars and mutters—
We know it works because it must—
*We, who are playing to-night!*

"Dirt is everlasting.—We never, never fear it.
Toil is never-ceasing.—We will play until we near it.
Tears are never-ending.—When once real tears have come;

"When we see our people as they are—
Our fathers—broken, dumb—
Our mothers—broken, dumb—
The weariest of women and of men;
Ah—then our eyes will lose their light—
Then we will never play again—
*We, who are playing to-night.*"


## THE SORCERESS!

I asked her, "Is Aladdin's lamp
Hidden anywhere?"
"Look into your heart," she said,
"Aladdin's lamp is there."

She took my heart with glowing hands.
It burned to dust and air
And smoke and rolling thistledown
Blowing everywhere.

"Follow the thistledown," she said,
"Till doomsday, if you dare,
Over the hills and far away.
Aladdin's lamp is there."

## THE AMARANTH

Ah, in the night, all music haunts me here. . . .
Is it for naught high Heaven cracks and yawns
And the tremendous Amaranth descends
Sweet with the glory of ten thousand dawns?

Does it not mean my God would have me say:—
"Whether you will or no, O city young,
Heaven will bloom like one great flower for you,
Flash and loom greatly all your marts among"?

Friends, I will not cease hoping though you weep.
Such things I see, and some of them shall come,
Though now or streets are harsh and ashen-gray,
Though our strong youths are strident now, or dumb.
Friends, that sweet town, that wonder-town, shall rise.
Naught can delay it.  Though it may not be
Just as I dream, it comes at last I know,
With streets like channels of an incense-sea.


## AN APOLOGY FOR THE BOTTLE VOLCANIC

Sometimes I dip my pen and find the bottle full of fire,
The salamanders flying forth I cannot but admire.
It's Etna, or Vesuvius, if those big things were small,
And then 'tis but itself again, and does not smoke at all.
And so my blood grows cold.  I say, "The bottle held but
  ink,
And, if you thought it otherwise, the worser for your think."
And then, just as I throw my scribbled paper on the floor,
The bottle says, "Fe, fi, fo, fum," and steams and shouts
  some more.

CONTENTS OF AN INK BOTTLE.

# THE VILLAGE IMPROVEMENT PARADE

O sad, deceiving ink, as bad as liquor in its way—
All demons of a bottle size have pranced from you to-day,
And seized my pen for hobby-horse as witches ride a broom,
And left a trail of brimstone words and blots and gobs of
    gloom.
And yet when I am extra good and say my prayers at night,
And mind my ma, and do the chores, and speak to folks
    polite,
My bottle spreads a rainbow-mist, and from the vapor fine
Ten thousands troops from fairyland come riding in a line.
I've seen them on their chargers race around my study chair,
They opened wide the window and rode forth upon the air,
The army widened as it went, and into myriads grew,
O how the lances shimmered, how the silvery trumpets blew!


## THE VILLAGE IMPROVEMENT PARADE

Guns salute, and crowds and pigeons fly,
Bronzed, Homeric bards go striding by,
Shouting "Glory" amid the cannonade:—
It is the cross-roads
Resurrection
Parade.

Actors, craftsmen, builders, join the throng,
Painters, sculptors, florists tramp along,
Farm-boys prance, in tinsel tin and jade:—
It is the cross-roads
Love and Laughter
Crusade.

The sun is blazing big as all the sky,
The mustard-plant with the sunflower climbing high,

With the Indian corn in fiery plumes arrayed:—
It is the cross-roads
Love and Beauty
Crusade.

Free and proud and mellow jamboree,
Roar and foam upon the prairie sea,
Tom turkeys sing the sun a serenade:—
It is the cross-roads
Resurrection
Parade.

Our sweethearts dance, with wands as white as milk,
With veils of gold and robes of silver silk,
Their caps in velvet pansy-patterns made:—
It is the cross-roads
Resurrection
Parade.

Wandering round the shrines we understand,
Waving oak-boughs cheap and close at hand,
And field-flowers fair, for which no man has paid:—
It is the cross-roads
Love and Beauty
Crusade.

Hieroglyphic marchers here we bring.
Rich inscriptions strut and talk and sing.
A scroll to read, a picture-word brigade:—
It is the cross-roads
Love and Laughter
Crusade.

Swans for symbols deck the banners rare,
Mighty acorn-signs command the air,

A HASTY PROSPERITY MAY BE RAW AND ABSURD A WELL-CONSIDERED POVERTY MAY BE EXQUISITE

WITHOUT AN EAGER PUBLIC ALL TEACHING IS VAIN

THE VILLAGE IMPROVEMENT PARADE.
SECTION III.

Wandering 'round the shrines we understand,
Waving oak-boughs cheap and close at hand,
And field-flowers fair, for which no man has paid :—
It is the cross-roads
Love and Beauty
Crusade.

Hieroglyphic marchers here we bring.
Rich inscriptions strut and talk and sing.
A scroll to read, a picture-word brigade:—
It is the cross-roads
Love and Laughter
Crusade.

For hearts of oak, by flying beauty swayed:—
It is the cross-roads
Resurrection
Parade.

The flags are big, like rainbows flashing round,
They spread like sails, and lift us from the ground,
Star-born ships, that have come in masquerade:—
It is the cross-roads
Resurrection
Parade.

## THE FAIRY FROM THE APPLE-SEED

O apple-seed I planted in a silly shallow place
In a bowl of wrought silver, with Sangamon earth within it,
O baby tree that came, without an apple on it,
A tree that grew a tiny height, but thickened on apace,
With bossy glossy arms, and leaves of trembling lace.

One night the trunk was rent, and the heavy bowl rocked
  round,
The boughs were bending here and there, with a curious
  locust sound,
And a tiny dryad came, from out the doll tree,
And held the boughs in ivory hands,
And waved her black hair round,
And climbed, and ate with merry words
The sudden fruit it bore.
And in the leaves she hides and sings
And guards my study door.

She guards it like a watchdog true
And robbers run away.

A LITTLE DRYAD

205

Her eyes are lifted spears all night,
But dove-eyes in the day.

And she is stranger, stronger
Than the funny human race.
Lovelier her form, and holier her face.
She feeds me flowers and fruit
With a quaint grace.
She dresses in the apple-leaves
As delicate as lace.
This girl that came from Sangamon earth
In a bowl of silver bright
From an apple-seed I planted in a silly shallow place.

## DANCING FOR A PRIZE

Three fairies by the Sangamon
    Were dancing for a prize.
The rascals were alike indeed
    As they danced with drooping eyes.
I gave the magic acorn
    To the one I loved the best,
The imp that made me think of her
    My heart's eternal guest,
My lady of the tea-rose, my lady far away,
    Queen of the fleets of No-Man's-Land
That sail to old Cathay.
    How did the trifler hint of her?
Ah, when the dance was done
    They begged me for the acorn,
Laughing every one.
    Two had eyes of midnight,
And one had golden eyes,
    And I gave the golden acorn

DANCING FOR A PRIZE.

THE PRESBYTERIAN CHURCH
Springfield, Illinois

## THE SOUL OF THE CITY

To the scamp with golden eyes.
    Confessor Dandelion,
My priest so gray and wise,
    Whispered when I gave it
To the girl with golden eyes:
    "She is like your Queen of Glory
On China's holy strand
    Who drove the coiling dragons
Like doves before her hand."


# THE SOUL OF THE CITY RECEIVES THE GIFT OF
# THE HOLY SPIRIT

### (A broadside distributed in Springfield, Illinois)

Censers are swinging
Over the town;
Censers are swinging,
Look overhead!
Censers are swinging,
Heaven comes down.
City, dead city,
Awake from the dead!

Censers, tremendous,
Gleam overhead.
Wind-harps are ringing,
Wind-harps unseen—
Calling and calling:—
"Wake from the dead.
Rise, little city,
Shine like a queen."

Soldiers of Christ
For battle grow keen.

Heaven-sent winds
Haunt alley and lane.
Singing of life
In town-meadows green
After the toil
And battle and pain.


Incense is pouring
Like the spring rain
Down on the mob
That moil through the street.
Blessed are they
Who behold it and gain
Power made more mighty
Thro' every defeat.


Builders, toil on.
Make all complete.
Make Springfield wonderful.
Make her renown
Worthy this day,
Till, at God's feet,
Tranced, saved forever,
Waits the white town.


Censers are swinging
Over the town,
Censers gigantic!
Look overhead!
Hear the winds singing:—
"Heaven comes down.
City, dead city,
Awake from the dead."

## THE ANGEL AND THE CLOWN

I saw wild domes and bowers
And smoking incense towers
And mad exotic flowers
In Illinois.
Where ragged ditches ran
Now springs of Heaven began
Celestial drink for man
In Illinois.

There stood beside the town
Beneath its incense-crown
An angel and a clown
In Illinois.
He was as Clowns are:
She was snow and star
With eyes that looked afar
In Illinois.

I asked, "How came this place
Of antique Asian grace
Amid our callow race
In Illinois?"
Said Clown and Angel fair:
"By laughter and by prayer,
By casting off all care
In Illinois."

## THE SONG OF THE STURDY SNAILS

Gristly bare-bone fingers
On my window-pane—
The drumbeat of a ghost
Louder than the rain!

Oh frail, storm-shaken hut—
No candle, not a spark
Of fire within the grate.
Oh the lonely dark!

Trembling by the window
I watched the lightning flash
And saw the little villains
Upon the outer sash

And other small musicians
Upon the window-pane—
Garden snails, a-dragging
Their shells amid the rain!

The thunder blew away.
My happiness began.
Over the dripping darkness
Rills of moonlight ran.

In the silence rich
The scratching of the shells
Became a crooning music
A lazy peal of bells.

So fearless in the night
My sluggard brothers bold!
Your fancies swift and glowing;
Your footsteps slow and cold!

My happy beggar brothers
Tuning all together
Playing on the pane
Praise of stormy weather!

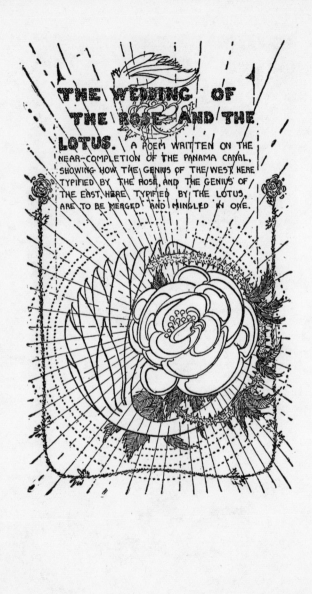

# THE WEDDING OF THE ROSE AND THE LOTUS.

A POEM WRITTEN ON THE NEAR-COMPLETION OF THE PANAMA CANAL, SHOWING HOW THE GENIUS OF THE WEST HERE TYPIFIED BY THE ROSE, AND THE GENIUS OF THE EAST, HERE TYPIFIED BY THE LOTUS, ARE TO BE MERGED AND MINGLED IN ONE.

NICHOLAS VACHEL LINDSAY.

Upon a ragged pillow
At last I laid my head
And watched the sparkling window,
And the wan light on my bed.

Through the glass came flying
Dream snails, with leafy wings—
Glided on the moonbeams—
And all the snails were kings!

With crowns of pollen yellow
And eyes of firefly gold
Behold—to crooning music
Their coiling wings unrolled!

These tiny kings I saw
Reigning over white
Bisque jars of fairy flowers
In sturdy proud delight.

These jars in fairyland
Await good snails that keep
Vigils on the windows
Of beggars fast asleep.

## THE WEDDING OF THE ROSE AND THE LOTUS

(A poem distributed to both houses of Congress by Secretary Franklin K. Lane on the opening day of the Panama-Pacific Exposition.)

Flags of the Pacific
And the Atlantic meet,
Captain calls to captain,
Fleet makes cheer with fleet.

Above the drownèd ages
A wind of wooing blows:—
The red rose woos the lotus,
The lotus woos the rose . . .

The lotus conquered Egypt.
   The rose was loved in Rome.
Great India crowned the lotus:
(Britain the rose's home).
Old China crowned the lotus,
They crowned it in Japan.
But Christendom adored the rose
Ere Christendom began . . .

The lotus speaks of slumber:
The rose is as a dart.
   The lotus is Nirvana:
The rose is Mary's heart.
The rose is deathless, restless,
The splendor of our pain:
   The flush and fire of labor
That builds, not all in vain. . . .

The genius of the lotus
Shall heal earth's too-much fret.
The rose, in blinding glory,
Shall waken Asia yet.
Hail to their loves, ye peoples!
Behold, a world-wind blows,
That aids the ivory lotus
To wed the red, red rose!

## THE TREE OF LAUGHING BELLS, OR THE WINGS OF THE MORNING

### A POEM FOR AVIATORS

#### *How the Wings Were Made*

From many morning-glories
That in an hour will fade,
From many pansy buds
Gathered in the shade,
From lily of the valley
And dandelion buds,
From fiery poppy-buds
   Are the Wings of the Morning made.

#### *The Indian Girl Who Made Them*

These, the Wings of the Morning,
An Indian Maiden wove,
Intertwining subtlely
Wands from a willow grove
Beside the Sangamon—
Rude stream of Dreamland Town.
She bound them to my shoulders
With fingers golden-brown.
The wings were part of me;
The willow-wands were hot.
Pulses from my heart
Healed each bruise and spot
Of the morning-glory buds,
Beginning to unfold
Beneath her burning song of suns untold.

213

## The Indian Girl Tells the Hero Where to Go to Get the Laughing Bell

"To the farthest star of all,
Go, make a moment's raid.
To the west—escape the earth
Before your pennons fade!
West! west! o'ertake the night
That flees the morning sun.
There's a path between the stars—
A black and silent one.
Oh, tremble when you near
The smallest star that sings:
Only the farthest star
Is cool for willow wings.

"There's a sky within the west—
There's a sky beyond the skies
Where only one star shines—
The Star of Laughing Bells—
In Chaos-land it lies;
Cold as morning-dew,
A gray and tiny boat
Moored on Chaos-shore,
Where nothing else can float
But the Wings of the Morning strong
And the lilt of laughing song
From many a ruddy throat:

"For the Tree of Laughing Bells
Grew from a bleeding seed
Planted mid enchantment
Played on a harp and reed:

214

# THE TREE OF LAUGHING BELLS

Darkness was the harp—
Chaos-wind the reed;
The fruit of the tree is a bell, blood-red—
The seed was the heart of a fairy, dead.
Part of the bells of the Laughing Tree
Fell to-day at a blast from the reed.
Bring a fallen bell to me.
Go!" the maiden said.
"For the bell will quench our memory,
Our hope,
Our borrowed sorrow;
We will have no thirst for yesterday,
No thought for to-morrow."

### The Journey Starts Swiftly

A thousand times ten thousand times
More swift than the sun's swift light
Were the Morning Wings in their flight
On—  On—
West of the Universe,
Thro' the West
To Chaos-night.

### He Nears the Goal

How the red bells rang
As I neared the Chaos-shore!
As I flew across to the end of the West
The young bells rang and rang
Above the Chaos roar,
And the Wings of the Morning
Beat in tune

215

And bore me like a bird along—
And the nearing star turned to a moon—
Gray moon, with a brow of red—
Gray moon with a golden song.
Like a diver after pearls
I plunged to that stifling floor.
It was wide as a giant's wheat-field
An icy, wind-washed shore.
O laughing, proud, but trembling star!
O wind that wounded sore!


*He Climbs the Hill Where the Tree Grows*

On—
Thro' the gleaming gray
I ran to the storm and clang—
To the red, red hill where the great tree swayed—
And scattered bells like autumn leaves.
How the red bells rang!
My breath within my breast
Was held like a diver's breath—
The leaves were tangled locks of gray—
The boughs of the tree were white and gray,
Shaped like scythes of Death.
The boughs of the tree would sweep and sway—
Sway like scythes of Death.
But it was beautiful!
I knew that all was well.
A thousand bells from a thousand boughs
Each moment bloomed and fell.
On the hill of the wind-swept tree
There were no bells asleep;
They sang beneath my training wings

216

Like rivers sweet and steep.
Deep rock-clefts before my feet
Mighty chimes did keep
And little choirs did keep.

## He Receives the Bells

*Honeyed, small and fair,*
*Like flowers, in flowery lands—*
*Like little maiden's hands—*
*Two bells fell in my hair,*
*Two bells caressed my hair.*
*I pressed them to my purple lips*
*In the strangling Chaos-air.*

## He Starts on the Return Journey

On desperate wings and strong,
Two bells within my breast,
I breathed again, I breathed again—
West of the Universe—
West of the skies of the West.
Into the black toward home,
And never a star in sight,
By Faith that is blind I took my way
With my two bosomed blossoms gay
Till a speck in the East was the Milky Way:
Till starlit was the night.
And the bells had quenched all memory—
All hope—
All borrowed sorrow:
I had no thirst for yesterday,
No thought for to-morrow.

Like hearts within my breast
The bells would throb to me
And down the siren stars
That sang enticingly;
My heart became a bell—
Three bells were in my breast,
Three hearts to comfort me.
We reached the daytime happily—
We reached the earth with glee.
In an hour, in an hour it was done!
The wings in their morning flight
Were a thousand times ten thousand times
More swift than beams of light.


### *He Gives What He Won to the Indian Girl*

I panted in the grassy wood;
I kissed the Indian Maid
As she took my wings from me:
With all the grace I could
I gave two throbbing bells to her
From the foot of the Laughing Tree.
And one she pressed to her golden breast
And one, gave back to me.

From Lilies of the valley—
See them fade.
From poppy-blooms all frayed,
From dandelions gray with care,
From pansy-faces, worn and torn,
From morning-glories—
See them fade—
From all things fragile, faint and fair
Are the Wings of the Morning made!

218

THE SPIDER AND THE GHOST OF THE FLY

## CRICKETS ON A STRIKE

THE FOOLISH QUEEN OF FAIRY-
LAND, FROM HER MILK-WHITE
THRONE IN A LILY-BELL, GAVE
COMMAND TO HER CRICKET-
BAND TO PLAY FOR HER WHEN
THE DEW-DROPS FELL.
BUT THE COLD DEW SPOILED
THEIR INSTRUMENTS, AND THEY
PLAY FOR THE FOOLISH QUEEN
NO MORE. INSTEAD, THOSE
STURDY MALCONTENTS PLAY
BROKEN TUNES IN THE
KITCHEN FLOOR.

THE SNAIL KING AND
QUEEN VISIT MAB.

N.V.L.
1910

NOTE: My painting of The Tree of Laughing Bells is hung on the mezzanine floor of the Davenport Hotel, Spokane, Washington, in the midst of the one thousand famous singing birds brought from all over the world by Louis M. Davenport. This recent honor I count a singularly fortunate interpretation of the symbolism of the painting.

## THE SPIDER AND THE GHOST OF THE FLY

Once I loved a spider
When I was born a fly,
A velvet-footed spider
With a gown of rainbow-dye.
She ate my wings and gloated.
She bound me with a hair.
She drove me to her parlor
Above her winding stair.
To educate young spiders
She took me all apart.
My ghost came back to haunt her.
I saw her eat my heart.

## CRICKETS ON A STRIKE

The foolish queen of fairyland
From her milk-white throne in a lily-bell,

219

Gave command to her cricket-band
To play for her when the dew-drops fell.

But the cold dew spoiled their instruments
And they play for the foolish queen no more.
Instead those sturdy malcontents
Play sharps and flats in my kitchen floor.

## THE VISIT TO MAB

When glad vacation time began
  A snail-king said to his dear spouse,
    "Come, let us lock our birch-bark house
And visit some important man.

"Each summer we have hoped to go
  To see the sultan Gingerbread
    Who wears chopped citron on his head
And currant love-locks in a row.

"And see his vizier Chocolate Bill
  And Popcorn Man, his pale young priest.
    They live twelve inches to the east
Behind the lofty brown-bread hill."

His wife said: "Simple elegance
  Is what we want. It is the mode
    To take the little western road
To where the blue-grass fairies dance.

"I think the queen will recognize
  Our atmosphere of wealth and ease.
    My steel-gray shell is sure to please,
And she will fear your fiery eyes."

## TO LADY JANE

And so they visited proud Mab.
  The firs were laughing overhead,
  The chattering roses burned deep-red.
The snails were queer and dumb and drab.

The contrast made them quite the thing.
  A setting spells success at times.
  Mab gave the queen a book of rhymes.
A tissue-cap she gave the king.

Like caps the children wear for sport.
  And vainer than he well could say
  He called gay Mab his "pride and stay,"
With pompous speeches to the court.

They journeyed home, made young indeed,
  But opening the book of song
  Each poem looked so deep and long
They could not bear to start to read.


## TO LADY JANE

(Written for Miss Jane Brown on her birthday)

Romance was always young.
You come to-day
Just eight years old
With marvellous dark hair.
Younger than Dante found you
When you turned
His heart into the way
That found the heavenly stair.

Perhaps we must be strangers.
I confess

221

My soul this hour is Dante's,
And your care
Should be for dolls
Whose painted hands caress
Your marvellous dark hair.

Romance, with moonflower face
And morning eyes,
And lips whose thread of scarlet prophesies
The canticles of a coming king unknown,
Remember, when you join him
On his throne,
Even me, your far-off troubadour,
And wear
For me some trifling rose
Beneath your veil,
Dying a royal death,
Happy and pale,
Choked by the passion,
The wonder and the snare,
The glory and despair
That still will haunt and own
Your marvellous dark hair.

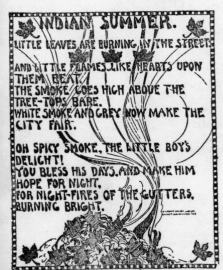

## AN INDIAN SUMMER DAY ON THE PRAIRIE

### IN THE BEGINNING

The sun is a huntress young,
The sun is a red, red joy,
The sun is an Indian girl,
Of the tribe of the Illinois.

222

# QUEEN MAB IN THE VILLAGE

## MID-MORNING

The sun is a smoldering fire,
That creeps through the high gray plain,
And leaves not a bush of cloud
To blossom with flowers of rain.

## NOON

The sun is a wounded deer,
That treads pale grass in the skies,
Shaking his golden horns,
Flashing his baleful eyes.

## SUNSET

The sun is an eagle old,
There in the windless west.
Atop of the spirit-cliffs
He builds him a crimson nest.

# QUEEN MAB IN THE VILLAGE

Once I loved a fairy,
Queen Mab it was. Her voice
Was like a little Fountain
That bids the birds rejoice.
Her face was wise and solemn,
Her hair was brown and fine.
Her dress was pansy velvet,
A butterfly design.

To see her hover round me
Or walk the hills of air,
Awakened love's deep pulses

COLLECTED POEMS

And boyhood's first despair;
A passion like a sword-blade
That pierced me thro' and thro':
Her fingers healed the sorrow
Her whisper would renew.
We sighed and reigned and feasted
Within a hollow tree,
We vowed our love was boundless,
Eternal as the sea.
She banished from her kingdom
The mortal boy I grew—
So tall and crude and noisy,
I killed grasshoppers too.
I threw big rocks at pigeons,
I plucked and tore apart
The weeping, wailing daisies,
And broke my lady's heart.
At length I grew to manhood,
I scarcely could believe
I ever loved the lady,
Or caused her court to grieve,
Until a dream came to me,
One bleak first night of Spring,
Ere tides of apple blossoms
Rolled in o'er everything,
While rain and sleet and snowbanks
Were still a-vexing men,
Ere robin and his comrades
Were nesting once again.

I saw Mab's Book of Judgment—
Its clasps were iron and stone,
Its leaves were mammoth ivory,
Its boards were mammoth bone,—
Hid in her seaside mountains,

Forgotten or unkept,
Beneath its mighty covers
Her wrath against me slept.
And deeply I repented
Of brash and boyish crime,
Of murder of things lovely
Now and in olden time.
I cursed my vain ambition,
My would-be worldly days,
And craved the paths of wonder,
Of dewy dawns and fays.
I cried, "Our love was boundless,
Eternal as the sea,
O Queen, reverse the sentence,
Come back and master me!"

The book was by the cliff-side
Upon its edge upright.
I laid me by it softly,
And wept throughout the night.
And there at dawn I saw it,
No book now, but a door,
Upon its panels written,
"Judgment is no more."
The bolt flew back with thunder,
I saw within that place
A mermaid wrapped in seaweed
With Mab's immortal face,
Yet grown now to a woman,
A woman to the knee.
She cried, she clasped me fondly,
We soon were in the sea.

Ah, she was wise and subtle,
And gay and strong and sleek,

225

We chained the wicked swordfish,
We played at hide and seek.
We floated on the water,
We heard the dawn-wind sing,
I made from ocean-wonders,
Her bridal wreath and ring.
All mortal girls were shadows,
All earth-life but a mist,
When deep beneath the maelstrom,
The mermaid's heart I kissed.

I woke beside the church-door
Of our small inland town,
Bowing to a maiden
In a pansy-velvet gown,
Who had not heard of fairies,
Yet seemed of love to dream.
We planned an earthly cottage
Beside an earthly stream.

Our wedding long is over,
With toil the years fill up,
Yet in the evening silence,
We drink a deep-sea cup.
Nothing the fay remembers,
Yet when she turns to me,
We meet beneath the whirlpool,
We swim the golden sea.

## THE MYSTERIOUS CAT

(A chant for a children's pantomime dance, suggested by
a picture painted by George Mather Richards)

I saw a proud, mysterious cat,
I saw a proud, mysterious cat,

226

Too proud to catch a mouse or rat—
Mew, mew, mew.

But catnip she would eat, and purr,
But catnip, she would eat, and purr.
And goldfish she did much prefer—
Mew, mew, mew.

I saw a cat—'twas but a dream,
I saw a cat—'twas but a dream
Who scorned the slave that brought her cream—
Mew, mew, mew.

Unless the slave were dressed in style,
Unless the slave were dressed in style,
And knelt before her all the while—
Mew, mew, mew.

Did you ever hear of a thing like that?
Did you ever hear of a thing like that?
Did you ever hear of a thing like that?
Oh, what a proud mysterious cat.
Oh, what a proud mysterious cat.
Oh, what a proud mysterious cat.
Mew . . . mew . . . mew.

# THE HUMBLE BUMBLE BEE.

THE WEATHER-MAN HAS PROMISED SNOW
AND SLEET.
NOW BUMBLE-BEE.
WHERE WILL
YOU WARM YOUR
FEET?

"BESIDE THE SANGAMON A HOLLOW
OAK
HAS BEEN MY WINTER WIGWAM;
'TIS THE CLOAK
THAT SHIELDS THE INDIAN
FAIRIES AND THEIR KING:
THEY SLEEP ON MOUSE-HIDES
IN A RAINBOW RING
OF BEES IN WAR-PAINT, CROUCHED
IN THICK ARRAY.
WHO SCARE THE CUT-WORMS
AND THE ANTS AWAY.
I LEAD THOSE BRAVES, COMMAND-
ING THEM TO KNEEL
AND BUZZ. AS ON THEIR WINGS
I PUT MY HEEL.
IN WINTER, FAIRYLAND BELONGS TO ME.
IN SUMMER, I'M A HUMBLE
BUMBLE-BEE."

# SECTION V

# MOON-POEMS

## TO GLORIANA

Girl with the burning golden eyes,
And red-bird song, and snowy throat:
I bring you gold and silver moons,
And diamond stars, and mists that float.
I bring you moons and snowy clouds,
I bring you prairie skies to-night
To feebly praise your golden eyes
And red-bird song, and throat so white.


## EUCLID

Old Euclid drew a circle
On a sand-beach long ago.
He bounded and enclosed it
With angles thus and so.
His set of solemn graybeards
Nodded and argued much
Of arc and of circumference,
Diameter and such.
A silent child stood by them
From morning until noon
Because they drew such charming
Round pictures of the moon.

231

## THE HAUGHTY SNAIL-KING

*(What Uncle William Told the Children)*

Twelve snails went walking after night.
They'd creep an inch or so,
Then stop and bug their eyes
And blow.
Some folks . . . are . . . deadly . . slow.
Twelve snails went walking yestereve,
Led by their fat old king.
They were so dull their princeling had
No sceptre, robe or ring—
Only a paper cap to wear
When nightly journeying.

This king-snail said: "I feel a thought
Within . . . It blossoms soon. . . .
O little courtiers of mine, . . .
I crave a pretty boon. . . .
Oh, yes . . . (High thoughts with effort come
And well-bred snails are ALMOST dumb.)
"I wish I had a yellow crown
As glistering . . . as . . . the moon."

## WHAT THE RATTLESNAKE SAID

The moon's a little prairie-dog.
He shivers through the night.
He sits upon his hill and cries
For fear that *I* will bite.

232

## WHAT THE GRAY-WINGED FAIRY SAID

The sun's a broncho.  He's afraid
Like every other thing,
And trembles, morning, noon and night,
Lest *I* should spring, and sting.


## DRYING THEIR WINGS

### (*What the Carpenter Said*)

The moon's a cottage with a door.
Some folks can see it plain.
Look, you may catch a glint of light,
A sparkle through the pane,
Showing the place is brighter still
Within, though bright without.
There, at a cosy open fire
Strange babes are grouped about.
The children of the wind and tide—
The urchins of the sky,
Drying their wings from storms and things
So they again can fly.


## WHAT THE GRAY-WINGED FAIRY SAID

The moon's a gong, hung in the wild,
Whose song the fays hold dear.
Of course you do not hear it, child.
It takes a FAIRY ear.

The full moon is a splendid gong
That beats as night grows still.
It sounds above the evening song
Of dove or whippoorwill.

## A SENSE OF HUMOR

No man should stand before the moon
To make sweet song thereon,
With dandified importance,
His sense of humor gone.

Nay, let us don the motley cap,
The jester's chastened mien,
If we would woo that looking-glass
And see what should be seen.

O mirror on fair Heaven's wall,
We find there what we bring.
So, let us smile in honest part
And deck our souls and sing.

Yea, by the chastened jest alone
Will ghosts and terrors pass,
And fays, or suchlike friendly things,
Throw kisses through the glass.


## WHAT THE CLOWN SAID

"The moon's a paper jumping hoop,"
    Went on the circus clown,
"A film of gilded nonsense
    For the games of Angel-town.

"If I could break those horses
    That gallop through my sleep,
I'd reach that aggravating hoop
    And make my finest leap.

"I climb upon their backs, and ride,
    But always slip too soon . . .
And fall and wake, when just one mile
    Remains to reach the moon."


## ON THE GARDEN WALL

Oh, once I walked a garden
In dreams. 'Twas yellow grass.
And many orange-trees grew there
In sand as white as glass.
The curving, wide wall-border
Was marble, like the snow.
I walked that wall a fairy-prince
And, pacing quaint and slow,
Beside me were my pages,
Two giant, friendly birds.
Half swan they were, half peacock.
They spake in courtier-words.
Their inner wings a chariot,
Their outer wings for flight,
They lifted me from dreamland.
We bade those trees good-night.
Swiftly above the stars we rode.
I looked below me soon.
The white-walled garden I had ruled
Was one lone flower—the moon.


## WRITTEN FOR A MUSICIAN

Hungry for music with a desperate hunger
I prowled abroad, I threaded through the town;

The evening crowd was clamoring and drinking,
Vulgar and pitiful—my heart bowed down—
Till I remembered duller hours made noble
By strangers clad in some surprising grace.
Wait, wait, my soul, your music comes ere midnight
Appearing in some unexpected place
With quivering lips, and gleaming, moonlit face.


## THE MOON IS A PAINTER

He coveted her portrait.
He toiled as she grew gay.
She loved to see him labor
In that devoted way.

And in the end it pleased her,
But bowed him more with care.
Her rose-smile showed so plainly,
Her soul-smile was not there.

That night he groped without a lamp
To find a cloak, a book,
And on the vexing portrait
By moonrise chanced to look.

The color-scheme was out of key,
The maiden rose-smile faint,
But through the blessed darkness
She gleamed, his friendly saint.

The comrade, white, immortal,
His bride, and more than bride—
The citizen, the sage of mind,
ᵂor whom he lived and died.

## THE ENCYCLOPÆDIA

"If I could set the moon upon
This table," said my friend,
"Among the standard poets
And brochures without end,
And noble prints of old Japan,
How empty they would seem,
By that encyclopædia
Of whim and glittering dream."


## WHAT THE MINER IN THE DESERT SAID

The moon's a brass-hooped water-keg,
A wondrous water-feast.
If I could climb the ridge and drink
And give drink to my beast;
If I could drain that keg, the flies
Would not be biting so,
My burning feet be spry again,
My mule no longer slow.
And I could rise and dig for ore,
And reach my fatherland,
And not be food for ants and hawks
And perish in the sand.


## WHAT THE COAL-HEAVER SAID

The moon's an open furnace door
Where all can see the blast,
We shovel in our blackest griefs,
Upon that grate are cast

Our aching burdens, loves and fears
And underneath them wait
Paper and tar and pitch and pine
Called strife and blood and hate.

Out of it all there comes a flame,
A splendid widening light.
Sorrow is turned to mystery
And Death into delight.

## WHAT THE MOON SAW

Two statesmen met by moonlight.
Their ease was partly feigned.
They glanced about the prairie.
Their faces were constrained.
In various ways aforetime
They had misled the state,
Yet did it so politely
Their henchmen thought them great.
They sat beneath a hedge and spake
No word, but had a smoke.
A satchel passed from hand to hand.
Next day, the deadlock broke.

## THE OLD HORSE IN THE CITY

The moon's a peck of corn.  It lies
Heaped up for me to eat.
I wish that I might climb the path
And taste that supper sweet.

## THE ROSE OF MIDNIGHT

Men feed me straw and scanty grain
And beat me till I'm sore.
Some day I'll break the halter-rope
And smash the stable-door,

Run down the street and mount the hill
Just as the corn appears.
I've seen it rise at certain times
For years and years and years.

## THE ROSE OF MIDNIGHT

### (*Set to music by Albert V. Davies*)

The moon is now an opening flower,
  The sky a cliff of blue.
The moon is now a silver rose;
  Her pollen is the dew.

Her pollen is the mist that swings
  Across her face of dreams:
Her pollen is the April rain,
  Filling the April streams.

Her pollen is eternal life,
  Endless ambrosial foam.
It feeds the swarming stars and fills
  Their hearts with honeycomb.

The earth is but a passion-flower
  With blood upon his crown.
And what shall fill his failing veins
  And lift his head, bowed down?

This cup of peace, this silver rose
  Bending with fairy breath
Shall lift that passion-flower, the earth,
  A million times from Death!

## THE PATH IN THE SKY

I sailed a little shallop
Upon a pretty sea
In blue and hazy mountains,
Scarce mountains unto me;
Their summits lost in wonder,
They wrapped the lake around,
And when my shallop landed
I trod on a vague ground,

And climbed and climbed toward heaven,
Though scarce before my feet
I found one step unveiled there
The blue-haze vast, complete,
Until I came to Zion
The gravel paths of God,
My endless trail pierced the thick veil
To flaming flowers and sod.
I rested, looked behind me
And saw where I had been.
*My little lake. It was the moon.*
Sky-mountains closed it in.


## WHAT THE HYENA SAID

The moon is but a golden skull,
She mounts the heavens now,
And Moon-Worms, mighty Moon-Worms
Are wreathed around her brow.

The Moon-Worms are a doughty race:
They eat her gray and golden face.

240

## WHAT THE SNOW MAN SAID

Her eye-sockets dead, and molding head:
These caverns are their dwelling-place.

The Moon-Worms, serpents of the skies,
From the great hollows of her eyes
Behold all souls, and they are wise:
With tiny, keen and icy eyes,
Behold how each man sins and dies.

When Earth in gold-corruption lies
Long dead, the moon-worm butterflies
On cyclone wings will reach this place—
Yea, rear their brood on earth's dead face.


## WHAT THE SNOW MAN SAID

The Moon's a snowball.  See the drifts
Of white that cross the sphere.
The Moon's a snowball, melted down
A dozen times a year.

Yet rolled again in hot July
When all my days are done
And cool to greet the weary eye
After the scorching sun.

The moon's a piece of winter fair
Renewed the year around,
Behold it, deathless and unstained,
Above the grimy ground!

It rolls on high so brave and white
Where the clear air-rivers flow,
Proclaiming Christmas all the time
And the glory of the snow!

241

## WHAT THE SCARECROW SAID

The dim-winged spirits of the night
Do fear and serve me well.
They creep from out the hedges of
The garden where I dwell.

I wave my arms across the walk.
The troops obey the sign,
And bring me shimmering shadow-robes
And cups of cowslip-wine.

Then dig a treasure called the moon,
A very precious thing,
And keep it in the air for me
Because I am a King.


## WHAT GRANDPA MOUSE SAID

The moon's a holy owl-queen.
She keeps them in a jar
Under her arm till evening,
Then sallies forth to war.

She pours the owls upon us.
They hoot with horrid noise
And eat the naughty mousie-girls
And wicked mousie-boys.

So climb the moonvine every night
And to the owl-queen pray:
Leave good green cheese by moonlit trees
For her to take away.

242

## THE BEGGAR SPEAKS

And never squeak, my children,
Nor gnaw the smoke-house door:
The owl-queen then will love us
And send her birds no more.


## THE BEGGAR SPEAKS

*(What Mister Moon Said to Me)*

Come, eat the bread of idleness,
Come, sit beside the spring:
Some of the flowers will keep awake,
Some of the birds will sing.

Come, eat the bread no man has sought
For half a hundred years:
Men hurry so they have no griefs,
Nor even idle tears:

They hurry so they have no loves:
They cannot curse nor laugh—
Their hearts die in their youth with neither
Grave nor epitaph.

My bread would make them careless,
And never quite on time—
Their eyelids would be heavy,
Their fancies full of rhyme:

Each soul a mystic rose-tree,
Or a curious incense tree:

.    .    .    .    .    .    .    .    .

Come, eat the bread of idleness,
Said Mister Moon to me.

## WHAT THE FORESTER SAID

The moon is but a candle-glow
That flickers thro' the gloom:
The starry space, a castle hall:
And Earth, the children's room,
Where all night long the old trees stand
To watch the streams asleep:
Grandmothers guarding trundle-beds:
Good shepherds guarding sheep.

## CAUGHT IN A NET

Upon her breast her hands and hair
  Were tangled all together.
The moon of June forbade me not—
The golden night time weather
In balmy sighs commanded me
  To kiss them like a feather.

Her looming hair, her burning hands,
  Were tangled black and white.
My face I buried there.  I pray—
  So far from her to-night—
For grace, to dream I kiss her soul
  Amid the black and white.

## MY LADY IN HER WHITE SILK SHAWL

My lady in her white silk shawl
  Is like a lily dim,

244

## BEYOND THE MOON

Within the twilight of the room
   Enthroned and kind and prim.

My lady! Pale gold is her hair.
   Until she smiles her face
Is pale with far Hellenic moods,
   With thoughts that find no place.

In our harsh village of the West
   Wherein she lives of late,
She's distant as far-hidden stars,
   And cold—almost!—as fate.

But when she smiles she's here again
   Rosy with comrade-cheer,
A Puritan Bacchante made
   To laugh around the year.

The merry gentle moon herself,
   Heart-stirring too, like her,
Wakening wild and innocent love
   In every worshipper.


## BEYOND THE MOON

### (Written to the Most Beautiful Woman in the World)

My Sweetheart is the TRUTH BEYOND THE MOON,
And never have I been in love with Woman,
Always aspiring to be set in tune
With one who is invisible, inhuman.

O laughing girl, cold TRUTH has stepped between,
Spoiling the fevers of your virgin face:

245

Making your shining eyes but lead and clay,
Mocking your brilliant brain and lady's grace.

TRUTH haunted me the day I wooed and lost,
The day I wooed and won, or wooed in play:
Tho' you were Juliet or Rosalind,
Thus shall it be, forever and a day.

I doubt my vows, tho' sworn on my own blood,
Tho' I draw toward you weeping, soul to soul,
I have a lonely goal beyond the moon;
Ay, beyond Heaven and Hell, I have a goal!

## WHAT SEMIRAMIS SAID

The moon's a steaming chalice
    Of honey and venom-wine.
A little of it sipped by night
    Makes the long hours divine.
But oh, my reckless lovers,
    They drain the cup and wail,
Die at my feet with shaking limbs
    And tender lips all pale.
Above them in the sky it bends
    Empty and gray and dread.
To-morrow night 'tis full again,
    Golden, and foaming red.

## WHAT THE GHOST OF THE GAMBLER SAID

Where now the huts are empty,
Where never a camp-fire glows,
In an abandoned cañon,
A Gambler's Ghost arose.

246

## WHAT THE SEXTON SAID

He muttered there, "The moon's a sack
Of dust." His voice rose thin:
"I wish I knew the miner-man.
I'd play, and play to win.
In every game in Cripple-creek
Of old, when stakes were high,
I held my own. Now I would play
For that sack in the sky.
The sport would not be ended there.
'Twould rather be begun.
I'd bet my moon against his stars,
And gamble for the sun.

## THE STRENGTH OF THE LONELY

*(What the Mendicant Said)*

The moon's a monk, unmated,
Who walks his cell, the sky.
His strength is that of heaven-vowed men
Who all life's flames defy.

They turn to stars or shadows,
They go like snow or dew—
Leaving behind no sorrow—
Only the arching blue.

## WHAT THE SEXTON SAID

Your dust will be upon the wind
Within some certain years,
Though you be sealed in lead to-day
Amid the country's tears.

When this idyllic churchyard
Becomes the heart of town,
The place to build garage or inn,
They'll throw your tombstone down.

Your name so dim, so long outworn,
Your bones so near to earth,
Your sturdy kindred dead and gone,
How should men know your worth?

So read upon the runic moon
Man's epitaph, deep-writ.
It says the world is one great grave.
For names it cares no whit.

It tells the folk to live in peace,
And still, in peace, to die.
At least so speaks the moon to me,
The tombstone of the sky.


## THE SCISSORS-GRINDER

### (An Unconscious Prophecy Written in 1913)

#### (*What the Tramp Said*)

The old man had his box and wheel
For grinding knives and shears.
No doubt his bell in village streets
Was joy to children's ears.
And I bethought me of my youth
When such men came around,

And times I asked them in, quite sure
The scissors should be ground.
The old man turned and spoke to me,
His face at last in view.
And then I thought those curious eyes
Were eyes that once I knew.

"The moon is but an emery-wheel
To whet the sword of God,"
He said. "And here beside my fire
I stretch upon the sod
Each night, and dream, and watch the stars
And watch the ghost-clouds go.
And see that sword of God in Heaven
A-waving to and fro.
I see that sword each century, friend.
It means the world-war comes
With all its bloody, wicked chiefs
And hate-inflaming drums.
Men talk of peace, but I have seen
That emery-wheel turn round.
The voice of Abel cries again
To God from out the ground.
The ditches must flow red, the plague
Go stark and screaming by
Each time that sword of God takes edge
Within the midnight sky.
And those that scorned their brothers here
And sowed a wind of shame
Will reap the whirlwind as of old
And face relentless flame."

And thus the scissors-grinder spoke,
His face at last in view.
*And there beside the railroad bridge*
*I saw the wandering Jew.*

# The Censer-Moon

### (What the Hermit Said)

The moon is but a censer swung
By angel hands unseen.
The earth has breathed the incense,
She is the angel queen.

The censer makes her drunk with hope,
She sees within the sky
A wild dominion she shall cross
Riding a chariot high.

Such hands as swing the censer
Shall grip the conquering steel
And hew and slay 'mid demon stars
But at the last shall heal.

They'll cast the crowns of conquered stars
On the proud queen's chariot-floor
And cry: "The whole sky loves you
And the great deep shall adore."

# SECTION VI

# INCENSE AND PRAISE, AND WHIM, AND GLORY

## THE STORM-FLOWER

THE STORM-FLOWER BLOOMS BY THE OUTER MOAT
OF MY CASTLE OF LOVE, WHILE THE PERILOUS RAIN
SHRIEKS AND BEATS AT THE GRANITE WALLS,
AT THE DOORS, AT EACH THICK WINDOW-PANE.
BUT IN THE KEEP, STILL, STILL, AND DEEP
MY SWEET LOVE WAITS IN IVORY ROOMS:
SHE WEARS NEW SILK FROM FAIRY LOOMS:
OUR LIPS BURN SWEETLY, WITHOUT FEAR:
OUR NEST IS STILL.  I HEAR HER SIGH,—
AND WHAT CARE I, IF THE STORM-FLOWER BLOOMS!

# HERE'S TO THE SPIRIT OF FIRE

Here's to the spirit of fire, wherever the flame is unfurled,
In the sun, it may be, as a torch to lead on and enlighten the
    world;
That melted the glacial streams, in the day that no memories
    reach,
That shimmered in amber and shell and weed on the earliest
    beach;
The genius of love and of life, the power that will ever
    abound,
That waits in the bones of the dead, who sleep till the judg-
    ment shall sound.
Here's to the spirit of fire, when clothed in swift music it
    comes,
The glow of the harvesting songs, the voice of the national
    drums;
The whimsical, various fire, in the rhymes and ideas of men,
Buried in books for an age, exploding and writhing again,
And blown a red wind round the world, consuming the lies
    in its mirth,
Then locked in dark volumes for long, and buried like coal in
    the earth.
Here's to the comforting fire in the joys of the blind and the
    meek,
In the customs of letterless lands, in the thoughts of the
    stupid and weak.
In the weariest legends they tell, in their cruellest, coldest
    belief,
In the proverbs of counter or till, in the arts of the priest or
    the thief.
Here's to the spirit of fire, that never the ocean can drown,

That glows in the phosphorent wave, and gleams in the sea-
    rose crown;
That sleeps in the sunbeam and mist, that creeps as the wise
    men know,
A wonder, an incense, a whim, a perfume, a fear and a glow,
Ensnaring the stars with a spell, and holding the earth in
    a net:
Yea, filling the nations with prayer, wherever man's pathway
    is set.


# BEING THE DEDICATION OF A MORNING

## To Hilda Conkling, Poet

Eyes of the eagle are yours, eyes of the dove are yours,
Heart of the robin is yours, heart of the woods is yours.
The long hair of Mab is yours. The long hair of Eve is yours.
And you are a cool clear river at play,
A river of light, that sweeps through the breast:—
Of healing and power,
That surely cures.
And I am young as Hilda today,
And all heavy years are hurried away,
And only the light and fire endures.


I am a trout in this river of light,
A cataract,
Or a pool,
A wave, or a thought, that curls and whirls,
Because of these magical silly reasons:—
You are all our birds, and all our seasons,
And all our hopes, and all little girls,
In one little lady, very polite,
The doll and the darling and boy of the forest,

254

## THE KNIGHT IN DISGUISE

The fern that is tallest, the dawn the heart fears,
All the stars of the morning in my sight.
Eyes of the eagle are yours. Eyes of the dove are yours,
Oh Hilda, singer, America bringer,
The prophets have told us ten thousand years—
Only the light of life endures
So I here deny sorrow,
And here denounce tears,
Only the light of life endures.

## THE KNIGHT IN DISGUISE

### (Concerning O. Henry [Sidney Porter])

"He could not forget that he was a Sidney."

Is this Sir Philip Sidney, this loud clown,
The darling of the glad and gaping town?

This is that dubious hero of the press
Whose slangy tongue and insolent address
Were spiced to rouse on Sunday afternoon
The man with yellow journals round him strewn.
We laughed and dozed, then roused and read again,
And vowed O. Henry funniest of men.
He always worked a triple-hinged surprise
To end the scene and make one rub his eyes .

He comes with vaudeville, with stare and leer.
He comes with megaphone and specious cheer.
His troupe, too fat or short or long or lean,
Step from the pages of the magazine
With slapstick or sombrero or with cane:
The rube, the cowboy or the masher vain.
They over-act each part. But at the height
Of banter and of canter and delight

255

The masks fall off for one queer instant there
And show real faces: faces full of care
And desperate longing: love that's hot or cold;
And subtle thoughts, and countenances bold.
The masks go back. 'Tis one more joke. Laugh on!
The goodly grown-up company is gone.

No doubt had he occasion to address
The brilliant court of purple-clad Queen Bess,
He would have wrought for them the best he knew
And led more loftily his actor-crew.
How coolly he misquoted. 'Twas his art—
Slave-scholar, who misquoted—from the heart.
So when we slapped his back with friendly roar
Aesop awaited him without the door,—
Aesop the Greek, who made dull masters laugh
With little tales of *fox* and *dog* and *calf*.
And be it said, mid these his pranks so odd
With something nigh to chivalry he trod
And oft the drear and driven would defend—
The little shopgirl's knight unto the end.
Yea, he had passed, ere we could understand
The blade of Sidney glimmered in his hand.
Yea, ere we knew, Sir Philip's sword was drawn
With valiant cut and thrust, and he was gone.

## THE WIZARD IN THE STREET

### (Concerning Edgar Allan Poe)

Who now will praise the Wizard in the street
With loyal songs, with humors grave and sweet—
This Jingle-man, of strolling players born,
Whom holy folk have hurried by in scorn,

# THE WIZARD IN THE STREET

This threadbare jester, neither wise nor good,
With melancholy bells upon his hood?

The hurrying great ones scorn his Raven's croak,
And well may mock his mystifying cloak
Inscribed with runes from tongues he has not read
To make the ignoramus turn his head.
The artificial glitter of his eyes
Has captured half-grown boys. They think him wise.
Some shallow player-folk esteem him deep,
Soothed by his steady wand's mesmeric sweep.

The little lacquered boxes in his hands
Somehow suggest old times and reverenced lands.
From them doll-monsters come, we know not how:
Puppets, with Cain's black rubric on the brow.
Some passing jugglers, smiling, now concede
That his best cabinet-work is made, indeed
By bleeding his right arm, day after day,
Triumphantly to seal and to inlay.
They praise his little act of shedding tears;
A trick, well learned, with patience, thro' the years.

I love him in this blatant, well-fed place.
Of all the faces, his the only face
Beautiful, tho' painted for the stage,
Lit up with song, then torn with cold, small rage,
Shames that are living, loves and hopes long dead,
Consuming pride, and hunger, real, for bread.

Here by the curb, ye Prophets thunder deep:
"What Nations sow, they must expect to reap,"

Or haste to clothe the race with truth and power,
With hymns and shouts increasing every hour.

Useful are you.   There stands the useless one
Who builds the Haunted Palace in the sun.
Good tailors, can you dress a doll for me
With silks that whisper of the sounding sea?
One moment, citizens,—the weary tramp
Unveileth Psyche with the agate lamp.
Which one of you can spread a spotted cloak
And raise an unaccounted incense smoke
Until within the twilight of the day
Stands dark Ligeia in her disarray,
Witchcraft and desperate passion in her breath
And battling will, that conquers even death?

And now the evening goes.   No man has thrown
The weary dog his well-earned crust or bone.
We grin and hie us home and go to sleep,
Or feast like kings till midnight, drinking deep.
He drank alone, for sorrow, and then slept,
And few there were that watched him, few that wept.
He found the gutter, lost to love and man.
Too slowly came the good Samaritan.

## THREE POEMS ABOUT MARK TWAIN

### I. The Raft

The whole world on a raft!   A King is here,
The record of his grandeur but a smear.
Is it his deacon-beard, or old bald plate
That makes the band upon his whims to wait?
Loot and mud-honey have his soul defiled.
Quack, pig, and priest, he drives camp-meetings wild
Until they shower their pennies like spring rain
That he may preach upon the Spanish main.
What landlord, lawyer, voodoo-man has yet
A better native right to make men sweat?

## THREE POEMS ABOUT MARK TWAIN

The whole world on a raft!  A Duke is here
At sight of whose lank jaw the muses leer.
Journeyman-printer, lamb with ferret eyes,
In life's skullduggery he takes the prize—
Yet stands at twilight wrapped in Hamlet dreams.
Into his eyes the Mississippi gleams.
The sandbar sings in moonlit veils of foam.
A candle shines from one lone cabin home.
The waves reflect it like a drunken star.

A banjo and a hymn are heard afar.
No solace on the lazy shore excels
The Duke's blue castle with its steamer-bells.
The floor is running water and the roof
The stars' brocade with cloudy warp and woof.

And on past sorghum fields the current swings.
To Christian Jim the Mississippi sings.
This prankish wave-swept barque has won its place,
A ship of jesting for the human race.
But do you laugh when Jim bows down forlorn
His babe, his deaf Elizabeth to mourn?
And do you laugh, when Jim, from Huck apart
Gropes through the rain and night with breaking heart?

But now that imp is here and we can smile
Jim's child and guardian this long-drawn while.
With knife and heavy gun, a hunter keen,
He stops for squirrel-meat in islands green.
The eternal gamin, sleeping half the day,
Then stripped and sleek, a river-fish at play.
And then well-dressed, ashore, he sees life spilt.
The river-bank is one bright crazy-quilt
Of patch-work dream, of wrath more red than lust,
Where long-haired feudist Hotspurs bite the dust . . .

This Huckleberry Finn is but the race,
America, still lovely in disgrace,
New childhood of the world, that blunders on
And wonders at the darkness and the dawn,
The poor damned human race, still unimpressed
With its damnation, all its gamin breast
Chorteling at dukes and kings with nigger Jim,
Then plotting for their fall, with jestings grim.

Behold a Republic
Where a river speaks to men
And cries to those that love its ways,
Answering again
When in the heart's extravagance
The rascals bend to say
"O singing Mississippi
Shine, sing for us today."

But who is this in sweeping Oxford gown
Who steers the raft, or ambles up and down,
Or throws his gown aside, and there in white
Stands gleaming like a pillar of the night?
The lion of high courts, with hoary mane,
Fierce jester that this boyish court will gain—
Mark Twain!
The bad world's idol:
Old Mark Twain!

He takes his turn as watchman with the rest,
With secret transports to the stars addressed,
With nightlong broodings upon cosmic law,
With daylong laughter at this world so raw.

All praise to Emerson and Whitman, yet
The best they have to say, their sons forget.

But who can dodge this genius of the stream,
The Mississippi Valley's laughing dream?
He is the artery that finds the sea
In this the land of slaves, and boys still free.
He is the river, and they one and all
Sail on his breast, and to each other call.

Come let us disgrace ourselves,
Knock the stuffed gods from their shelves,
And cinders at the schoolhouse fling.
Come let us disgrace ourselves,
And live on a raft with gray Mark Twain
And Huck and Jim
And the Duke and the King.

## II. When the Mississippi Flowed in Indiana

(Inscribed to Bruce Campbell, who read "Tom Sawyer" with
me in the old house)

Beneath Time's roaring cannon
Many walls fall down.
But though the guns break every stone,
Level every town:—
Within our Grandma's old front hall
Some wonders flourish yet:—
The Pavement of Verona,
Where stands young Juliet,
The roof of Blue-beard's palace,
And Kubla Khan's wild ground,
The cave of young Aladdin,
Where the jewel-flowers were found,

261

And the garden of old Sparta
Where little Helen played,
The grotto of Miranda
That Prospero arrayed.
And the cave, by the Mississippi,
Where Becky Thatcher strayed.

On that Indiana stairway
Gleams Cinderella's shoe.
Upon that mighty mountainside
Walks Snow-white in the dew.
Upon that grassy hillside
Trips shining Nicolette:—
That stairway of remembrance
Time's cannon will not get—
That chattering slope of glory
Our little cousins made,
That hill by the Mississippi
Where Becky Thatcher strayed.

Spring beauties on that cliffside,
Love in the air,
While the soul's deep Mississippi
Sweeps on, forever fair.
And he who enters in the cave,
Nothing shall make afraid,
The cave by the Mississippi
Where Tom and Becky strayed.

### III. Mark Twain and Joan of Arc

When Yankee soldiers reach the barricade
Then Joan of Arc gives each the accolade.

## THE LION

For she is there in armor clad, today,
All the young poets of the wide world say.

Which of our freemen did she greet the first,
Seeing him come against the fires accurst?

Mark Twain, our Chief with neither smile nor jest,
Leading to war our youngest and our best.

The Yankee to King Arthur's court returns.
The sacred flag of Joan above him burns.

For she has called his soul from out the tomb.
And where she stands, there he will stand till doom.

.    .    .    .    .    .    .    .    .

But I, I can but mourn, and mourn again
At bloodshed caused by angels, saints, and men.


## THE LION

The Lion is a kingly beast.
He likes a Hindu for a feast.
And if no Hindu he can get,
The lion-family is upset.

He cuffs his wife and bites her ears
Till she is nearly moved to tears.
Then some explorer finds the den
And all is family peace again.

263

## AN EXPLANATION OF THE GRASSHOPPER

The Grasshopper, the grasshopper,
I will explain to you:—
He is the Brownies' racehorse,
The fairies' Kangaroo.

## THE DANGEROUS LITTLE BOY FAIRIES

In fairyland the little boys
Would rather fight than eat their meals.
They like to chase a gauze-winged fly
And catch and beat him till he squeals.
Sometimes they come to sleeping men
Armed with the deadly red-rose thorn,
And those that feel its fearful wound
Repent the day that they were born.

## THE MOUSE THAT GNAWED THE OAK-TREE DOWN

The mouse that gnawed the oak-tree down
Began his task in early life.
He kept so busy with his teeth
He had no time to take a wife.

He gnawed and gnawed through sun and rain
When the ambitious fit was on,
Then rested in the sawdust till
A month of idleness had gone.

He did not move about to hunt
The coteries of mousie-men.

# THE SONG OF THE GARDEN-TOAD

He was a snail-paced, stupid thing
Until he cared to gnaw again.

The mouse that gnawed the oak-tree down,
When that tough foe was at his feet—
Found in the stump no angel-cake
Nor buttered bread, nor cheese nor meat—
The forest-roof let in the sky.
"This light is worth the work," said he.
"I'll make this ancient swamp more light,"
And started on another tree.

## THE SONG OF THE GARDEN-TOAD

Down, down beneath the daisy beds,
O hear the cries of pain!
And moaning on the cinder-path
They're blind amid the rain.
Can murmurs of the worms arise
To higher hearts than mine?
I wonder if that gardener hears
Who made the mold all fine
And packed each gentle seedling down
So carefully in line?

I watched the red rose reaching up
To ask him if he heard
Those cries that stung the evening earth
Till all the rose-roots stirred.
She asked him if he felt the hate
That burned beneath them there.
She asked him if he heard the curse
Of worms in black despair.
He kissed the rose. What did it mean?

What of the rose's prayer?
Down, down where rain has never come
They fight in burning graves,
Bleeding and drinking blood
Within those venom-caves.
Blaspheming still the gardener's name,
They live and hate and go.
I wonder if the gardener heard
The rose that told him so?

## FACTORY WINDOWS ARE ALWAYS BROKEN

Factory windows are always broken.
Somebody's always throwing bricks,
Somebody's always heaving cinders,
Playing ugly Yahoo tricks.

Factory windows are always broken.
Other windows are let alone.
No one throws through the chapel-window
The bitter, snarling, derisive stone.

Factory windows are always broken.
Something or other is going wrong.
Something is rotten—I think, in Denmark.
*End of the factory-window song.*

## IN PRAISE OF SONGS THAT DIE

(After having read a great deal of good current poetry in
the magazines and newspapers)

Ah, they are passing, passing by,
Wonderful songs, but born to die!

## TO EVE, MAN'S DREAM OF WIFEHOOD

Cries from the infinite human seas,
Waves thrice-winged with harmonies.
Here I stand on a pier in the foam
Seeing the songs to the beach go home,
Dying in sand while the tide flows back,
As it flowed of old in its fated track.
O hurrying tide that will not hear
Your own foam-children dying near:
Is there no refuge-house of song,
No home, no haven where songs belong?
O precious hymns that come and go!
You perish, and I love you so!


## TO EVE, MAN'S DREAM OF WIFEHOOD
## AS DESCRIBED BY MILTON

Darling of Milton—when that marble man
Saw you in shadow, coming from God's hand
Serene and young, did he not chant for you
Praises more quaint than he could understand?

"To justify the ways of God to man"—
So, self-deceived, his printed purpose runs.
His love for you is the true key to him,
And Uriel and Michael were your sons.

Your bosom nurtured his Urania.
Your meek voice, piercing through his midnight sleep
Shook him far more than silver chariot wheels
Or rattling shields, or trumpets of the deep.

Titan and lover, could be content
With Eden's narrow setting for your spell?

267

You wound soft arms around his brows. He smiled
And grimly for your home built Heaven and Hell.
That was his posy. A strange gift, indeed.
We bring you what we can, not what is fit.
Eve, dream of wifehood! Each man in his way
Serves you with chants according to his wit.


## EDEN IN WINTER

(Supposed to be chanted to some rude instrument at a
modern fireplace)

Chant we the story now
Tho' in a house we sleep;
Tho' by a hearth of coals
Vigil to-night we keep.
Chant we the story now,
Of the vague love we knew
When I from out the sea
Rose to the feet of you.

Bird from the cliffs you came,
Flew thro' the snow to me,
Facing the icy blast
There by the icy sea.
How did I reach your feet?
Why should I—at the end
Hold out half-frozen hands
Dumbly to you my friend?
Ne'er had I woman seen,
Ne'er had I seen a flame.
There you piled fagots on,
Heat rose—the blast to tame.

268

There by the cave-door dark,
Comforting me you cried—
Wailed o'er my wounded knee,
Wept for my rock-torn side.

Up from the South I trailed—
Left regions fierce and fair!
Left all the jungle-trees,
Left the red tiger's lair.
Dream-led, I scarce knew why,
Into your North I trod—
Ne'er had I known the snow,
Or the frost-blasted sod.

O how the flakes came down!
O how the fire burned high!
Strange thing to see he was,
Thro' his dry twigs would fly,
Creep there awhile and sleep—
Then wake and bark for fight—
Biting if I too near
Came to his eyes so bright.
Then with a will you fed
Wood to his hungry tongue.

Then he did leap and sing—
Dancing the clouds among,
Turning the night to noon,
Stinging my eyes with light,
Making the snow retreat,
Making the cave-house bright.

There were dry fagots piled,
Nuts and dry leaves and roots,
Stores there of furs and hides,
Sweet-barks and grains and fruits.

There wrapped in fur we lay,
Half-burned, half-frozen still—
Ne'er will my soul forget
All the night's bitter chill.
We had not learned to speak,
I was to you a strange
Wolfling or wounded fawn,
Lost from his forest-range.

Thirsting for bloody meat,
Out at the dawn we went.
Weighed with our prey at eve,
Home-came we all forspent.
Comrades and hunters tried
Ere we were maid and man —
Not till the spring awoke
Laughter and speech began.

Whining like forest dogs,
Rustling like budding trees,
Bubbling like thawing springs,
Humming like little bees,
Crooning like Maytime tides,
Chattering parrot words,
Crying the panther's cry,
Chirping like mating birds—
Thus, thus, we learned to speak,
Who mid the snows were dumb,
Nor did we learn to kiss
Until the Spring had come.

## GENESIS

I was but a half-grown boy,
You were a girl-child slight.

# GENESIS

Ah, how weary you were!
You had led in the bullock-fight . . .
We slew the bullock at length
With knives and maces of stone.
And so your feet were torn,
Your lean arms bruised to the bone.

Perhaps 'twas the slain beast's blood
We drank, or a root we ate,
Or our revelling evening bath
In the fall by the garden gate,
But you turned to a witching thing,
Side-glancing, and frightened me;
You purred like a panther's cub,
You sighed like a shell from the sea.

We knelt. I caressed your hair
By the light of the leaping fire:
Your fierce eyes blinked with smoke,
Pine-fumes, that enhanced desire.
I helped to unbraid your hair
In wonder and fear profound:
You were humming your hunting tune
As it swept to the grassy ground.

Our comrades, the shaggy bear,
The tiger with velvet feet,
The lion, crept to the light
Whining for bullock meat.
We fed them and stroked their necks . . .
They took their way to the fen
Where they hunted or hid all night;
No enemies, they, of men.

Evil had entered not
The cobra, since defiled.

He watched, when the beasts had gone,
Our kissing and singing wild.
Beautiful friend he was,
Sage, not a tempter grim.
Many a year should pass
Ere Satan should enter him.

He danced while the evening dove
And the nightingale kept in tune.
I sang of the angel sun:
You sang of the angel-moon:
We sang of the *angel-chief*
Who blew thro' the trees strange breath,
Who helped in the hunt all day
And granted the bullock's death.

O Eve with the fire-lit breast
And child-face red and white!
I heaped the great logs high!
That was our bridal night.

## THE PERFECT MARRIAGE

I hate this yoke; for the world's sake here put it on:
Knowing 'twill weigh as much on you till life is gone.
Knowing you love your freedom dear, as I love mine—
Knowing that love unchained has been our life's great wine:
Our one great wine (yet spent too soon, and serving none;
Of the two cups free love at last the deadly one).

We grant our meetings will be tame, not honey-sweet,
No longer turning to the tryst with flying feet.
We know the toil that now must come will spoil the bloom
And tenderness of passion's touch, and in its room

# THE PERFECT MARRIAGE

Will come tame habit, deadly calm, sorrow and gloom.
Oh, how the battle scars the best who enter life!
Each soldier comes out blind or lame from the black strife.
Mad or diseased or damned of soul the best may come—
It matters not how merrily now rolls the drum,
The fife shrills high, the horn sings loud, till no steps lag—
And all adore that silken flame, Desire's great flag.

We will build strong our tiny fort, strong as we can—
Holding one inner room beyond the sword of man.
Love is too wide, it seems to-day, to hide it there.
It seems to flood the fields of corn, and gild the air—
It seems to breathe from every brook, from flowers to sigh—
It seems a cataract poured down from the great sky;
It seems a tenderness so vast no bush but shows
Its haunting and transfiguring light where wonder glows.
It wraps us in a silken snare by shadowy streams,
And wildering sweet and stung with joy your white soul
      seems
A flame, a flame, conquering day, conquering night,
Brought from our God, a holy thing, a mad delight.
But love when all things beat it down, leaves the wide air,
The heavens are gray, and men turn wolves, lean with despair.
Ah, when we need love most, and weep, when all is dark,
Love is a pinch of ashes gray with one live spark—
Yet on the hope to keep alive that treasure strange
Hangs all earth's struggle, strife and scorn, and desperate
      change.

Love? . . . we will scarcely love our babes full many a time—
Knowing their souls and ours too well, and all our grime—
And there beside our holy hearth we'll hide our eyes—
Lest we should flash what seems disdain without disguise.
Yet there shall be no wavering there in that deep trial—
And no false fire or stranger hand or traitor vile—

We'll fight the gloom and fight the world with strong sword
    play,
Entrenched within our block-house small, ever at bay—
As fellow-warriors, underpaid, wounded and wild,
True to their battered flag, their faith still undefiled!


## DARLING DAUGHTER OF BABYLON

Too soon you wearied of our tears.
And then you danced with spangled feet,
Leading Belshazzar's chattering court
A-tinkling through the shadowy street.
With mead they came, with chants of shame.
DESIRE's red flag before them flew.
And Istar's music moved your mouth
And Baal's deep shames rewoke in you.

Now you could drive the royal car;
Forget our Nation's breaking load:
Now you could sleep on silver beds—
(Bitter and dark was our abode).
And so, for many a night you laughed,
And knew not of my hopeless prayer,
Till God's own spirit whipped you forth
From Istar's shrine, from Istar's stair.

Darling daughter of Babylon—
Rose by the black Euphrates flood—
Again your beauty grew more dear
Than my slave's bread, than my heart's blood.
We sang of Zion, good to know,
Where righteousness and peace abide . . .

## LIFE TRANSCENDENT

What of your second sacrilege
Carousing at Belshazzar's side?

Once, by a stream, we clasped tired hands—
Your paint and henna washed away.
Your place, you said, was with the slaves
Who sewed the thick cloth, night and day.
You were a pale and holy maid
Toil-bound with us.  One night you said:—
"Your God shall be my God until
I slumber with the patriarch dead."

Pardon, daughter of Babylon,
If, on this night remembering
Our lover walks under the walls
Of hanging gardens in the spring,
A venom comes from broken hope,
From memories of your comrade-song
Until I curse your painted eyes
And do your flower-mouth too much wrong.


## LIFE TRANSCENDENT

This being the name of praise given to a fair lady

I used to think, when the corn was blowing
Of my lost lady, *Life Transcendent*,
Of her valiant way, of her pride resplendent:
For the corn swayed round, like her warrior-band
When I knelt by the blades to kiss her hand.
But now the green of the corn is going,
And winter comes and a springtime sowing
Of other grain, on the plains we knew.
So I walk on air, where the clouds are blowing,

And kiss her hand, where the gods are sowing
Stars for corn, in the star-fields new.

## WITH A ROSE, TO BRUNHILDE

Brunhilde, with the young Norn soul
That has no peace, and grim as those
That spun the thread of life, give heed:
Peace is concealed in every rose.
And in these petals peace I bring:
A jewel clearer than the dew:
A perfume subtler than the breath
Of Spring with which it circles you.

Peace I have found, asleep, awake,
By many paths, on many a strand.
Peace overspreads the sky with stars.
Peace is concealed within your hand.
And when at night I clasp it there
I wonder how you never know
The strength you shed from finger-tips:
The treasure that consoles me so.

Begin the art of finding peace,
Beloved:—it is art, no less.
Sometimes we find it hid beneath
The orchards in their springtime dress:
Sometimes one finds it in oak woods,
Sometimes in dazzling mountain-snows;
In books, sometimes. But pray begin
By finding it within a rose.

# SUNSHINE

### (For a very little girl, not a year old)

CATHERINE FRAZEE WAKEFIELD

The sun gives not directly
  The coal, the diamond crown;
Not in a special basket
  Are these from Heaven let down.

The sun gives not directly
  The plough, man's iron friend;
Not by a path or stairway
  Do tools from Heaven descend.

Yet sunshine fashions all things
  That cut or burn or fly;
And corn that seems upon the earth
  Is made in the hot sky.

The gravel of the roadbed,
  The metal of the gun,
The engine of the airship
  Trace somehow from the sun.

And so your soul, my lady
  (Mere sunshine, nothing more),
Prepares me the contraptions
  I work with or adore.

Within me cornfields rustle,
  Niagaras roar their way,

277

Vast thunderstorms and rainbows
   Are in my thought to-day.

Ten thousand anvils sound there
   By forges flaming white,
And many books I read there,
   And many books I write;

And freedom's bells are ringing,
   And bird-choirs chant and fly—
The whole world works in me to-day
   And all the shining sky,

Because of one small lady
   Whose smile is my chief sun.
She gives not any gift to me
   Yet all gifts, giving one. . . .
                                    Amen.


## TWO EASTER STANZAS

### I. THE HOPE OF THE RESURRECTION

Though I have watched so many mourners weep
O'er the real dead, in dull earth laid asleep—
Those dead seemed but the shadows of my days
That passed and left me in the sun's bright rays.
Now though you go on smiling in the sun
Our love is slain, and love and you were one.
You are the first, you I have known so long,
Whose death was deadly, a tremendous wrong.

278

Therefore I seek the faith that sets it right
Amid the lilies and the candle-light.
I think on Heaven, for in that air so clear
We two may meet, confused and parted here.
Ah, when man's dearest dies, 'tis then he goes
To that old balm that heals the centuries' woes.
Then Christ's wild cry in all the streets is rife:—
"I am the Resurrection and the Life."

## II. WE MEET AT THE JUDGMENT AND I FEAR IT NOT

Though better men may fear that trumpet's warning,
I meet you, lady, on the Judgment morning,
With golden hope my spirit still adorning.

Our God who made you all so fair and sweet
Is three times gentle, and before his feet
Rejoicing I shall say:—"The girl you gave
Was my first Heaven, an angel bent to save.
O God, her maker, if my ingrate breath
Is worth this rescue from the Second Death,
Perhaps her dear proud eyes grow gentler too
That scorned my graceless years and trophies few.
Gone are those years, and gone ill-deeds that turned
Her sacred beauty from my songs that burned.
We now as comrades through the stars may take
The rich and arduous quests I did forsake.
Grant me a seraph-guide to thread the throng
And quickly find that woman-soul so strong.
I dream that in her deeply-hidden heart
Hurt love lived on, though we were far apart,
A brooding secret mercy like your own
That blooms to-day to vindicate your throne."

# ALONE IN THE WIND, ON THE PRAIRIE

I know a seraph who has golden eyes,
And hair of gold, and body like the snow.
Here in the wind I dream her unbound hair
Is blowing round me, that desire's sweet glow
Has touched her pale keen face, and willful mien
And though she steps as one in manner born
To tread the forests of fair Paradise,
Dark memory's wood she chooses to adorn.
Here with bowed head, bashful with half-desire
She glides into my yesterday's deep dream,
All glowing by the misty ferny cliff
Beside the far forbidden thundering stream.
Within my dream I shake with the old flood.
I fear its going, ere the spring days go.
Yet pray the glory may have deathless years,
And kiss her hair, and sweet throat like the snow.

# THIS SECTION IS A CHRISTMAS TREE

This section is a Christmas tree:
Loaded with pretty toys for you.
Behold the blocks, the Noah's arks,
The popguns painted red and blue.
No solemn pine-cone forest-fruit,
But silver horns and candy sacks
And many little tinsel hearts
And cherubs pink, and jumping-jacks.
For every child a gift, I hope.
The doll upon the topmost bough

## THIS SECTION IS A CHRISTMAS TREE

Is mine. But all the rest are yours.
And I will light the candles now.


### I. THE DOLL UPON THE TOPMOST BOUGH

This doll upon the topmost bough,
This playmate-gift, in Christmas dress,
Was taken down and brought to me
One sleety night most comfortless.

Her hair was gold, her dolly-sash
Was gray brocade, most good to see.
The dear toy laughed, and I forgot
The ill the new year promised me.


### II. ON SUDDENLY RECEIVING A CURL LONG REFUSED

Oh, saucy gold circle of fairyland silk—
Impudent, intimate, delicate treasure;
A noose for my heart and a ring for my finger:—
Here in my study you sing me a measure.

Whimsy and song in my little gray study!
Words out of wonderland, praising her fineness,
Touched with her pulsating, delicate laughter,
Saying, "The girl is all daring and kindness!"

Saying, "Her soul is all feminine gameness,
Trusting her insights, ardent for living;
She would be weeping with me and be laughing
A thoroughbred, joyous receiving and giving!"

281

## III. On Receiving One of Gloriana's Letters

Your pen needs but a ruffle
To be Pavlova whirling.
It surely is a scalawag
A-scamping down the page.
A pretty little May-wind
The morning buds uncurling.
And then the white sweet Russian,
The dancer of the age.

Your pen's the Queen of Sheba,
Such serious questions bringing,
That merry rascal Solomon
Would show a sober face:—
And then again Pavlova
To set our spirits singing,
The snowy-swan bacchante
All glamour, glee and grace.

## IV. In Praise of Gloriana's Remarkable Golden Hair

The gleaming head of one fine friend
Is bent above my little song,
So through the treasure-pits of Heaven
In fancy's shoes, I march along.

I wander, seek and peer and ponder
In Splendor's last ensnaring lair—
'Mid burnished harps and burnished crowns
Where noble chariots gleam and flare:

282

Amid the spirit-coins and gems,
The plates and cups and helms of fire—
The gorgeous treasure-pits of Heaven—
Where angel-misers slake desire!

O endless treasure-pits of gold
Where silly angel-men make mirth—
I think that I am there this hour,
Though walking in the ways of earth!

## TO A GOLDEN-HAIRED GIRL IN A LOUISIANA TOWN

You are a sunrise,
If a star should rise instead of the sun.
You are a moonrise,
If a star should come, in the place of the moon.
You are the Spring,
If a face should bloom,
Instead of an apple-bough.
You are my love
If your heart is as kind
As your young eyes now.

## KALAMAZOO

Once, in the city of Kalamazoo,
The gods went walking, two and two,
With the friendly phœnix, the stars of Orion,
The speaking pony and singing lion.
For in Kalamazoo in a cottage apart
Lived the girl with the innocent heart.

Thenceforth the city of Kalamazoo
Was the envied, intimate chum of the sun.
He rose from a cave by the principal street.
The lions sang, the dawn-horns blew,
And the ponies danced on silver feet.
He hurled his clouds of love around;
Deathless colors of his old heart
Draped the houses and dyed the ground.
O shrine of that wide young Yankee land,
Incense city of Kalamazoo,
That held, in the midnight, the priceless sun
As a jeweller holds an opal in hand!

From the awkward city of Oshkosh came
Love, (the bully no whip shall tame),
Bringing his gang of sinners bold.
And I was the least of his Oshkosh men;
But none were reticent, none were old.
And we joined the singing phœnix then,
And shook the lilies of Kalamazoo
All for one hidden butterfly.
Bulls of glory, in cars of war
We charged the boulevards, proud to die
For her ribbon sailing there on high.
Our blood set gutters all aflame,
Where the sun slept without any shame,
Cold rock till he must rise again.
She made great poets of wolf-eyed men—
The dear queen-bee of Kalamazoo,
With her crystal wings, and her honey heart.
We fought for her favors a year and a day
(Oh, the bones of the dead, the Oshkosh dead,
That were scattered along her pathway red!)
And then, in her harum-scarum way,
She left with a passing traveller-man—

# THE CELESTIAL CIRCUS

With a singing Irishman
Went to Japan.

Why do the lean hyenas glare
Where the glory of Artemis had begun—
Of Atalanta, Joan of Arc,
Lorna Doone, Rosy O'Grady,
And Orphant Annie all in one?
Who burned this city of Kalamazoo
Till nothing was left but a ribbon or two—
One scorched phœnix that mourned in the dew,
Acres of ashes, a junk-man's cart,
A torn-up letter, a dancing shoe
(And the bones of the valiant dead)?
Who burned this city of Kalamazoo—
Love-town Troy-town Kalamazoo?

A harum-scarum innocent heart.


## THE CELESTIAL CIRCUS

In Heaven, if not on earth,
You and I will be dancing.
I will whirl you over my head,
A torch and a flag and a bird,
A hawk that loves my shoulder,
A dove with plumes outspread.
We will whirl for God when the trumpets
Speak the millennial word.

We will howl in praise of God,
Dervish and young cyclone.
We will ride in the joy of God
On circus horses white.

Your feet will be white lightning,
Your spangles white and regal,
We will leap from the horses' backs
To the cliffs of day and night.

We will have our rest in the pits of sleep
When the darkness leaps upon us,
And buries us for æons
Till we rise like grass in the spring.
We will come like dandelions,
Like buttercups and crocuses,
And all the winter of our sleep
But make us storm and sing.

We will tumble like swift foam
On the wave-crests of old ghostland,
And dance on the crafts of doom,
And wrestle on the moon.
And Saturn and his triple ring
Will be our tinsel circus,
Till all sad wraiths of yesterday
With the stars rejoice and croon.

O dancer, love undying,
My soul, my swan, my eagle,
The first of our million dancing years
Dawns, dawns soon.

## HARPS IN HEAVEN

I will bring you great harps in Heaven,
Made of giant shells
From the jasper sea.
With a thousand burnt-up years behind,

## A KIND OF SCORN

What then of the gulf from you to me?
It will be but the width of a thread,
Or the narrowest leaf of our sheltering tree.

You dare not refuse my harps in Heaven.
Or angels will mock you, and turn away.
Or with angel wit,
Will praise your eyes,
And your pure Greek lips and bid you play,
And sing of the love from them to you,
And then of my poor flaming heart
In the far-off earth, when the years were new.

I will bring you such harps in Heaven
That they will shake at your touch and breath,
Whose threads are rainbows,
Seventy times seven,
Whose voice is life, and silence death.


## A KIND OF SCORN

You do not know my pride
Or the storm of scorn I ride.

I am too proud to kiss you and leave you
Without wonders
Spreading round you like flame.
I am too proud to leave you
Without love
Haunting your very name:
Until you bear the Grail
Above your head in splendor
O child, dear and pale.

I am too proud to leave you
Though we part forevermore
Till all your thoughts
Go up toward Glory's door.

Oh, I am but a sinner proud and poor,
Utterly without merit
To help you climb in wonder
A stair toward Heaven's door—
Except that I have prayed my God,
And He will give the Grail,
And you will mourn no longer,
Beset, confused, and pale.
And God will lift you far on high,
The while I pray and pray
Until the hour I die.
The effectual fervent prayer availeth much.
And my first prayer ascends this proud harsh day.


## MY LADY IS COMPARED TO A YOUNG TREE

When I see a young tree
In its white beginning,
With white leaves
And white buds
Barely tipped with green,
In the April weather,
In the weeping sunshine—
Then I see my lady,
My democratic queen,
Standing free and equal
With the youngest woodland sapling
Swaying, singing in the wind,

# THE DRUNKARDS IN THE STREET

Delicate and white:
Soul so near to blossom,
Fragile, strong as death;
A kiss from far-off Eden,
A flash of Judgment's trumpet—
April's breath.

## IN MEMORY OF A CHILD

The angels guide him now,
And watch his curly head,
And lead him in their games,
The little boy we led.

He cannot come to harm,
He knows more than we know,
His light is brighter far
Than daytime here below.

His path leads on and on,
Through pleasant lawns and flowers,
His brown eyes open wide
At grass more green than ours.

With playmates like himself,
The shining boy will sing,
Exploring wondrous woods,
Sweet with eternal spring.

## THE DRUNKARDS IN THE STREET

The Drunkards in the street are calling one another,
Heeding not the night-wind, great of heart and gay,—

Publicans and wantons—
Calling, laughing, calling,
While the Spirit bloweth Space and Time away.

Why should I feel the sobbing, the secrecy, the glory,
This comforter, this fitful wind divine?
I the cautious Pharisee, the scribe, the whited sepulchre—
I have no right to God, he is not mine.

\*     \*     \*     \*     \*     \*

Within their gutters, drunkards dream of Hell.
I say my prayers by my white bed to-night,
With the arms of God about me, with the angels singing,
     singing,
Until the grayness of my soul grows white.

## SECTION VII

## RUNES OF THE ROAD

*Being rhymes that have to do with "Adventures While
Preaching the Gospel of Beauty"*

# A Song in July

A little bird has told me that today will appear
The lost land of Atlantis, so drowned for many a year.
With blue harbors for you, and mountain peaks for me.
Atlantis, Atlantis, the lost land of Atlantis,
Rising again from the sea!

There storms of raining attar drench
And drug the isle with calm.
And dawn will bring us cloud cups heaped
With lightning, spice and balm.
There we will rest from all old things,
From hot and long endeavor,
Two sages lost in glorious thought
And ocean dreams forever.
Come sail, O Sinbad, we shall tame
The waves between, in Allah's name.
Coral palaces for you,
Fog chalices for me,
Mohammed's girls for you
And Mab's girls for me,
Soft shore winds for you,
And mountain streams for me,
In Atlantis, Atlantis, the lost land of Atlantis,
Rising again from the sea!

# I WANT TO GO WANDERING

I want to go wandering. Who shall declare
I will regret if I dare?

    To the rich days of age—
      To some mid-afternoon—
    A wide fenceless prairie,
      A lonely old tune,
    Ant-hills and sunflowers,
      And sunset too soon.

    Behind the brown mountain
      The sun will go down;
    I shall climb, I shall climb,
      To the sumptuous crown;
    To the rocks of the summit,
      And find some strange things:—
    Some echo of echoes
      When the thunder-wind sings;
    Old Spanish necklaces,
      Indian rings,
    Or a feeble old eagle
      With great, dragging wings.
    He may leave me and soar;
      But if he shall die,
    I shall bury him deep
      While the thunder-winds cry.

And there, as the last of my earth-nights go:
What is the thing I shall know?

With a feather cast off from his wings
I shall write, be it revel or psalm,
Or whisper of redwood, or cypress, or palm,—
The treasure of dream that he brings.

The soul of the eagle will call,
Whether he lives or he dies:—
The cliff and the prairie call,
The sagebrush and starlight sing,
And the songs of my far-away Sangamon call
From the plume of the bird of the Rockies,
And midnight's omnipotent wing—
The last of my earth-nights will ring
With cries from a far haunted river,
And all of my wandering,
      Wandering,
      Wandering,
      Wandering. . . .


## PROLOGUE TO "RHYMES TO BE TRADED FOR BREAD"

### (A Private Publication Out of Print)

Even the shrewd and bitter,
Gnarled by the old world's greed,
Cherished the stranger softly
Seeing his utter need.
Shelter and patient hearing,
These were their gifts to him,
To the minstrel chanting, begging,
As the sunset-fire grew dim.
The rich said "You are welcome."

## BY THE SPRING AT SUNSET

Yea, even the rich were good.
How strange that in their feasting
His songs were understood!
The doors of the poor were open,
The poor who had wandered too,
Who slept with never a roof-tree
Under the wind and dew.
The minds of the poor were open,
There dark mistrust was dead:
They loved his wizard stories,
They bought his rhymes with bread.

Those were his days of glory,
Of faith in his fellow-men.
Therefore, to-day the singer
Turns beggar once again.


## BY THE SPRING AT SUNSET

Sometimes we remember kisses,
Remember the dear heart-leap when they came:
Not always, but sometimes we remember
The kindness, the dumbness, the good flame
Of laughter and farewell.

                        Beside the road
Afar from those who said "Good-by" I write,
Far from my city task, my lawful load.

Sun in my face, wind beside my shoulder,
Streaming clouds, banners of new-born night
Enchant me now.  The splendors growing bolder
Make bold my soul for some new wise delight.

I write the day's event, and quench my drouth,
Pausing beside the spring with happy mind.
And now I feel those kisses on my mouth,
Hers most of all, one little friend most kind.


## ON THE ROAD TO NOWHERE

On the road to nowhere
What wild oats did you sow
When you left your father's house
With your cheeks aglow?
Eyes so strained and eager
To see what you might see?
Were you thief or were you fool
Or most nobly free?

Were the tramp-days knightly,
True sowing of wild seed?
Did you dare to make the songs
Vanquished workmen need?
Did you waste much money
To deck a leper's feast?
Love the truth, defy the crowd
Scandalize the priest?
On the road to nowhere
What wild oats did you sow?
Stupids find the nowhere-road
Dusty, grim and slow.

Ere their sowing's ended
They turn them on their track,
Look at the caitiff craven wights
Repentant, hurrying back!

296

Grown ashamed of nowhere,
Of rags endured for years,
Lust for velvet in their hearts,
Pierced with Mammon's spears,
All but a few fanatics
Give up their darling goal,
Seek to be as others are,
Stultify the soul.
Reapings now confront them,
Glut them, or destroy.
Curious seeds, grain or weeds
Sown with awful joy.
Hurried is their harvest,
They make soft peace with men.
Pilgrims pass. They care not,
Will not tramp again.

O nowhere, golden nowhere!
Sages and fools go on
To your chaotic ocean,
To your tremendous dawn.
Far in your fair dream-haven,
Is nothing or is all . . .
They press on, singing, sowing
Wild deeds without recall!

## THE BEGGAR'S VALENTINE

Kiss me and comfort my heart
    Maiden honest and fine.
I am the pilgrim boy
    Lame, but hunting the shrine;

Fleeing away from the sweets,
  Seeking the dust and rain,
Sworn to the staff and road,
  Scorning pleasure and pain;

Nevertheless my mouth
  Would rest like a bird an hour
And find in your curls a nest
  And find in your breast a bower:

Nevertheless my eyes
  Would lose themselves in your own,
Rivers that seek the sea,
  Angels before the throne:

Kiss me and comfort my heart,
  For love can never be mine;
Passion, hunger and pain,
  These are the only wine

Of the pilgrim bound to the road.
  He would rob no man of his own.
Your heart is another's, I know,
  Your honor is his alone.

The feasts of a long-drawn love,
  The feasts of a wedded life,
The harvests of patient years,
  And hearthstone and children and wife:

These are your lords, I know.
  These can never be mine—
This is the price I pay
  For the foolish search for the shrine:

# THE WOULD-BE MERMAN

This is the price I pay
  For the joy of my midnight prayers,
Kneeling beneath the moon
  With hills for my altar stairs;

This is the price I pay
  For the throb of the mystic wings.
When the dove of God comes down
  And beats round my heart and sings;

This is the price I pay
  For the light I shall some day see
At the ends of the infinite earth
  When truth shall come to me.

And what if my body die
  Before I meet the truth?
The road is dear, more dear
  Than love or life or youth.

The road, it is the road,
  Mystical, endless, kind,
Mother of visions vast,
  Mother of soul and mind;

Mother of all of me
  But the blood that cries for a mate—
That cries for a farewell kiss
  From the child of God at the gate.


## THE WOULD-BE MERMAN

Mobs are like the Gulf Stream,
Like the vast Atlantic.

29ª

In your fragile boats you ride.
Conceited folk at ease.
Far beneath are dancers,
Mermen wild and frantic,
Circling round the giant glowing
Sea-anemones.

"Crude, ill-smelling voters,—
Herds," to you in seeming.
But to me their draggled clothes
Are scales of gold and red.
Ah, the pink sea-horses,
Green sea-dragons gleaming,
And knights that chase the dragons
And spear them till they're dead!

Wisdom waits the diver
In the social ocean—
Rainbow shells of wonder,
Piled into a throne.
I would go exploring
Through the wide commotion,
Building under some deep cliff
A pearl-throne all my own.

Yesterday I dived there,
Grinned at all the roaring,
Clinging to the corals for a flash,
Defying death.
Mermen came rejoicing,
In procession pouring,
Yet I lost my feeble grip
And came above for breath.

I would be a merman.
Not in desperation

## WHY I VOTED THE SOCIALIST TICKET

A momentary diver
Blue for lack of air.
But with gills deep-breathing
Swim amid the nation—
Finny feet and hands forsooth,
Sea-laurels in my hair.

## HONOR AMONG SCAMPS

We are the smirched.  Queen Honor is the spotless.
We slept thro' wars where Honor could not sleep.
We were faint-hearted.  Honor was full-valiant.
We kept a silence Honor could not keep.

Yet this late day we make a song to praise her.
We, codeless, will yet vindicate her code.
She who was mighty, walks with us, the beggars.
The merchants drive her out upon the road.

She makes a throne of sod beside our campfire.
We give the maiden-queen our rags and tears.
A battered, rascal guard have rallied round her,
To keep her safe until the better years.

## WHY I VOTED THE SOCIALIST TICKET

I am unjust, but I can strive for justice.
My life's unkind, but I can vote for kindness.
I, the unloving, say life should be lovely.
I, that am blind, cry out against my blindness.

Man is a curious brute—he pets his fancies—
Fighting mankind, to win sweet luxury.
So he will be, tho' law be clear as crystal,
Tho' all men plan to live in harmony.

Come let us vote against our human nature,
Crying to God in all the polling places
To heal our everlasting sinfulness
And make us sages with transfigured faces.


## GALAHAD, KNIGHT WHO PERISHED

(A Poem dedicated to all Crusaders against the International and Interstate Traffic in Young Girls)

Galahad . . . soldier that perished . . . ages ago,
Our hearts are breaking with shame, our tears overflow.
Galahad . . . knight who perished . . . awaken again,
Teach us to fight for immaculate ways among men.
Soldiers fantastic, we pray to the star of the sea,
We pray to the mother of God that the bound may be free.
Rose-crowned lady from heaven, give us thy grace,
Help us the intricate, desperate battle to face,
Till the leer of the trader is seen nevermore in the land,
Till we bring every maid of the age to one sheltering hand.
Ah, they are priceless, the pale and the ivory and red!
Breathless we gaze on the curls of each glorious head!
Arm them with strength mediæval, thy marvellous dower,
Blast now their tempters, shelter their steps with thy power.
Leave not life's fairest to perish—stranger to thee,
Let not the weakest be shipwrecked, oh, star of the sea!

## THE TRAP

She was taught desire in the street,
Not at the angels' feet.
By the good no word was said
Of the worth of the bridal bed.
The secret was learned from the vile,
Not from her mother's smile.
Home spoke not. And the girl
Was caught in the public whirl.
Do you say, "She gave consent:
Life drunk, she was content
With beasts that her fire could please"?
But she did not choose disease
Of mind and nerves and breath.
She was trapped to a slow, foul death.
The door was watched so well,
That the steep dark stair to hell
Was the only escaping way . . .
"She gave consent," you say?

Some think she was meek and good,
Only lost in the wood
Of youth, and deceived in man
When the hunger of sex began
That ties the husband and wife
To the end in a strong fond life.
Her captor, by chance, was one
Of those whose passion was done,
A cold fierce worm of the sea
Enslaving for you and me.
The wages the poor must take
Have forced them to serve this snake.

303

Yea, half-paid girls must go
For bread to his pit below.
What hangman shall wait his host
Of butchers from coast to coast,
New York to the Golden Gate—
The merger of death and fate,
Lust-kings with a careful plan
Clean-cut, American?

In liberty's name we cry
For these women about to die.

O mothers who failed to tell
The mazes of heaven and hell,
Who failed to advise, implore
Your daughters at Love's strange door,
What will you do this day?
Your dear ones are hidden away,
As good as chained to the bed,
Hid like the mad, or the dead:—
The glories of endless years
Drowned in their harlot-tears:
The children they hoped to bear,
Grandchildren strong and fair,
The life for ages to be,
Cut off like a blasted tree,
Murdered in filth in a day,
Somehow by the merchant gay!

In liberty's name we cry
For these women about to die.

What shall be said of a state
Where traps for the white brides wait?

## THE GAMBLERS

Of sellers of drink who play
The game for the extra pay?
Of statesmen in league with all
Who hope for the girl-child's fall?
Of banks where hell's money is paid
And Pharisees all afraid
Of panders that help them sin?
When will our wrath begin?


## THE GAMBLERS

Life's a jail where men have common lot.
Gaunt the one who has, and who has not.
All our treasures neither less nor more,
Bread alone comes thro' the guarded door.
Cards are foolish in this jail, I think,
Yet they play for shoes, for drabs and drink.
She, my lawless, sharp-tongued gypsy maid
Will not scorn with me this jail-bird trade,
Pets some fox-eyed boy who turns the trick,
Tho' he win a button or a stick,
Pencil, garter, ribbon, corset-lace—
*His* the glory, *mine* is the disgrace.

Sweet, I'd rather lose than win despite
Love of hearty words and maids polite.
"Love's a gamble," say you. I deny.
Love's a gift. I love you till I die.
Gamblers fight like rats. I will not play.
All I ever had I gave away.
All I ever coveted was peace
Such as comes if we have jail release.

Cards are puzzles, tho' the prize be gold,
Cards help not the bread that tastes of mold,
Cards dye not your hair to black more deep.
Cards make not the children cease to weep.

Scorned, I sit with half-shut eyes all day—
Watch the cataract of sunshine play
Down the wall, and dance upon the floor.
Sun, come down and break the dungeon door!
Of such gold dust could I make a key,—
Turn the bolt—how soon we would be free!
Over borders we would hurry on
Safe by sunrise farms, and springs of dawn,
Wash our wounds and jail stains there at last,
Azure rivers flowing, flowing past.
*God has great estates just past the line,*
*Green farms for all, and meat and corn and wine.*

## IN THE IMMACULATE CONCEPTION CHURCH

Hunted by friends who think that life is play,
Shaken by holy loves, more feared than foes,
By beauty's amber cup, that overflows,
And pride of place that leads me more astray:—

Here I renew my vows, and this chief vow—
To seek each year this shrine of deathless power,
Keeping my springtime cornland thoughts in flower,
While labor-gnarled gray Christians round me bow.

Arm me against great towns, strong spirits old!
St. Francis keep me road-worn, music-fed.
Help me to look upon the poorhouse bed
As a most fitting death, more dear than gold.

THE IMMACULATE CONCEPTION CHURCH
SPRINGFIELD, ILLINOIS

## STAR OF MY HEART

Help me to seek the sunburned groups afield
The iron folk, the pioneers free-born.
Make me to voice the tall men in the corn.
Let boyhood's wildflower days a bright fruit yield.

Scourge me, a slave that brings unhallowed praise
To you, stern Virgin in this church so sweet,
If I desert the ways wherein my feet
Were set by Heaven, in prenatal days.

## STAR OF MY HEART

Star of my heart, I follow from afar.
Sweet Love on high, lead on where shepherds are,
Where Time is not, and only dreamers are.
Star from of old, the Magi-Kings are dead
And a foolish Saxon seeks the manger-bed.
Oh, lead me to Jehovah's child
Across this dreamland lone and wild,
Then will I speak this prayer unsaid,
And kiss his little haloed head—
"My star and I, we love thee, little child."

Except the Christ be born again to-night
In dreams of all men, saints and sons of shame,
The world will never see his kingdom bright.
Stars of all hearts, lead onward thro' the night
Past death-black deserts, doubts without a name,
Past hills of pain and mountains of new sin
To that far sky where mystic births begin
Where dreaming ears the angel-song shall win.
Our Christmas shall be rare at dawning there,

And each shall find his brother fair,
Like a little child within:
All hearts of the earth shall find new birth
And wake, no more to sin.

## LOOK YOU, I'LL GO PRAY

Look you, I'll go pray
My shame is crying,
My soul is gray and faint,
My faith is dying.
Look you, I'll go pray—
"Sweet Mary, make me clean,
Thou rainstorm of the soul,
Thou wine from worlds unseen."

## A PRAYER TO ALL THE DEAD AMONG MINE OWN PEOPLE

Are these your presences, my clan from Heaven?
Are these your hands upon my wounded soul?
Mine own, mine own, blood of my blood be with me,
Fly by my path till you have made me whole!

## AT MASS

No doubt to-morrow I will hide
My face from you, my King.
Let me rejoice this Sunday noon.
And kneel while gray priests sing.

## THE CITY THAT WILL NOT REPENT

It is not wisdom to forget.
But since it is my fate
Fill thou my soul with hidden wine
To make this white hour great.

My God, my God, this marvellous hour
I am your son I, know.
Once in a thousand days your voice
Has laid temptation low.


## THE DANDELION

O dandelion, rich and haughty,
King of village flowers!
Each day is coronation time,
You have no humble hours.
I like to see you bring a troop
To beat the blue-grass spears,
To scorn the lawn-mower that would be
Like fate's triumphant shears,
Your yellow heads are cut away,
It seems your reign is o'er.
By noon you raise a sea of stars
More golden than before.


## THE CITY THAT WILL NOT REPENT

Climbing the heights of Berkeley
Nightly I watch the West.
There lies new San Francisco,
Sea-maid in purple dressed,

Wearing a dancer's girdle
All to inflame desire:
Scorning her days of sackcloth,
Scorning her cleansing fire.

See, like a burning city
Sets now the red sun's dome.
See, mystic firebrands sparkle
There on each store and home.
See how the golden gateway
Burns with the day to be—
Torch-bearing fiends of portent
Loom o'er the earth and sea.

Not by the earthquake daunted
Nor by new fears made tame,
Painting her face and laughing
Plays she a new-found game.
Here on her half-cool cinders
'Frisco abides in mirth,
Planning the wildest splendor
Ever upon the earth.

Here on this crumbling rock-ledge
'Frisco her all will stake,
Blowing her bubble-towers,
Swearing they will not break,
Rearing her Fair transcendent,
Singing with piercing art,
Calling to Ancient Asia,
Wooing young Europe's heart.
Here where her God has scourged her
Wantoning, singing sweet:
Waiting her mad bad lovers
Here by the judgment-seat!

# THE VOICE OF ST. FRANCIS OF ASSISI

'Frisco, God's doughty foeman,
Scorns and blasphemes him strong.
Tho' He again should smite her
She would not slack her song.
Nay, she would shriek and rally—
'Frisco would ten times rise!
Not till her last tower crumbles,
Not till her last rose dies,
Not till the coast sinks seaward,
Not till the cold tides beat
Over the high white Shasta,
'Frisco will cry defeat.

God loves this rebel city,
Loves foemen brisk and game,
Tho', just to please the angels,
He may send down his flame.
God loves the golden leopard
Tho' He may spoil her lair.
God smites, yet loves the lion.
God makes the panther fair.

Dance then, wild guests o' 'Frisco,
Yellow, bronze, white and red!
Dance by the golden gateway—
Dance, tho' He smite you dead!


# THE VOICE OF ST. FRANCIS OF ASSISI

I saw St. Francis by a stream
Washing his wounds that bled.
The aspens quivered overhead.
The silver doves flew round.

311

Weeping and sore dismayed
"Peace, peace," St. Francis prayed.

But the soft doves quickly fled.
Carrion crows flew round.
An earthquake rocked the ground.

"War, war," the west wind said.


# THE GOLDEN WHALES OF CALIFORNIA

(Inscribed to Isadora Bennett Reed)

## I. A SHORT WALK ALONG THE COAST

Yes, I have walked in California,
And the rivers there are blue and white.
Thunderclouds of grapes hang on the mountains.
Bears in the meadows pitch and fight.
(*Limber, double-jointed lords of fate,*
*Proud native sons of the Golden Gate.*)
And flowers burst like bombs in California,
Exploding on tomb and tower.
And the panther-cats chase the red rabbits,
Scatter their young blood every hour.
Both the cattle and the swine of California,
On the hills or in the holes:—
Have ears of silk and velvet,
Have tusks like long white poles.
And the cattle and the swine, big hearted,
Walk with pride to their doom
For they feed on the sacred raisins
Where the great black agates loom.

312

Goshawfuls are Burbanked with the grizzly bears.
At midnight their children come clanking up the stairs.
They wiggle up the canyons,
Nose into the caves,
And swallow the papooses and the Indian braves.
The trees climb so high the crows are dizzy
Flying to their nests at the top.
While the jazz-birds screech, and storm the brazen beach
And the sea-stars turn flip flop.
The solid Golden Gate soars up to Heaven.
Perfumed cataracts are hurled
From the zones of silver snow
To the ripening rye below,
To the land of the lemon and the nut
And the biggest ocean in the world.
While the Native Sons, like lords tremendous,
Lift up their heads with chants sublime,
And the band-stands sound the trombone, the saxophone and
      xylophone
And the whales roar in perfect tune and time.
And the chanting of the whales of California
I have set my heart upon.
It is sometimes a play by Belasco,
Sometimes a tale of Prester John.

## II. THE CHANTING OF THE WHALES

North to the Pole, south to the Pole
The whales of California wallow and roll.
They dive and breed and snort and play
And the sun-struck feed them every day
Boatloads of citrons, quinces, cherries,
Of bloody strawberries, plums and beets,
Hogsheads of pomegranates, vats of sweets,

313

And the he-whales' chant like a cyclone blares,
Proclaiming the California noons
So gloriously hot some days
The snake is fried in the desert
And the flea no longer plays.
There are ten gold suns in California
When all other lands have one,
For the Golden Gate must have due light
And persimmons be well-done.
And the hot whales slosh and cool in the wash
And the fume of the hollow sea.
Rally and roam in the loblolly foam
And whoop that their souls are free.
(*Limber, double-jointed lords of fate,
Proud native sons of the Golden Gate.*)
And they chant of the forty-niners
Who sailed round the cape for their loot
With guns and picks and washpans
And a dagger in each boot.
How the richest became the King of England,
The poorest became the King of Spain,
The bravest a colonel in the army,
And a mean one went insane.

The ten gold suns are so blasting
The sunstruck scoot for the sea
And turn to mermen and mermaids
And whoop that their souls are free.
(*Limber, double-jointed lords of fate,
Proud native sons of the Golden Gate.*)
And they take young whales for their bronchos
And old whales for their steeds,
Harnessed with golden seaweeds,
And driven with golden reeds.

They dance on the shore throwing rose-leaves.
They kiss all night throwing hearts.
They fight like scalded wildcats
When the least bit of fighting starts.
They drink, these belly-busting devils
And their tremens shake the ground.
And then they repent like whirlwinds
And never were such saints found.
They will give you their plug tobacco.
They will give you the shirts off their backs,
They will cry for your every sorrow,
Put ham in your haversacks.
And they feed the cuttlefishes, whales and skates
With dates and figs in bales and crates:—
Shiploads of sweet potatoes, peanuts, rutabagas,
Honey in hearts of gourds;
Grapefruits and oranges barrelled with apples,
And spices like sharp sweet swords.

### III. St. Francis of San Francisco

But the surf is white, down the long strange coast
With breasts that shake with sighs,
And the ocean of all oceans
Holds salt from weary eyes.

St. Francis comes to his city at night
And stands in the brilliant electric light
And his swans that prophesy night and day
Would soothe his heart that wastes away:
The giant swans of California
That nest on the Golden Gate
And beat through the clouds serenely
And on St. Francis wait.

315

But St. Francis shades his face in his cowl
And stands in the street like a lost gray owl.
He thinks of *gold . . . gold.*
He sees on far redwoods
Dewfall and dawning:
Deep in Yosemite
Shadows and shrines:
He hears from far valleys
Prayers by young Christians,
He sees their due penance
So cruel, so cold;
He sees them made holy,
White-souled like young aspens
With whimsies and fancies untold:—
*The opposite of gold.*
And the mighty mountain swans of California
Whose eggs are like mosque domes of Ind,
Cry with curious notes
That their eggs are good for boats
To toss upon the foam and the wind.
He beholds on far rivers
The venturesome lovers
Sailing for the sea
All night
In swanshells white.
He sees them far on the ocean prevailing
In a year and a month and a day of sailing
Leaving the whales and their whoop unfailing
On through the lightning, ice and confusion
North of the North Pole,
South of the South Pole,
And west of the west of the west of the west,
To the shore of Heartache's Cure,
*The opposite of gold,*
On and on like Columbus
With faith and eggshell sure.

## IV. The Voice of the Earthquake

But what is the earthquake's cry at last
Making St. Francis yet aghast:—

"Oh the flashing cornucopia of haughty California
Is *gold, gold, gold.*
Their brittle speech and their clutching reach
Is *gold, gold, gold.*
*What* is the fire-engine's ding dong bell?
The burden of the burble of the bullfrog in the well?
*Gold, gold, gold.*
*What* is the color of the cup and plate
And knife and fork of the chief of state?
*Gold, gold, gold.*
*What* is the flavor of the Bartlett pear?
*What* is the savor of the salt sea air?
*Gold, gold, gold.*
*What* is the color of the sea-girl's hair?
*Gold, gold, gold.*
In the church of Jesus and the streets of Venus:—
*Gold, gold, gold.*
What color are the cradle and the bridal bed?
What color are the coffins of the great gray dead?
*Gold, gold, gold.*
What is the hue of the big whales' hide?
*Gold, gold, gold.*
What is the color of their guts' inside?
*Gold, gold, gold.*

"What is the color of the pumpkins in the moonlight?
*Gold, gold, gold.*

*From here on, the audience joins in the refrain:— "gold, gold, gold."*

317

The color of the moth and the worm in the starlight?
*Gold, gold, gold.*"


## I WENT DOWN INTO THE DESERT

I went down into the desert
To meet Elijah—
Arisen from the dead.
I thought to find him in an echoing cave;
*For so my dream had said.*

I went down into the desert
To meet John the Baptist.
I walked with feet that bled,
Seeking that prophet lean and brown and bold.
*I spied foul fiends instead.*

I went down into the desert
To meet my God.
By him be comforted.
I went down into the desert
To meet my God.
*And I met the devil in red.*

I went down into the desert
To meet my God.
O Lord my God, awaken from the dead!
I see you there, your thorn-crown on the ground,
I see you there, half-buried in the sand.
I see you there, your white bones glistening bare
*The carrion-birds a-wheeling round your head.*

# POEMS SPEAKING OF BUDDHA, PRINCE SIDDARTHA

## I. WITH A BOUQUET OF TWELVE ROSES

I saw Lord Buddha towering by my gate  
Saying: "Once more, good youth, I stand and wait."  
Saying: "I bring you my fair Law of Peace  
And from your withering passion full release;  
Release from that white hand that stabbed you so.  
The road is calling. With the wind you go,  
Forgetting her imperious disdain—  
Quenching all memory in the sun and rain."

"Excellent Lord, I come. But first," I said,  
"Grant that I bring her these twelve roses red.  
Yea, twelve flower kisses for her rose-leaf mouth,  
And then indeed I go in bitter drouth  
To that far valley where your river flows  
In Peace, that once I found in every rose."

## II. THE FIREMEN'S BALL

### Section One

"Give the engines room,  
Give the engines room."  
Louder, faster  
The little band-master  
Whips up the fluting,  
Hurries up the tooting.  
He thinks that he stands,  
The reins in his hands,  
In the fire-chief's place  
In the night alarm chase.

*To be read, or chanted, with the heavy buzzing bass of*

319

The cymbals whang,
The kettledrums bang:—
"Clear the street,
Clear the street,
Clear the street—Boom, boom.
In the evening gloom,
In the evening gloom,
Give the engines room,
Give the engines room,
Lest souls be trapped
In a terrible tomb."
The sparks and the pine-brands
Whirl on high
From the black and reeking alleys
To the wide red sky.
Hear the hot glass crashing,
Hear the stone steps hissing.
Coal-black streams
Down the gutters pour.
There are cries for help
From a far fifth floor.
For a longer ladder
Hear the fire-chief call.
Listen to the music
Of the firemen's ball.
Listen to the music
Of the firemen's ball.
" 'Tis the
NIGHT
Of doom."
Say the ding-dong doom-bells.
"NIGHT
Of doom."
Say the ding-dong doom-bells.

*fire-engines pumping.*

*In this passage the reading or chanting is shriller and higher.*

*To be read or chanted in a heavy bass.*

Faster, faster
The red flames come.
"Hum grum," say the engines,
"Hum grum grum."
"Buzz, buzz,"                                   *Shriller and*
Says the crowd.                                 *higher.*
"See, see,"
Calls the crowd.
"Look out,"
Yelps the crowd
And the high walls fall:—
Listen to the music
Of the firemen's ball.
Listen to the music
Of the firemen's ball.
" 'Tis the                                      *Heavy bass.*
NIGHT
Of doom,"
Say the ding-dong doom-bells.
NIGHT
Of doom,
Say the ding-dong doom-bells.
Whangaranga, whangaranga,
Whang, whang, whang,
Clang, clang, clangaranga,
Clang, clang, clang.                            *Bass, much*
Clang—a—ranga—                                  *slower.*
Clang—a—ranga—
Clang—a—ranga—
Clang,
Clang,
Clang.
Listen — to — the — music —
Of the firemen's ball—

321

## Section Two

"Many's the heart that's breaking
If we could read them all
After the ball is over."   (An old song.)

Scornfully, gaily
The bandmaster sways,
Changing the strain
That the wild band plays.
With a red and royal intoxication,
A tangle of sounds
And a syncopation,
Sweeping and bending
From side to side,
Master of dreams,
With a peacock pride.
A lord of the delicate flowers of delight
He drives compunction
Back through the night.
Dreams he's a soldier
Plumed and spurred,
And valiant lads
Arise at his word,
Flaying the sober
Thoughts he hates,
Driving them back
From the dream-town gates.
How can the languorous
Dancers know
The red dreams come
When the good dreams go?
" 'Tis the
NIGHT

*To be read or
sung slowly
and softly, in
the manner of
lustful, insinu-
ating music.*

*To be read
or chanted
slowly and
softly in the*

322

Of love,"
Call the silver joy-bells,
"NIGHT
Of love,"
Call the silver joy-bells.
Honey and wine,
Honey and wine.
Sing low, now, violins,
Sing, sing low,
Blow gently, wood-wind,
Mellow and slow.
Like midnight poppies
The sweethearts bloom.
Their eyes flash power,
Their lips are dumb.
Faster and faster
Their pulses come,
Though softer now
The drum-beats fall.
Honey and wine,
Honey and wine.
'Tis the firemen's ball,
'Tis the firemen's ball.

*manner of lustful, insinuating music*

"I am slain,"
Cries true-love
There in the shadow.
"And I die,"
Cries true-love,
There laid low.
"When the fire-dreams come,
The wise dreams go."

*With a climax of whispered mourning.*

BUT HIS CRY IS DROWNED
BY THE PROUD BAND-MASTER.
And now great gongs whang,

*Suddenly interrupting. To be read or sung in a heavy*

Sharper, faster,
And kettledrums rattle
And hide the shame
With a swish and a swirk
In dead love's name.
Red and crimson
And scarlet and rose
Magical poppies
The sweethearts bloom.
The scarlet stays
When the rose-flush goes,
And love lies low
In a marble tomb.
" 'Tis the
NIGHT
Of doom,"
Call the ding-dong doom-bells.
"NIGHT
Of Doom,"
Call the ding-dong doom-bells.

*bass. First eight lines as harsh as possible. Then gradually musical and sonorous.*

    Hark how the piccolos still make cheer.
      " 'Tis a moonlight night in the spring
        of the year."

*Sharply interrupting in a very high key*

CLANGARANGA, CLANGARANGA,
CLANG . . . CLANG . . . CLANG.
CLANG . . . CLANG . . . RANGA . . .
CLANG . . . A . . . RANGA . . .
CLANG . . . CLANG . . . CLANG . . .
LISTEN . . . TO . . . THE . . . MUSIC . . .
OF . . . THE . . . FIREMEN'S BALL . . .
LISTEN . . . TO . . . THE . . . MUSIC . . .
OF . . . THE . . . FIREMEN'S . . . BALL . . .

*Heavy bass.*

324

### Section Three

In Which, contrary to Artistic Custom, the moral of the piece is placed before the reader.

(From the first Khandaka of the Mahavagga: "There Buddha thus addressed his disciples: 'Everything, O mendicants, is burning. With what fire is it burning? I declare unto you it is burning with the fire of passion, with the fire of anger, with the fire of ignorance. It is burning with the anxieties of birth, decay and death, grief, lamentation, suffering and despair. . . . A disciple, . . . becoming weary of all that, divests himself of passion. By absence of passion he is made free.'")

I once knew a teacher,
Who turned from desire,
Who said to the young men
"Wine is a fire."
Who said to the merchants:—
"Gold is a flame
That sears and tortures
If you play at the game."
I once knew a teacher
Who turned from desire
Who said to the soldiers,
"Hate is a fire."
Who said to the statesmen:—
"Power is a flame
That flays and blisters
If you play at the game."
I once knew a teacher
Who turned from desire,
Who said to the lordly,

*To be intoned after the manner of a priestly service.*

"Pride is a fire."
Who thus warned the revellers:—
"Life is a flame.
Be cold as the dew
Would you win at the game
With hearts like the stars,
With hearts like the stars."
So BEWARE,
So BEWARE,
So BEWARE OF THE FIRE.

*Interrupting
very loudly
for the last
time.*

Clear the streets,
BOOM, BOOM,
Clear the streets,
BOOM, BOOM,
GIVE THE ENGINES ROOM,
GIVE THE ENGINES ROOM,
LEST SOULS BE TRAPPED
IN A TERRIBLE TOMB.
SAYS THE SWIFT WHITE HORSE
TO THE SWIFT BLACK HORSE:—
"THERE GOES THE ALARM,
THERE GOES THE ALARM.
THEY ARE HITCHED, THEY ARE OFF,
THEY ARE GONE IN A FLASH,
AND THEY STRAIN AT THE DRIVER'S IRON ARM."
CLANG . . . A . . . RANGA. . . . CLANG . . . A
    . . . RANGA. . . .
CLANG . . . CLANG . . . CLANG. . . .
CLANG . . . A . . . RANGA. . . . CLANG . . . A
    . . . RANGA. . . .
CLANG . . . CLANG . . . CLANG. . . .
CLANG . . . A . . . RANGA. . . . CLANG . . . A
    . . . RANGA. . . .
CLANG . . . CLANG . . . *CLANG.* . . .

### III. To Buddha

Awake again in Asia, Lord of Peace,
Awake and preach, for her far swordsmen rise.
And would they sheathe the sword before you, friend,
Or scorn your way, while looking in your eyes?

Good comrade and philosopher and prince,
Thoughtful and thoroughbred and strong and kind,
Dare they to move against your pride benign,
Lord of the Law, high chieftain of the mind?

\*     \*     \*     \*     \*     \*     \*

But what can Europe say, when in your name
The throats are cut, the lotus-ponds turn red?
And what can Europe say, when with a laugh
Old Asia heaps her hecatombs of dead?

## THE COMET OF PROPHECY

I had hold of the comet's mane
A-clinging like grim death.
I passed the dearest star of all,
The one with violet breath:
The blue-gold-silver Venus star,
And almost lost my hold. . . .
Again I ride the chaos-tide,
Again the winds are cold.

I look ahead, I look above,
I look on either hand.

327

I cannot sight the fields I seek,
The holy No-Man's-Land.
And yet my heart is full of faith.
My comet splits the gloom,
His red mane slaps across my face,
His eyes like bonfires loom.

My comet smells the far-off grass
Of valleys richly green.
My comet sights strange continents
My sad eyes have not seen,
We gallop through the whirling mist.
My good steed cannot fail.
And we shall reach that flowery shore,
And wisdom's mountain scale.

And I shall find my wizard cloak
Beneath that alien sky
And touching black soil to my lips
Begin to prophesy.
While chaos sleet and chaos rain
Beat on an Indian Drum
There in to-morrow's moon I will stand,
And speak the age to come.


## THE TRAMP'S REFUSAL

### ON BEING ASKED BY A BEAUTIFUL GYPSY TO JOIN HER GROUP OF STROLLING PLAYERS

Lady, I cannot act, though I admire
God's great chameleons Booth-Barret men.
But when the trees are green, my thoughts may be
October-red. December comes again

328

# THE FLOWER OF MENDING

And snowy Christmas there within my breast
Though I be walking in the August dust.
Often my lone contrary sword is bright
When every other soldier's sword is rust.
Sometimes, while churchly friends go up to God
On wings of prayer to altars of delight
I walk and talk with Satan, call him friend,
And greet the imps with converse most polite.
When hunger nips me, then at once I knock
At the near farmer's door and ask for bread.
I must, when I have wrought a curious song
Pin down some stranger till the thing is read.
When weeds choke up within, then look to me
To show the world the manners of a weed.
I cannot change my cloak except my heart
Has changed and set the fashion for the deed.
When love betrays me I go forth to tell
The first kind gossip that too-patent fact.
I cannot pose at hunger, love or shame.
It plagues me not to say: "I cannot act."
I only mourn that this unharnessed *me*
Walks with the devil far too much each day.
I would be chained to angel-kings of fire.
And whipped and driven up the heavenly way.


## THE FLOWER OF MENDING

**(To Eudora, after I had had certain dire adventures)**

When Dragon-fly would fix his wings,
When Snail would patch his house,
When moths have marred the overcoat
Of tender Mister Mouse,

329

The pretty creatures go with haste
To the sunlit blue-grass hills
Where the Flower of Mending yields the wax
And webs to help their ills.

The hour the coats are waxed and webbed
They fall into a dream,
And when they wake the ragged robes
Are joined without a seam.

My heart is but a dragon-fly,
My heart is but a mouse,
My heart is but a haughty snail
In a little stony house.

Your hand was honey-comb to heal,
Your voice a web to bind.
You were a Mending Flower to me
To cure my heart and mind.


# EPILOGUE TO THE ADVENTURES WHILE
## PREACHING THE GOSPEL OF BEAUTY

(Written to all young lovers about to set up homes of their own—but especially to those of some far-distant day, and those of my home-village)

Lovers, O lovers, listen to my call.
    Give me kind thoughts. I woo you on my knees.
Lovers, pale lovers, when the wheat grows tall,
    When willow trees are Eden's incense trees:—

## EPILOGUE TO ADVENTURES

I would be welcome as the rose in flower
  Or busy bird in your most secret fane.
I would be read in your transcendent hour
  When book and rhyme seem for the most part vain.

I would be read, the while you kiss and pray.
  I would be read, ere the betrothal ring
Circles the slender finger and you say
  Words out of Heaven, while your pulses sing.

O lovers, be my partisans and build
  Each home with a great fireplace as is meet.
When there you stand, with royal wonder filled,
  In bridal peace, and comradeship complete,

While each dear heart beats like a fairy drum—
  Then burn a new-ripe wheat-sheaf in my name.
Out of the fire my spirit-bread shall come
  And my soul's gospel swirl from that red flame.

## SECTION VIII

# HOME TOWN

*Being verses that carry further the metaphors of*
*"The Golden Book of Springfield"*

A MAP OF THE UNIVERSE ISSUED IN 1909. THIS MAP IS ONE BEGINNING OF THE GOLDEN BOOK OF SPRINGFIELD.

# AFTER READING THE SAD STORY OF THE FALL
## OF BABYLON

O Lady, my city, and new flower of the prairie
What have we to do with this long time ago?
O lady love,
Bud of tomorrow,
With eyes that hold the hundred years
Yet to ebb and flow,
And breasts that burn
With great-great-grandsons
All their valor, all their tears,
A century hence shall know,
What have we to do
With this long time ago?


## TO REFORMERS IN DESPAIR

'Tis not too late to build our young land right,
Cleaner than Holland, courtlier than Japan,
Devout like early Rome with hearths like hers,
Hearths that will recreate the breed called man.


## THE CORNFIELDS

The cornfields rise above mankind,
Lifting white torches to the blue,

Each season not ashamed to be
Magnificently decked for you.

What right have you to call them yours,
And in brute lust of riches burn
Without some radiant penance wrought,
Some beautiful, devout return?

# KING ARTHUR'S MEN HAVE COME AGAIN

*(Written while a field-worker in the Anti-Saloon League of Illinois)*

King Arthur's men have come again.
They challenge everywhere
The foes of Christ's Eternal Church.
Her incense crowns the air.
The heathen knighthood cower and curse
To hear the bugles ring,
*But spears are set, the charge is on,*
*Wise Arthur shall be king!*

And Cromwell's men have come again,
I meet them in the street.
Stern but in this—no way of thorns
Shall snare the children's feet.
The revelling foemen wreak but waste,
A sodden poisonous band.
*Fierce Cromwell builds the flower-bright towns,*
*And a more sunlit land!*

And Lincoln's men have come again.
Up from the South he flayed,

# DRINK FOR SALE.

"WHAT BLOSSOMS ARE YOU STEWING, WHAT
ROOTS AND CREEPING THINGS?"
HE ANSWERED:"IN MY CALDRON ARE THREADS
FROM COMETS WINGS,
THE VIOLETS OF THE ANGELS, AND DEW
FROM EDENS HILL,
AND GRAPES OF OLD ENGEDI; GOOD BROTHER
DRINK YOUR FILL.
ONE CUP WILL WARM YOUR HEART WITH LOVE:
THE PRICE, A PIECE OF GOLD"

I WAITED TILL THE FLAME WAS DEAD,
THE LIQUOR CLEAR AND COLD:
IN THE BOTTOM OF THE CALDRON WERE
THE HEADS OF DOGS AND MEN,
AND WINGS OF LARKS AND ROBINS WHO WILL
NEVER SING AGAIN.
ABOVE THE CUP HE FILLED, I SAW THE SOULS OF
RATS IN FLIGHT,
SO I DID NOT BUY HIS LIQUOR, AND I BADE
THE DWARF GOODNIGHT.

NICHOLAS VACHEL LINDSAY, RHYMER AND DESIGNER

SAID THIRST TO HUNGER
ONE DAY,
WHY DO WE ALWAYS MEET?
I WISH YOU WOULD
GO AND PLAY
ON THE OTHER SIDE OF THE STREET."

NICHOLAS VACHEL LINDSAY 190

HUNGER
AND
THIRST.

## ON READING OMAR KHAYYAM

The grandsons of his foes arise
In his own cause arrayed.
They rise for freedom and clean laws
High laws, that shall endure.
*Our God establishes his arm*
*And makes the battle sure!*

## ON READING OMAR KHAYYAM

(During an anti-saloon campaign, in central Illinois)

In the midst of the battle I turned
(For the thunders could flourish without me)
And hid by a rose-hung wall,
Forgetting the murder about me;
And wrote, from my wound on the stone,
In mirth, half prayer, half play:—
"Send me a picture book,
Send me a song, today."

I saw him there by the wall
When I scarce had written the line,
In the enemy's colors dressed
And the serpent-standard of wine
Writhing its withered length
From his ghostly hands o'er the ground,
And there by his shadowy breast
The glorious poem I found.

This was his world-old cry:
Thus read the famous prayer:
"Wine, wine, wine and flowers
And cup-bearers always fair!"

337

'Twas a book of the snares of earth
Bordered in gold and blue,
And I read each line to the wind
And read to the roses too:
And they nodded their womanly heads
And told to the wall just why
For wine of the earth men bleed,
Kingdoms and empires die.
I envied the grape-stained sage
(The roses were praising him):
The ways of the world seemed good
And the glory of heaven dim.
I envied the endless kings
Who found great pearls in the mire,
Who bought with the nation's life
The cup of delicious fire.

But the wine of God came down,
And I drank it out of the air.
(Fair is the serpent-cup,
But the cup of God more fair.)
The wine of God came down
That makes no drinker to weep.
And I went back to battle again
Leaving the singer asleep.


# FOREIGN MISSIONS IN BATTLE ARRAY

An endless line of splendor,
These troops with heaven for home,
With creeds they go from Scotland,
With incense go from Rome.

# A RHYME ABOUT AN ELECTRICAL ADVERTISING SIGN

These, in the name of Jesus,
Against the dark gods stand,
They gird the earth with valor,
They heed their King's command.

Onward the line advances,
Shaking the hills with power,
Slaying the hidden demons,
The lions that devour.
No bloodshed in the wrestling,—
But souls new-born arise—
The nations growing kinder,
The child-hearts growing wise.

What is the final ending?
The issue, can we know?
Will Christ outlive Mohammed?
Will Kali's altar go?
This is our faith tremendous,—
Our wild hope, who shall scorn,—
That in the name of Jesus
The world shall be reborn!


# A RHYME ABOUT AN ELECTRICAL
ADVERTISING SIGN

I look on the specious electrical light
Blatant, mechanical, crawling and white,
Wickedly red or malignantly green
Like the beads of a young Senegambian queen.
Showing, while millions of souls hurry on,
The virtues of collars, from sunset till dawn,
By dart or by tumble of whirl within whirl,

339

Starting new fads for the shame-weary girl,
By maggoty motions in sickening line
Proclaiming a hat or a soup or a wine,
While there far above the steep cliffs of the street

The stars sing a message elusive and sweet.
Now man cannot rest in his pleasure and toil
His clumsy contraptions of coil upon coil
Till the thing he invents, in its use and its range,
Leads on to the marvellous CHANGE BEYOND CHANGE
Some day this old Broadway shall climb to the skies,
As a ribbon of cloud on a soul-wind shall rise.
And we shall be lifted, rejoicing by night,
Till we join with the planets who choir their delight.
The signs in the street and the signs in the skies
Shall make a new Zodiac, guiding the wise,
And Broadway make one with that marvellous stair
That is climbed by the rainbow-clad spirits of prayer.


# AN ARGUMENT

## I. The Voice of the Man Impatient with Visions and Utopias

We find your soft Utopias as white
As new-cut bread, and dull as life in cells,
O scribes who dare forget how wild we are,
How human breasts adore alarum bells.
You house us in a hive of prigs and saints
Communal, frugal, clean and chaste by law.
I'd rather brood in bloody Elsinore
Or be Lear's fool, straw-crowned amid the straw.
Promise us all our share in Agincourt

**THE OLD HIGH SCHOOL BUILDING**
SPRINGFIELD, ILLINOIS

# BLACKSMITH

aristocracy is a permanent ideal of the American nation, so thoroughly established by the founders of the Constitution, that modern mammonites and Marxians rave at it in vain. In a special sense the dream of its triumph in 2018 haunts the cottage hearths of those in Springfield who revere Abraham Lincoln and Andrew Jackson alike as vindicators of the ideal. Many of the State House Politicians and all of the Country Club people utterly abhor this ideal, of the self-respecting blacksmith forge, yet they constantly invoke it for certain political and festival reasons. Their bitterest sneer and deepest hate are for those who take the ideal seriously, and all their fruitless devices are to circumvent it.

But those who look into the little cottage hearthfires of Springfield see rising a show of anvils with tremendous wings of fire. These anvils, whose wings will sweep the earth, stand for the craftsman ideal, in no narrow sense. Just as there may be in Switzerland a hereditary family pride in the making of a certain type of Swiss watch, which puts the family utterly beyond the domination of either riches or poverty, and the blood is blue and proud, as long as the watch is made well in that house, century after century, so the Springfield craftsmen will hammer out other things than horseshoes on these anvils for the next hundred years.

EDITORIAL FROM THE VILLAGE MAGAZINE

## AN ARGUMENT

Say that our clerks shall venture scorns and death,
That future ant-hills will not be too good
For Henry Fifth, or Hotspur, or Macbeth.
Promise that through tomorrow's spirit-war
Man's deathless soul will hack and hew its way,
Each flaunting Cæsar climbing to his fate
Scorning the utmost steps of yesterday.
Never a shallow jester any more!
Let not Jack Falstaff spill the ale in vain.
Let Touchstone set the fashions for the wise
And Ariel wreak his fancies through the rain.

## II. THE RHYMER'S REPLY: INCENSE AND SPLENDOR

Incense and Splendor haunt me as I go.
Though my good works have been, alas, too few,
Though I do naught, High Heaven comes down to me,
And future ages pass in tall review.
I see the years to come as armies vast,
Stalking tremendous through the fields of time.
Man is unborn. Tomorrow he is born,
Flame-like to hover o'er the moil and grime,
Striving, aspiring till the shame is gone,
Sowing a million flowers where now we mourn—
Laying new, precious pavements with a song,
Founding new shrines the good streets to adorn.
I have seen lovers by those new-built walls
Clothed like the dawn in orange, gold and red.
Eyes flashing forth the glory-light of love
Under the wreath that crowned each royal head.
Life was made greater by their sweetheart prayers.
Passion was turned to civic strength that day—
Piling the marbles, making fairer domes
With zeal that else had burned bright youth away.

341

COLLECTED POEMS

I have seen priestesses of life go by,
Gliding in samite through the incense-sea—
Innocent children marching with them there,
Singing in flowered robes, "THE EARTH IS FREE":
While on the fair, deep-carved unfinished towers
Sentinels watched in armor, night and day—
Guarding the brazier-fires of hope and dream—
Wild was their peace, and dawn-bright their array!


## THE NORTH STAR WHISPERS TO THE
## BLACKSMITH'S SON

The North Star whispers: "You are one
Of those whose course no chance can change.
You blunder, but are not undone,
Your spirit-task is fixed and strange.

"When here you walk, a bloodless shade,
A singer all men else forget.
Your chants of hammer, forge and spade
Will move the prairie-village yet.

"That young, stiff-necked, reviling town
Beholds your fancies on her walls,
And paints them out or tears them down,
Or bars them from her feasting-halls.

"Yet shall the fragments still remain;
Yet shall remain some watch-tower strong
That ivy-vines will not disdain,
Haunted and trembling with your song.

342

## THE PRAIRIE BATTLEMENTS

"Your flambeau in the dusk shall burn,
Flame high in storms, flame white and clear;
Your ghost in gleaming robes return
And burn a deathless incense here."


## THE PRAIRIE BATTLEMENTS

(To Edgar Lee Masters, with great respect)

Here upon the prairie
Is our ancestral hall.
Agate is the dome,
Cornelian the wall.
Ghouls are in the cellar,
But fays upon the stairs.
And here lived old King Silver Dreams,
Always at his prayers.

Here lived gray Queen Silver Dreams,
Always singing psalms,
And haughty Grandma Silver Dreams,
Throned with folded palms.
Here played cousin Alice.
Her soul was best of all.
And every fairy loved her,
In our ancestral hall.

Alice has a prairie grave.
The King and Queen lie low,
And aged Grandma Silver Dreams
Four tombstones in a row.
But still in snow and sunshine
Stands our ancestral hall.

343

Agate is the dome,
Cornelian the wall.
And legends walk about,
And proverbs, with proud airs.
Ghouls are in the cellar,
But fays upon the stairs.


# THE DREAM OF ALL THE SPRINGFIELD WRITERS

I'll haunt this town, though gone the maids and men,
The darling few, my friends and loves today.
My ghost returns, bearing a great sword-pen
When far-off children of their children play.

That pen will drip with moonlight and with fire.
I'll write upon the church-doors and the walls.
And reading there, young hearts shall leap the higher
Though drunk already with their own love-calls.

Still led of love and arm in arm, strange gold
Shall find in tracing the far-speeding track
The dauntless war-cries that my sword-pen bold
Shall carve on terraces and tree-trunks black—

On tree-trunks black beneath the blossoms white:—
Just as the phosphorent merman, bound for home
Jewels his fire-path in the tides at night
While hurrying sea-babes follow through the foam.

And in December when the leaves are dead
And the first snow has carpeted the street
While young cheeks flush a healthful Christmas red
And young eyes glisten with youth's fervor sweet—

344

## THE HEARTH ETERNAL

My pen shall cut in winter's snowy floor
Cries that in channeled glory leap and shine,
My Village Gospel, living evermore
Amid rejoicing, loyal friends of mine.


## THE HEARTH ETERNAL

There dwelt a widow learned and devout,
Behind our hamlet on the eastern hill.
Three sons she had, who went to find the world.
They promised to return, but wandered still.
The cities used them well, they won their way:
Rich gifts they sent, to still their mother's sighs.
Worn out with honors and apart from her,
They died as many a self-made exile dies.
The mother had a hearth that would not quench,
The deathless embers fought the creeping gloom.
She said to us who came with wondering eyes—
"This is a magic fire, a magic room."
The pine burned out, but still the coals glowed on.
Her grave grew old beneath the pear-tree shade,
And yet her crumbling home enshrined the light.
The neighbors peering in were half afraid.
Then sturdy beggars, needing fagots, came,
One at a time, and stole the walls and floor.
They left a naked stone, but how it blazed!
And in the thunderstorm it flared the more.
And now it was that men were heard to say,
"This light should be beloved by all the town."
At last they made the slope a place of prayer,
Where marvellous thoughts from God came sweeping
        down.
They left their churches crumbling in the sun,

They met on that soft hill, one brotherhood;
One strength and valor only, one delight,
One laughing, brooding genius great and good.
Now many gray-haired prodigals come home.
The place out-flames the cities of the land,
And twice-born Brahmans reach us from afar,
With subtle eyes prepared to understand.
Higher and higher burns the eastern steep,
Showing the roads that march from every place,
A steady beacon o'er the weary leagues,
At dead of night it lights the traveller's face!
Thus has the widow conquered half the earth,
She who increased in faith, though all alone,
Who kept her empty house a magic place,
Has made the town a holy angel's throne.

## THE TOWN OF AMERICAN VISIONS

### (Springfield, Illinois)

Is it for naught that where the tired crowds see
Only a place for trade, a teeming square,
Doors of high portent open unto me
Carved with great eagles, and with hawthorns rare?

Doors I proclaim, for there are rooms forgot
Ripened through æons by the good and wise:
Walls set with Art's own pearl and amethyst
Angel-wrought hangings there, and heaven-hued dyes:—

Dazzling the eye of faith, the hope-filled heart:
Rooms rich in records of old deeds sublime:
Books that hold garnered harvests of far lands,
Pictures that tableau Man's triumphant climb:

346

THE STATE FAIR DOME
SPRINGFIELD, ILLINOIS

# THE SPRINGFIELD OF THE FAR FUTURE

Statues so white, so counterfeiting life,
Bronze so ennobled, so with glory fraught
That the tired eyes must weep with joy to see
And the tired mind in Beauty's net be caught.

Come enter there, and meet Tomorrow's Man,
Communing with him softly day by day.
Ah, the deep vistas he reveals, the dream
Of angel-bands in infinite array—

Bright angel-bands, that dance in paths of earth
When our despairs are gone, long overpast—
When men and maidens give fair hearts to Christ
And white streets flame in righteous peace at last.

## THE SPRINGFIELD OF THE FAR FUTURE

Some day our town will grow old.
"She is wicked and raw," men say,
"Awkward and brash and profane."
But the years have a healing way.
The years of God are like bread,
Balm of Gilead and sweet.
And the soul of this little town
Our Father will make complete.

Some day our town will grow old,
Filled with the fullness of time,
Treasure on treasure heaped
Of beauty's tradition sublime.
Proud and gay and gray
Like Hannah with Samuel blest.
Humble and girlish and white
Like Mary, the manger guest.

347

Like Mary the manger queen
Bringing the God of Light
Till Christmas is here indeed
And earth has no more of night,
And hosts of Magi come,
The wisest under the sun
Bringing frankincense and praise
For her gift of the Infinite One.

## OUR GUARDIAN ANGELS AND THEIR CHILDREN

Where a river roars in rapids
And doves in maples fret,
Where peace has decked the pastures
Our guardian angels met.

Long they had sought each other
In God's mysterious name,
Had climbed the solemn chaos tides
Alone, with hope aflame:

Amid the demon deeps had wound
By many a fearful way.
As they beheld each other
Their shout made glad the day.

No need of purse delayed them,
No hand of friend or kin—
Nor menace of the bell and book,
Nor fear of mortal sin.

You did not speak, my girl,
At this, our parting hour.

348

Long we held each other
And watched their deeds of power.

They made a curious Eden.
We saw that it was good.
We thought with them in unison.
We proudly understood

Their amaranth eternal,
Their roses strange and fair,
The asphodels they scattered
Upon the living air.

They built a house of clouds
With skilled immortal hands.
They entered through the silver doors.
Their wings were wedded brands.

I labored up the valley
To granite mountains free.
You hurried down the river
To Zidon by the sea.

But at their place of meeting
They keep a home and shrine.
Your angel twists a purple flax,
Then weaves a mantle fine.

My angel, her defender
Upstanding, spreads the light
On painted clouds of fancy
And mists that touch the height.

Their sturdy babes speak kindly
And fly and run with joy,

Shepherding the helpless lambs—
A Grecian girl and boy.

These children visit Heaven
Each year and make of worth
All we planned and wrought in youth
And all our tears on earth.

From books our God has written
They sing of high desire.
They turn the leaves in gentleness.
Their wings are folded fire.


## THE EMPTY BOATS

Why do I see these empty boats, sailing on airy seas?
One haunted me the whole night long, swaying with every
    breeze,
Returning always near the eaves, or by the skylight glass:
There it will wait me many weeks, and then, at last, will
    pass.
Each soul is haunted by a ship in which that soul might
    ride
And climb the glorious mysteries of Heaven's silent tide
In voyages that change the very metes and bounds of Fate—
O empty boats, we all refuse, that by our windows wait!


## HOW I WALKED ALONE IN THE JUNGLES OF HEAVEN

Oh, once I walked in Heaven, all alone
Upon the sacred cliffs above the sky.
God and the angels and the gleaming saints
Had journeyed out into the stars to die.

# HOW I WALKED ALONE IN THE JUNGLES OF HEAVEN

They had gone forth to win far citizens,
Bought at great price, bring happiness for all:
By such a harvest make a holier town
And put new life within old Zion's wall.

Each chose a far-off planet for his home,
Speaking of love and mercy, truth and right,
Envied and cursed, thorn-crowned and scourged in time
Each tasted death on his appointed night.

Then resurrection day from sphere to sphere
Sped on, with all the POWERS arisen again,
While with them came in clouds recruited hosts
Of sun-born strangers and of earth-born men.

And on that day gray prophet saints went down
And poured atoning blood upon the deep,
Till every warrior of old Hell flew free
And all the torture fires were laid asleep.

And Hell's lost company I saw return
Clear-eyed, with plumes of white, the demons bold
Climbed with the angels now on Jacob's stair,
And built a better Zion than the old.

.    .    .    .    .    .    .    .    .    [.`

And yet I walked alone on azure cliffs
A lifetime long, and loved each untrimmed vine:
The rotted harps, the swords of rusted gold,
The jungles of all Heaven then were mine.

Oh mesas and throne-mountains that I found!
Oh strange and shaking thoughts that touched me there,
Ere I beheld the bright returning wings
That came to spoil my secret, silent lair!

## ALEXANDER CAMPBELL

"The present material universe, yet unrevealed in all
its area, in all its tenantries, in all its riches, beauty and
grandeur, will be wholly regenerated. Of this fact we
have full assurance since He that now sits upon the
throne of the Universe has pledged His word for it, saying: 'Behold I will create all things new,' consequently, 'new
heavens, new earth,' consequently, new tenantries, new em-
ployments, new pleasures, new joys, new ecstasies. There is
a fullness of joy, a fullness of glory, and a fullness of bless-
edness of which no living man however enlightened, however
enlarged, however gifted, ever formed or entertained one
adequate conception."

The above is the closing paragraph in Alexander Campbell's last essay in the *Millennial Harbinger,* which he had
edited thirty-five years. This paragraph appeared November, 1865, four months before his death.

## I. My Fathers Came from Kentucky

I was born in Illinois,—
Have lived there many days.
And I have Northern words,
And thoughts,
And ways.

But my great-grandfathers came
To the west with Daniel Boone,
And taught his babes to read,
And heard the redbird's tune;

And heard the turkey's call,
And stilled the panther's cry,

252

And rolled on the blue-grass hills,
And looked God in the eye.

And feud and Hell were theirs;
Love, like the moon's desire,
Love like a burning-mine,
Love like rifle-fire.

I tell tales out of school
Till these Yankees hate my style.
Why should the young cad cry,
Shout with joy for a mile?

Why do I faint with love
Till the prairies dip and reel?
My heart is a kicking horse
Shod with Kentucky steel.

No drop of my blood from north
Of Mason and Dixon's line.
And this racer in my breast
Tears my ribs for a sign.

But I ran in Kentucky hills
Last week. They were hearth and home.
And the church at Grassy Springs,
Under the redbird's wings
Was peace and honeycomb.


## II. WRITTEN IN A YEAR WHEN MANY OF MY PEOPLE DIED

I have begun to count my dead.
They wave green branches
Around my head,
Put their hands upon my shoulders,

353

Stand behind me,
Fly above me —
Presences that love me.
They watch me daily,
Murmuring, gravely, gaily,
Praising, reproving, readily.
And every year that company
Grows the greater steadily.
And every day I count my dead
In robes of sunrise, blue and red.


## III. A RHYMED ADDRESS TO ALL RENEGADE CAMPBELLITES, EXHORTING THEM TO RETURN

### I

O prodigal son, O recreant daughter,
When broken by the death of a child
You called for the graybeard Campbellite elder,
Who spoke as of old in the wild.
His voice held echoes of the deep woods of Kentucky.
He towered in apostolic state,
While the portrait of Campbell emerged from the dark:
That genius beautiful and great.
And millennial trumpets poised, half lifted,
Millennial trumpets that wait.


### II

Like the woods of old Kentucky
The memories of childhood
Arch up to where gold chariot wheels go ringing,
To where the precious airs are terraces and roadways

354

**THE DISCIPLES CHURCH**
SPRINGFIELD, ILLINOIS

**The Disciples Denomination Was Founded**
by Alexander Campbell

For witnesses to God, forever singing.
Like Mammoth Cave, Kentucky, the memories of childhood
Go in and in forever underground
To river and fountain of whispering and mystery
And many a haunted hall without a sound.
To Indian hoards and carvings and graveyards unexplored.
To pits so deep a torch turns to a star
Whirling 'round and going down to the deepest rocks of
    earth,
To the fiery roots of forests brave and far.


### III


As I built cob-houses with small cousins on the floor:
(The talk was not meant for me).
Daguerreotypes shone.  The back log sizzled
And my grandmother traced the family tree.
Then she swept to the proverbs of Campbell again.
And we glanced at the portrait of that most benign of men
Looking down through the evening gleam
With a bit of Andrew Jackson's air,
More of Henry Clay
And the statesmen of Thomas Jefferson's day:
With the face of age,
And the flush of youth,
And that air of going on, forever free.


For once upon a time . . .
Long, long ago . . .
In the holy forest land
There was a jolly pre-millennial band,
When that text-armed apostle, Alexander Campbell
Held deathless debate with the wicked "infi-del."
The clearing was a picnic ground.

Squirrels were barking.
The seventeen-year locust charged by.
Wild turkeys perched on high.
And millions of wild pigeons
Broke the limbs of trees,
Then shut out the sun, as they swept on their way.
But ah, the wilder dove of God flew down
To bring a secret glory, and to stay,
With the proud hunter-trappers, patriarchs that came
To break bread together and to pray
And oh the music of each living throbbing thing
When Campbell arose,
A pillar of fire,
The great high priest of the Spring.

He stepped from out the Brush Run Meeting House
To make the big woods his cathedrals,
The river his baptismal font,
The rolling clouds his bells,
The storming skies his waterfalls,
His pastures and his wells.
Despite all sternness in his word
Richer grew the rushing blood
Within our fathers' coldest thought.
Imagination at the flood
Made flowery all they heard.
The deep communion cup
Of the whole South lifted up.

Who were the witnesses, the great cloud of witnesses
With which he was compassed around?
The heroes of faith from the days of Abraham
Stood on that blue-grass ground —
While the battle-ax of thought
Hewed to the bone

356

That the utmost generation
Till the world was set right
Might have an America their own.
For religion Dionysian
Was far from Campbell's doctrine.

He preached with faultless logic
An American Millennium:
The social order
Of a realist and farmer
With every neighbor
Within stone wall and border.
And the tongues of flame came down
Almost in spite of him.
And now all but that Pentecost is dim.


IV

I walk the forest by the Daniel Boone trail.
By guide posts quaint.
And the blazes are faint
In the rough old bark
Of silver poplars
And elms once slim,
Now monoliths tall.
I walk the aisle,
The cathedral hall
That is haunted still
With chariots dim,
Whispering still
With debate and call.

I come to you from Campbell,
Turn again, prodigal

Haunted by his name!
Artist, singer, builder,
The forest's son or daughter!
You, the blasphemer
Will yet know repentance,
And Campbell old and gray
Will lead you to the dream-side
Of a pennyroyal river.
While your proud heart is shaken
Your confession will be taken
And your sins baptized away.

You, statesman-philosopher,
Sage with high conceit
Who speak of revolutions, in long words,
And guide the little world as best you may:
I come to you from Campbell
And say he rides your way
And will wait with you the coming of his day.
His horse still threads the forest,
Though the storm be roaring down. . . .
Campbell enters now your log-house door.
Indeed you make him welcome, after many years,
While the children build cob-houses on the floor.

Let a thousand prophets have their due.
Let each have his boat in the sky.
But you were born for his secular millennium
With the old Kentucky forest blooming like Heaven,
And the redbirds flying high.

## THE TALE OF THE TIGER TREE

A Fantasy, dedicated to the little poet Alice Oliver Henderson, ten years old.

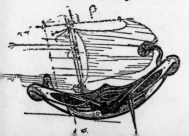

# THE TALE OF THE TIGER TREE

The Fantasy shows how tiger-hearts are the cause of war in all ages. It shows how the mammoth forces may be either friends or enemies of the struggle for peace. It shows how the dream of peace is unconquerable and eternal.

## I

Peace-of-the-Heart, my own for long,
Whose shining hair the May-winds fan,
Making it tangled as they can,
A mystery still, star-shining yet,
Through ancient ages known to me
And now once more reborn with me:—

This is the tale of the Tiger Tree
A hundred times the height of a man,
Lord of the race since the world began.

This is my city Springfield,
My home on the breast of the plain.
The state house towers to heaven,
By an arsenal gray as the rain . . .
And suddenly all is mist,
And I walk in a world apart,
In the forest-age when I first knelt down
At your feet, O Peace-of-the-Heart.

This is the wonder of twilight:
Three times as high as the dome
Tiger-striped trees encircle the town,
Golden geysers of foam.
While giant white parrots sail past in their pride.
The roofs now are clouds and storms that they ride.
And there with the huntsmen of mound-builder days
Through jungle and meadow I stride.

And the Tiger Tree leaf is falling around
As it fell when the world began:
Like a monstrous tiger-skin, stretched on the ground,
Or the cloak of a medicine man.
A deep-crumpled gossamer web,
Fringed with the fangs of a snake.
The wind swirls it down from the leperous boughs.
It shimmers on clay-hill and lake,
With the gleam of great bubbles of blood,
Or coiled like a rainbow shell. . . .
I feast on the stem of the Leaf as I march.
I am burning with Heaven and Hell.


## II

The gray king died in his hour.
Then we crowned you, the prophetess wise:
Peace-of-the-Heart we deeply adored
For the witchcraft hid in your eyes.
Gift from the sky, overmastering all,
You sent forth your magical parrots to call
The plot-hatching prince of the tigers,
To your throne by the red-clay wall.

Thus came that genius insane:
Spitting and slinking,
Sneering and vain,
He sprawled to your grassy throne, drunk on The Leaf,
The drug that was cunning and splendor and grief.
He had fled from the mammoth by day,
He had blasted the mammoth by night,
War was his drunkenness,
War was his dreaming,
War was his love and his play.

# THE TALE OF THE TIGER TREE

And he hissed at your heavenly glory
While his councillors snarled in delight,
Asking in irony: "What shall we learn
From this whisperer, fragile and white?"

And had you not been an enchantress
They would not have loitered to mock
Nor spared your white parrots who walked by their paws
With bantering venturesome talk.

You made a white fire of The Leaf.
You sang while the tiger-chiefs hissed.
You chanted of "Peace to the wonderful world."
And they saw you in dazzling mist.
And their steps were no longer insane,
Kindness came down like the rain,
They dreamed that like fleet young ponies they feasted
On succulent grasses and grain.

.    .    .    .    .    .    .    .    .

Then came the black-mammoth chief:
Long-haired and shaggy and great,
Proud and sagacious he marshalled his court:
(You had sent him your parrots of state.)
His trunk in rebellion upcurled,
A curse at the tiger he hurled.
Huge elephants trumpeted there by his side,
And mastodon-chiefs of the world.
But higher magic began.
For the turbulent vassals of man.
You harnessed their fever, you conquered their ire,
Their hearts turned to flowers through holy desire,
For their darling and star you were crowned,
And their raging demons were bound.

You rode on the back of the yellow-streaked king,
His loose neck was wreathed with a mistletoe ring.
Primordial elephants loomed by your side,
And our clay-painted children danced by your path,
Chanting the death of the kingdoms of wrath.
You wrought until night with us all.
The fierce brutes fawned at your call,
Then slipped to their lairs, song-chained.
And thus you sang sweetly, and reigned:
"Immortal is the inner peace, free to beasts and men.
Beginning in the darkness, the mystery will conquer,
And now it comforts every heart that seeks for love again.
And now the mammoth bows the knee,
We hew down every Tiger Tree,
We send each tiger bound in love and glory to his den,
Bound in love . . . and wisdom . . . and glory, . . . to his
      den."

## III

"Beware of the trumpeting swine,"
Came the howl from the northward that night:—
Twice-rebel tigers warning us still
If we held not beside them it boded us ill.
From the parrots translating the cry,
And the apes in the trees came the whine:
"Beware of the trumpeting swine.
Beware of the faith of a mammoth."

"Beware of the faith of a tiger,"
Came the roar from the southward that night.
Trumpeting mammoths warning us still
If we held not beside them it boded us ill.
The frail apes wailed to us all,
The parrots re-echoed the call:

362

"Beware of the faith of a tiger."
From the heights of the forest the watchers could see
The tiger-cats crunching the Leaf of the Tree
Lashing themselves, and scattering foam,
Killing our huntsmen, hurrying home.
The chiefs of the mammoths our mastery spurned,
And eastward restlessly fumed and burned.
The peacocks squalled out the news of their drilling
And told how they trampled, maneuvered, and turned.
Ten thousand man-hating tigers
Whirling down from the north, like a flood!
Ten thousand mammoths oncoming
From the south as avengers of blood!
Our child-queen was mourning, her magic was dead,
The roots of the Tiger Tree reeking with red.


IV


This is the tale of the Tiger Tree
A hundred times the height of a man,
Lord of the race since the world began.

We marched to the mammoths,
We pledged them our steel,
And scorning you, sang:—
"We are men,
We are men."
We mounted their necks,
And they stamped a wide reel.
We sang:
"We are fighting the hell-cats again,
We are mound-builder men,
We are elephant men."
We left you there, lonely,

Beauty your power,
Wisdom your watchman,
To hold the clay tower.
While the black-mammoths boomed —
"You are elephant men,
Men,
Men,
Elephant men."
The dawn-winds prophesied battles untold.
While the Tiger Trees roared of the glories of old,
Of the masterful spirits and hard.

The drunken cats came in their joy
In the sunrise, a glittering wave.
"We are tigers, are tigers," they yowled.
"Down,
Down,
Go the swine to the grave."
But we tramp
Tramp
Trampled them there,
Then charged with our sabres and spears.
The swish of the sabre,
The swish of the sabre,
Was a marvellous tune in our ears.
We yelled "We are men,
We are men."
As we bled to death in the sun. . . .
Then staunched our horrible wounds
With the cry that the battle was won. . . .
And at last,
When the black-mammoth legion
Split the night with their song :—
"Right is braver than wrong,
Right is stronger than wrong,"

The buzzards came taunting:
"Down from the north
Tiger-nations are sweeping along."

.    .    .    .    .    .

Then we ate of the ravening Leaf
As our savage fathers of old.
No longer our wounds made us weak,
No longer our pulses were cold.
Though half of my troops were afoot
(For the great who had borne them were slain),
We dreamed we were tigers, and leaped
And foamed with that vision insane.
We cried, "We are soldiers of doom,
Doom,
Sabres of glory and doom."
We wreathed the king of the mammoths
In the tiger-leaves' terrible bloom.
We flattered the king of the mammoths,
Loud-rattling sabres and spears.
The swish of the sabre,
The swish of the sabre,
Was a marvellous tune in his ears.

### V

This was the end of the battle.
The tigers poured by in a tide
Over us all with their caterwaul call,
"We are the tigers,"
They cried.
"We are the sabres,"
They cried.

But we laughed while our blades swept wide,
While the dawn-rays stabbed through the gloom.
"We are suns on fire" was our yell—
"Suns on fire." . . .
But man-child and mastodon fell,
Mammoth and elephant fell.
The fangs of the devil-cats closed on the world,
Plunged it to blackness and doom.
The desolate red-clay wall
Echoed the parrots' call:—
"Immortal is the inner peace, free to beasts and men.
Beginning in the darkness, the mystery will conquer,
And now it comforts every heart that seeks for love again,
And now the mammoth bows the knee,
We hew down every Tiger Tree,
We send each tiger bound in love and glory to his den,
Bound in love . . . and wisdom . . . and glory, . . . to
     his den."

A peacock screamed of his beauty
On that broken wall by the trees,
Chiding his little mate,
Spreading his fans in the breeze . . .
And you, with eyes of a bride,
Knelt on the wall at my side,
The deathless song in your mouth . . .
A million new tigers swept south . . .
As we laughed at the peacock, and died.

This is my vision in Springfield:
Three times as high as the dome,
Tiger-striped trees encircle the town,
Golden geysers of foam;—
Though giant white parrots sail past, giving voice,
Though I walk with Peace-of-the-Heart and rejoice.

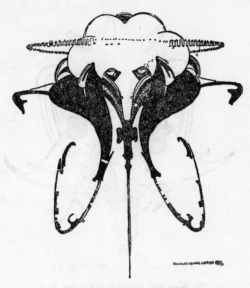

## THE SOUL OF A SPIDER

The thing that eats the rotting' stars
  On the black sea-beach of shame
Is a giant spider's deathless soul,
  And Mammon is its name.

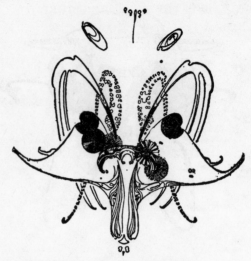

## THE SOUL OF A BUTTERFLY

The thing that breaks Hell's prison bars,
  And heals the sea of shame,
Is a fragile butterfly's great soul
  And Beauty is its name.

## HEART OF GOD

O great heart of God,
Once vague and lost to me,
Why do I throb with your throb tonight,
In this land, eternity?

O little heart of God,
Sweet intruding stranger,
You are laughing in my human breast,
A Christ-child in a manger.

Heart, dear heart of God,
Beside you now I kneel,
Strong heart of faith.  O heart not mine,
Where God has set His seal.

Wild thundering heart of God
Out of my doubt I come,
And my foolish feet with prophets' feet,
March with the prophets' drum.

## SEW THE FLAGS TOGETHER

(Written for William Stanley Braithwaite's Victory Anthology issued at once, after Armistice Day, November,
1918)

Great wave of youth, ere you be spent,
Sweep over every monument
Of caste, smash every high imperial wall
That stands against the new World State,

And overwhelm each ravening hate,
And heal, and make blood-brothers of us all.
Nor let your clamor cease
Till ballots conquer guns.
Drum on for the world's peace
Till the Tory power is gone.
Envenomed lame old age
Is not our heritage,
But springtime's vast release, and flaming dawn.

Peasants, rise in splendor
And your accounting render
Ere the lords unnerve your hand!
Sew the flags together.
Do not tear them down.
Hurl the worlds together.
Dethrone the wallowing monster
And the clown.
Resolving: —
"Only that shall grow
In Balkan furrow, Chinese row,
That blooms, and is perpetually young."
That only be held fine and dear
That brings heart-wisdom year by year
And puts this thrilling word upon the tongue:
"The United States of Europe, Asia, and the World."

"Youth will be served," now let us cry.
Hurl the referendum.
Your fathers, five long years ago,
Resolved to strike, too late.
Now
Sun-crowned crowds
Innumerable,
Of boys and girls

# I HEARD IMMANUEL SINGING

Imperial,
With your patchwork flag of brotherhood
On high,
With every silk
In one flower-banner whirled—
Rise,
Citizens of one tremendous state,
The United States of Europe, Asia, and the World.

The dawn is rose-drest and impearled.
The guards of privilege are spent.
The blood-fed captains nod.
So Saxon, Slav, French, German,
Rise,
Yankee, Chinese, Japanese,
All the lands, all the seas,
With the blazing rainbow flag unfurled,
Rise, rise,
Take the sick dragons by surprise,
Highly establish,
In the name of God,
The United States of Europe, Asia, and the World.


## I HEARD IMMANUEL SINGING

The poem shows the Master with his work done, singing to free his heart in Heaven.

This poem is intended to be half said, half sung, very softly, to the well-known tune:—

"Last night I lay a-sleeping,
There came a dream so fair,
I stood in Old Jerusalem
Beside the temple there,—" etc.

Yet this tune is not to be fitted on, arbitrarily. It is here given to suggest the manner of handling rather than determine it.

I heard Immanuel singing
Within his own good lands,
I saw him bend above his harp.
I watched his wandering hands
Lost amid the harp-strings;
Sweet, sweet I heard him play.
His wounds were altogether healed.
Old things had passed away.

*To be sung.*

All things were new, but music.
The blood of David ran
Within the Son of David,
Our God, the Son of Man.
He was ruddy like a shepherd.
His bold young face, how fair.
Apollo of the silver bow
Had not such flowing hair.

I saw Immanuel singing
On a tree-girdled hill.
The glad remembering branches
Dimly echoed still
The grand new song proclaiming
The Lamb that had been slain.
New-built, the Holy City
Gleamed in the murmuring plain.

*To be read very
softly, but in
spirited
response.*

The crowning hours were over.
The pageants all were past.
Within the many mansions
The hosts, grown still at last,

# I HEARD IMMANUEL SINGING

In homes of holy mystery
Slept long by crooning springs
Or waked to peaceful glory,
A universe of Kings.

*To be sung.*

He left his people happy.
He wandered free to sigh
Alone in lowly friendship
With the green grass and the sky.
He murmured ancient music
His red heart burned to sing
Because his perfect conquest
Had grown a weary thing.

No chant of gilded triumph—
His lonely song was made
Of Art's deliberate freedom;
Of minor chords arrayed
In soft and shadowy colors
That once were radiant flowers:—
The Rose of Sharon, bleeding
In Olive-shadowed bowers:—

And all the other roses
In the songs of East and West
Of love and war and worshipping,
And every shield and crest
Of thistle or of lotus
Or sacred lily wrought
In creeds and psalms and palaces
And temples of white thought:—

All these he sang, half-smiling
And weeping as he smiled,
Laughing, talking to his harp
As to a new-born child:—

*To be read very
softly, yet in
spirited
response.*

371

As though the arts forgotten
But bloomed to prophecy
These careless, fearless, harp-strings,
New-crying in the sky.
"When this his hour of sorrow      *To be sung.*
For flowers and Arts of men
Has passed in ghostly music,"
I asked my wild heart then—
What will he sing tomorrow,
What wonder, all his own
Alone, set free, rejoicing
With a green hill for his throne?
What will he sing tomorrow
What wonder all his own
Alone, set free, rejoicing,
With a green hill for his throne?

# SECTION IX

# POLITICS

# THE JINGO AND THE MINSTREL

## An Argument for the Maintenance of Peace and Goodwill with the Japanese People

Glossary for the uninstructed and the hasty: Jimmu Tenno, ancestor of all the Japanese Emperors; Nikko, Japan's loveliest shrine; Iyeyasu, her greatest statesman; Bushido, her code of knighthood; The Forty-seven Ronins, her classic heroes; Nogi, her latest hero; Fuji, her most beautiful mountain. The Pendragon flag is King Arthur's Banner (see Tennyson).

"Now do you know of Avalon *The minstrel*
  That sailors call Japan? *speaks.*
She holds as rare a chivalry
  As ever bled for man.
King Arthur sleeps at Nikko hill
  Where Iyeyasu lies,
And there the broad Pendragon flag
  In deathless splendor flies."

"*Nay, minstrel, but the great ships come* *The jingo*
  *From out the sunset sea.* *answers.*
*We cannot greet the souls they bring*
  *With welcome high and free.*
*How can the Nippon nondescripts,*
  *That weird and dreadful band,*
*Be aught but what we find them here:—*
  *The blasters of the land?*"

375

"First race, first men from anywhere
  To face you, eye to eye.
For *that* do you curse Avalon
  And raise a hue and cry?
These toilers cannot kiss your hand,
  Or fawn with hearts bowed down.
Be glad for them, and Avalon,
  And Arthur's ghostly crown.

*The minstrel replies.*

"No doubt your guests, with sage debate,
  In grave things gentlemen,
Will let your trade and farms alone,
  And turn them back again.
But why should brawling braggarts rise
  With hasty words of shame,
To drive them back, like dogs and swine,
  Who in due honor came?"

*"We cannot give them honor, sir.
  We give them scorn for scorn.
And Rumor steals around the world,
  All white-skinned men to warn
Against this sleek silk-merchant here
  And viler coolie-man,
And wrath within the courts of war
  Brews on against Japan!"*

*The jingo answers.*

"Must Avalon, with hope forlorn,
  Her back against the wall,
Have lived her brilliant life in vain
  While ruder tribes take all?
Must Arthur stand with Asian Celts,
  A ghost with spear and crown,
Behind the great Pendragon flag
  And be again cut down?

*The minstrel replies.*

376

"Tho' Europe's self shall move against
  High Jimmu Tenno's throne,
The Forty-seven Ronin Men
  Will not be found alone.
For Percival and Bedivere
  And Nogi side by side
Will stand,—with mourning Merlin there,
  Tho' all go down in pride.

"But has the world the envious dream—
  Ah, such things cannot be,—
To tear their fairy-land like silk
  And toss it in the sea?
Must this day rob the future day,
  The ultimate world-man,
Of rare Bushido, code of codes,
  The fair heart of Japan?

"Go, be the guest of Avalon.
  Believe me it lies there
Behind the mighty gray sea-wall
  Where heathen bend in prayer:
Where peasants lift adoring eyes
  To Fuji's crown of snow.
King Arthur's knights will be your hosts.
  So cleanse your heart, and go.

"And you will find but gardens sweet
  Prepared beyond the seas,
And you will find but gentlefolk
  Beneath the cherry-trees.
So walk you worthy of your Christ
  The church bells do not sound,
And weave the bands of brotherhood
  On Jimmu Tenno's ground."

## YANKEE DOODLE

This poem is intended as a description of a sort of Blash-field mural painting on the sky. To be sung to the tune of Yankee Doodle, yet in a slower, more orotund fashion. It is presumably an exercise for an entertainment on the evening of Washington's Birthday.

Dawn this morning burned all red;
Watching then, in wonder
There I saw our spangled flag
Divide the clouds asunder.
Then there followed Washington.
Ah, he rode from glory,
Cold and mighty as his name
And stern as Freedom's story.
Unsubdued by burning dawn
Led his continentals.
Vast they were, and strange to see
In gray old regimentals:—
Marching still with bleeding feet,
Bleeding feet and jesting—
Marching from the judgment throne
With energy unresting.
How their merry quickstep played—
Silver, sharp, sonorous,
Piercing through with prophecy
The demons' rumbling chorus—
Behold the ancient powers of sin
And slavery before them!—
Sworn to stop the glorious dawn,
The pit-black clouds hung o'er them.
Plagues that rose to blast the day
Fiend and tiger faces,

378

## YANKEE DOODLE

Monsters plotting bloodshed for
The patient toiling races.
Round the dawn their cannon raged,
Hurling bolts of thunder,
Yet before our spangled flag
Their host was cut asunder.
Like a mist they fled away. . . .
Ended wrath and roaring.
Still our restless soldier-host
From East to West went pouring.

High beside the sun of noon
They bore our banner splendid.
All its days of stain and shame
And heaviness were ended.
Men were swelling now the throng
From great and lowly station—
Valiant citizens today
Of every tribe and nation.
Not till night their rear-guard came,
Down the west went marching,
And left behind the sunset-rays
In beauty overarching.
War-god banners lead us still,
Rob, enslave and harry
Let us rather choose today
The flag the angels carry—
Flag we love, but brighter far —
Soul of it made splendid:
Let its days of stain and shame
And heaviness be ended.
Let its fifes fill all the sky,
Redeemed souls marching after,
Hills and mountains shake with song,
While seas roll on in laughter.

## THE TIGER ON PARADE

The Sparrow and the Robin on a toot
Drunk on honey-dew and violet's breath
Came knocking at the brazen bars of Death.
And Death, no other than a tiger caged,
In a street parade that had no ending,
Roared at them and clawed at them and raged—
Whose chirping was the height of their offending.
His paws too big—their fluttering bodies small
Escaped unscathed above the City Hall.

They learned new dances, scattering birdy laughter,
And filled again their throats with honey-dew.
A Maltese kitten killed them, two days after.
But they had had their fill. It was enough:—
Had quarrelled, made up, on many a lilac swayed,
Darted through sunny thunder-clouds and rainbows,
High above that tiger on parade.

## TO JANE ADDAMS AT THE HAGUE

(Two poems, written on the sinking of the Lusitania,
appearing in the Chicago *Herald,* May 11, 1915)

### I. SPEAK NOW FOR PEACE

Lady of Light, and our best woman, and queen,
Stand now for peace (though anger breaks your heart),
Though naught but smoke and flame and drowning is seen.

380

Lady of Light, speak, though you speak alone,
Though your voice may seem as a dove's in this howling
 flood,
It is heard tonight by every senate and throne.

Though the widening battle of millions and millions of men
Threatens tonight to sweep the whole of the earth,
Back of the smoke is the promise of kindness again.


## II. Tolstoi Is Plowing Yet

Tolstoi is plowing yet. When the smoke-clouds break,
High in the sky shines a field as wide as the world.
There he toils for the Kingdom of Heaven's sake.

Ah, he is taller than clouds of the little earth.
Only the congress of planets is over him,
And the arching path where new sweet stars have birth.

Wearing his peasant dress, his head bent low,
Tolstoi, that angel of Peace, is plowing yet;
Forward across the field, his horses go.


## A CURSE FOR KINGS

A curse upon each king who leads his state,
No matter what his plea, to this foul game,
And may it end his wicked dynasty,
And may he die in exile and black shame.

If there is vengeance in the Heaven of Heavens,
What punishment could Heaven devise for these
Who fill the rivers of the world with dead,
And turn their murderers loose on all the seas!

Put back the clock of time a thousand years,
And make our Europe, once the world's proud Queen,
A shrieking strumpet, furious fratricide,
Eater of entrails, wallowing obscene

In pits where millions foam and rave and bark,
Mad dogs and idiots, thrice drunk with strife;
While Science towers above;—a witch, red-winged:
Science we looked to for the light of life.

Curse me the men who make and sell iron ships,
Who walk the floor in thought, that they may find
Each powder prompt, each steel with fearful edge,
Each deadliest device against mankind.

Curse me the sleek lords with their plumes and spurs,
May Heaven give their land to peasant spades,
Give them the brand of Cain, for their pride's sake,
And felon's stripes for medals and for braids.

Curse me the fiddling, twiddling diplomats,
Haggling here, plotting and hatching there,
Who make the kind world but their game of cards,
Till millions die at turning of a hair.

What punishment will Heaven devise for these
Who win by others' sweat and hardihood,
Who make men into stinking vultures' meat,
Saying to evil still "Be thou my good"?

Ah, he who starts a million souls toward death
Should burn in utmost hell a million years!
—Mothers of men go on the destined wrack
To give them life, with anguish and with tears:—

## ABOVE THE BATTLE'S FRONT

Are all those childbed sorrows sneered away?
Yea, fools laugh at the humble christenings,
And cradle-joys are mocked of the fat lords:
These mothers' sons made dead men for the Kings!

All in the name of this or that grim flag,
No angel-flags in all the rag-array—
Banners the demons love, and all Hell sings
And plays wild harps. Those flags march forth today!


## ABOVE THE BATTLE'S FRONT

St. Francis, Buddha, Tolstoi, and St. John—
Friends, if you four, as pilgrims, hand in hand,
Returned, the hate of earth once more to dare,
And walked upon the water and the land,

If you, with words celestial, stopped these kings
For sober conclave, ere their battle great,
Would they for one deep instant then discern
Their crime, their heart-rot, and their fiend's estate?

If you should float above the battle's front,
Pillars of cloud, of fire that does not slay,
Bearing a fifth within your regal train,
The Son of David in his strange array—

If, in his majesty, he towered toward Heaven,
Would they have hearts to see or understand?
. . . Nay, for he hovers there tonight, we know,
Thorn-crowned above the water and the land.

## WHO KNOWS?

They say one king is mad.  Perhaps.  Who knows?
They say one king is doddering and gray.
They say one king is slack and sick of mind,
A puppet for hid strings that twitch and play.

Is Europe then to be their sprawling-place?
Their madhouse, till it turns the wide world's bane?
Their place of maudlin, slavering conference
Till every far-off farmstead goes insane?

## THE UNPARDONABLE SIN

This is the sin against the Holy Ghost:—
To speak of bloody power as right divine,
And call on God to guard each vile chief's house,
And for such chiefs, turn men to wolves and swine:—

To go forth killing in White Mercy's name,
Making the trenches stink with spattered brains,
Tearing the nerves and arteries apart,
Sowing with flesh the unreaped golden plains.

In any Church's name, to sack fair towns,
And turn each home into a screaming sty,
To make the little children fugitive,
And have their mothers for a quick death cry,—

This is the sin against the Holy Ghost:
This is the sin no purging can atone:—
To send forth rapine in the name of Christ:—
To set the face, and make the heart a stone.

## IN WHICH ROOSEVELT IS COMPARED TO SAUL

## THE MERCIFUL HAND

(Written to Miss Alice L. F. Fitzgerald, Edith Cavell memorial nurse, going to the front)

Your fine white hand is Heaven's gift
To cure the wide world, stricken sore,
Bleeding at the breast and head,
Tearing at its wounds once more.

Your white hand is a prophecy,
A living hope that Christ shall come
And make the nations merciful,
Hating the bayonet and drum.

Each desperate burning brain you soothe,
Or ghastly broken frame you bind,
Brings one day nearer our bright goal,
The love-alliance of mankind.

WELLESLEY,
February, 1916.

## IN WHICH ROOSEVELT IS COMPARED TO SAUL

(Written and published in 1913, and republished five years later, in the Boston *Transcript,* on the death of Roosevelt)

Where is David? . . . Oh God's people
Saul has passed, the good and great.
Mourn for Saul, the first anointed,
Head and shoulders o'er the state.

385

He was found among the prophets:
Judge and monarch, merged in one.
But the wars of Saul are ended,
And the works of Saul are done.

Where is David, ruddy shepherd,
God's boy-king for Israel?
Mystic, ardent, dowered with beauty,
Singing where still waters dwell?

Prophet, find that destined minstrel
Wandering on the range today,
Driving sheep, and crooning softly
Psalms that cannot pass away.

"David waits," the prophet answers,
"In a black, notorious den,
In a cave upon the border,
With four hundred outlaw men.

"He is fair and loved of women,
Mighty-hearted, born to sing:
Thieving, weeping, erring, praying,
Radiant royal rebel-king.

"He will come with harp and psaltry,
Quell his troop of convict swine,
Quell his mad-dog roaring rascals,
Witching them with tunes divine.

"They will ram the walls of Zion.
They will win us Salem hill,
All for David, shepherd David,
Singing like a mountain rill."

## HAIL TO THE SONS OF ROOSEVELT

"Out of the eater came forth meat, and out of the strong came forth sweetness."—Samson's riddle.

There is no name for brother
Like the name of Jonathan
The son of Saul.
And so we greet you all:
The sons of Roosevelt—
The sons of Saul.

Four brother Jonathans went out to battle.
Let every Yankee poet sing their praise
Through all the days—
What David sang of Saul
And Jonathan, beloved more than all.

God grant such sons, begot of our young men,
To make each generation glad again.
Let sons of Saul be springing up again:
Out of the eater, fire and power again.
From the lost lion, honey for all men.

I hear the sacred Rocky Mountains call,
I hear the Mississippi Jordan call:
*"Stand up, America, and praise them all,
Living and dead, the fine young sons of Saul!"*

# IN MEMORY OF MY FRIEND, JOYCE KILMER, POET AND SOLDIER

(Written Armistice Day, November eleventh, 1918)

I hear a thousand chimes,
I hear ten thousand chimes,

I hear a million chimes
In Heaven.
I see a thousand bells,
I see ten thousand bells,
I see a million bells
In Heaven.

Listen, friends and companions,
Through the deep heart,
Sweetly they toll.

I hear the chimes
Of tomorrow ring,
The azure bells
Of eternal love. . . .
I see the chimes
Of tomorrow swing:
On unseen ropes
They gleam above.

Rejoice, friends and companions.
Through the deep heart
Sweetly they toll.

They shake the sky
They blaze and sing.
They fill the air
Like larks a-wing,
Like storm-clouds
Turned to blue-bell flowers.
Like Spring gone mad,
Like stars in showers.

Join the song,
Friends and companions.

Through the deep heart
Sweetly they toll.

And some are near,
And touch my hand,
Small whispering blooms
From Beulah Land.
Giants afar
Still touch the sky,
Still give their giant
Battle-cry.

Join hands, friends and companions.
Through the deep heart
Sweetly they toll.

And every bell
Is voice and breath
Of a spirit
Who has conquered death,
In this great war
Has given all,
Like Kilmer
Heard the hero-call.

Join hands,
Poets,
Friends,
Companions.
Through the deep heart
Sweetly they toll!

# WHERE IS THE REAL NON-RESISTANT?

## (Matthew V, 38-48.)

Who can surrender to Christ, dividing his best with the
    stranger,
Giving to each what he asks, braving the uttermost danger
All for the enemy, MAN? Who can surrender till death
His words and his works, his house and his lands,
His eyes and his heart and his breath?

Who can surrender to Christ? Many have yearned toward
    it daily.
Yet they surrender to passion, wildly or grimly or gaily:
Yet they surrender to pride, counting her precious and
    queenly;
Yet they surrender to knowledge, preening their feathers
    serenely.

Who can surrender to Christ? Where is the man so tran-
    scendent,
So heated with love of his kind, so filled with the spirit
    resplendent
That all of the hours of his day his song is thrilling and
    tender,
And all of his thoughts to our white cause of peace
           Surrender, surrender, surrender?

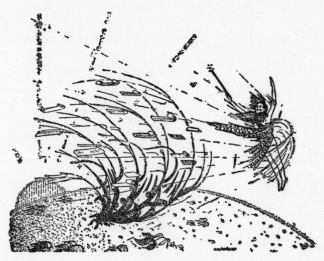

# THE WIZARD WIND

THE WIZARD WIND'S A FRIEND OF MINE—MOST INTIMATE IN TRUTH!
HE WHISTLES SORROW HALF AWAY, HE GIVES ME GOLDEN YOUTH.
AND FREE AS THAT SMALL BIRD THAT EATS THE WHEAT EAR IN THE SHEAF
I AM NO LONGER MAN, BUT CLOUD, OR TUMBLED MAPLE LEAF.
ONCE HE TRANSFORMED ME TO A BEE, HUNGRY FOR HONEY DEW.
HE BLEW ME TO A WINDLAND BUSH; WITH SPEED AND JOY WE FLEW.
THE GREAT BUSH BLOOMED WITH PARCHMENTS FINE, OR SONGS THAT FEED THE SOUL,
ALL NEW, THAT OUR DEAR EARTH SHALL HEAR, WHEN POETS REACH THEIR GOAL:
WHEN OUR GROWN CHILDREN, BREATHING FIRE SHALL JUSTIFY ALL TIME
BY HYMNS OF LIVING SILVER, SONGS WITH SUNRISE IN THE RHYME.
I WISH THAT I HAD LEARNED BY HEART SOME LYRICS READ THAT DAY.
I KNEW NOT 'TWAS A GIANT HOUR, AND SPENT IT ALL IN PLAY.
WINDLAND GLEAMS SO DEWY-WHITE, SO FULL OF CRYSTAL PEACE!
AND EVERY LEAF A SILKEN HARP, WHOSE MURMURS WILL NOT CEASE!
I GORGED THE HONEY FROM THE CUPS OF WILD FLOWERS ALL ABOUT;
LAUGHING WHEN THE WIZARD LAUGHED AND PUT THE GNATS TO ROUT.
I READ ONCE MORE, THEN SLEPT AWHILE, THEN WOKE ON EARTH AGAIN.
I WISH THOSE SCROLLS WERE MINE, THAT I MIGHT BRING THEM UNTO MEN.
I WISH THE VILLAGE MAGAZINE HELD ONLY SONGS AS RARE
EACH WORD A SPIRIT-WONDERLAND OF PERFUME FIRE AND AIR.

## SECTION X

## SONGS BASED ON
## CARTOONS, BILL-BOARDS, AND
## AMERICAN HIEROGLYPHICS, AND
## MOTION-PICTURES

# ROOSEVELT

(Written for the Illinois State Teachers' Association,
printed as a broadside, and read, and distributed the same
day: April 4, 1924.)

When the stuffed prophets quarrel, when the sawdust comes
       out, I think of Roosevelt's genuine sins.
Once more my rash love for that cinnamon bear,
   *Begins!*

His sins were better than their sweetest goodness.
His blows were cleaner than their plainest kindness.
He saw more than they all, in his hours of black blindness.
The hour of his pitiful spiritual fall
He was more of an angel than all of this host,
When with Lucifer's pride his soul was burnt out,
When, still in the game, he gave up the ghost.

His yarns were nearer the sky than their truth.
His wildest tales, in his fish-story hour,
Nearer true than their truth.
When with art and with laughter he held supreme power,
He was white as the moon, and as honest as youth.

And now their sworn word is but barnyard mud.
And their highest pride is to hide in a hole.
They talk of "dollars" and "dollars" and "dollars"
And "dollars" and "dollars," and hate his clean soul.

(Oh money, money—that *never* can think,
Money, money, that *never* can rule,
Always an anarchist, always an idiot,
Always King Log—never King Stork,
Always rotting, reeking:—always a fool.)

Roosevelt was proud like a singer.
Roosevelt's pride was that of a scribe,
Or the pride of a father, the pride of a ruler,
The pride of the thoroughbred chief of a tribe,
The pride of Confucius, the pride of a student!
He hated a coward, he hated a fool,
He knew that money is always a fool.

When they tear each others' newspaper-hearts
I think of Theodore's genuine code.
He hated the paste-board, the smeary, the fake.
He hated the snake, the frog and the toad.

Oh a moose with sharp antlers!
Oh a panther of panthers—Oh a fox of foxes
Often caught in tight boxes!
Yet we know he would always bark out the truth.
He loved the curious political game:—
But we know he loved better:—truth, God, and *youth.*

A peacock of peacocks! An eagle of eagles!
Defeating, within himself, the quick fox.
A buffalo roaring—a world-lion roaring!
Defeating within himself the bright fox,—
Then ranging out through the wilderness trail,
Killing the jackal—felling the ox.

Megalomaniac, envious, glorious,
Envying only the splendors of worth.

Emulating the cleanest on earth,
(Those who were, therefore, the strongest on earth.)
Emulating thoroughbreds—always.
Peacock! Lion! Cinnamon bear!
Skyscrapers—steeples and plains for abode!
He was mostly the world's fine cinnamon bear,

# ROOSEVELT

He was mostly our glittering cinnamon bear,
Sitting there in an old rocking chair,
In the White House yard, taking the air.

He told us Aesop's new fables, each day—
President seven big glorious years!
Seven years of wonder. Must they all fade away,
In the quarrels of the rat with the loud-voiced cootie
Told by the zinc-throated, varnished "loud-speaker,"
Told by wireless, while the world sits breathless,
Or by megaphone,
By line-o'-type, or by letter ripe:—
The quarrels of the angle-worm with the toad?

Who elected these pole-cats rulers of men?

Let us start a gay nation over again!
Let us start a circus as honest as Barnum's,
With three clean rings, and plenty to see,
Athletes, not snakes, on the trapeze tree.

Let us start our nation over again,
In the names of legitimate rulers of men,
In the names of the great, and the famous dead:—
Yes, the name of the glittering cinnamon bear,
Never so wicked or sore in the head,
But he fed the children honey and bread.
He taught them the names of the great and the dead,
From the Irish Sagas, to Carson and Boone.

He loved the villages, Deadwood, Medora,
Tuskeegee and Tuscarora,
Mexicali and Farmington,
Calexico and Bennington,
Arlington and Lexington,
Oyster Bay, Mount Vernon.

He loved the cities Denver, Manhattan,
And the wide great spaces
From the Amazon to Saskatoon—
He loved the heroes, Columbus, Whitman, Lincoln,
He loved the heroes! He loved George Washington!—
Who was honest as youth and white as the moon.

"Great-heart!" Roosevelt! Father of men!
He fed the children honey and bread.
He taught them the Ten Commandments and prayer,
Rocking there in his old rocking chair,
Or riding the storms of dream that he rode.

Join hands, poets, friends, companions!
Let us start a new world on the Roosevelt Code!

Let us start our nation over again
In the name of the honest, proud cinnamon bear,
Rocking there in his old rocking chair
Or riding the terrible storms that he rode!

The most-quoted phrase from the first edition of this book is
on page 2—"*That this whole book is a weapon in a strenuous
battlefield.*" So this section starts with two broadsides, carrying
out that idea, one on Roosevelt, one on Sandburg. "Roosevelt"
was written, printed and issued in one day, after reading of
the behavior of two middle western governors, that morning. I
read the poem that night in East St. Louis for the Illinois
State Teachers' Association, three thousand strong. It was
distributed by the Doubleday Page Book Shop, St. Louis. I
read it in the loudest voice I could muster, holding the broadside up before the convention like a banner. It was an occasion
of some humor, but of even more seriousness, and the New
Republic telegraphed for a copy of the broadside at once, and
reissued it in abbreviated form. In this form it was quoted with
apparent approval by the Philadelphia *North American*, and sent
for by the Roosevelt Memorial Association to be fastened on their
walls. And the same day it was politically attacked by the earnest Providence (Rhode Island) *Journal.*

# BABYLON, BABYLON, BABYLON THE GREAT

## (Inscribed to Carl Sandburg)

This poem is based on the episode of "Lincoln's Lost Speech," too dangerous to print at the time, at Cooper Union, his first appearance in the East.

Isaiah, the country-boy, marched against the jazz—
Babylon the shrewd and slick, Babylon the great.
Jeremiah, Ezekiel, Daniel, walked alone,
Alone against Babylon, alone against fate.
St. Paul walked alone, St. Peter walked alone,
Against that town to marvel on, Babylon the great.

Lincoln at Cooper Union, improvised and chanted,
Threw away his speech, and told tales out of school,
Changed from politician to God's divine fool.
Beside himself, beyond himself, set his old heart free,
The flame spread, the flame spread, every suppressed word
      was said,
Isaiah's voice from the dead;
Lincoln's great lost speech, nowhere written down,
But it burned every gate of the famous old town.

Lincoln at Cooper Union, called down fire from Heaven,
Overthrew jazz—Babylon, Babylon the great.

I have seen the burning of Babylon's gardens,
Many and many a noble day.
I have watched the ashes of that beautiful lost city,
Blown through many a year away.

Statesmen have torn down Babylon. . . . The gophers have
    buried Babylon. . . .
Coyotes lope through Babylon. . . . Prairie dogs bore the
    clay and sand. . . .
Texas cattle have trampled Babylon deeper in dung and
    dust. . . .
But forever stands Babylon, fresh in the sunrise, . . .
Foam upon the ocean . . . or granite on the land,
As new as the Devil, and the Devil's lust.

How our tales of Babylon multiply upon the ranges!
How old memories of victory renew!
Except for the warfare of the youngsters against Babylon,
The campfire songs would be few.

Troubadour!—March with bleeding feet against Babylon!—
(So, keep going to the sun! So, keep going to the sun!)
—If you would be a man.—As these have done before!
As lonely as Lincoln, dazed in Babylon,
Plod, plod, with a heartache, through the Devil's own door!
Tear up your set speeches, improvise once more!

War must begin against that city's music,
So—sing a silly song. Say:—"The sky is blue."
Sing a song of rainbow gems, unknown to Babylon.
Then improvise a song of the mick who lifts the hod,
Of the mick who sets in concrete the steel truss and rod,
Who builds the auto highways across the prairie sod—
(So, keep going to the sun! So, keep going to the sun!)
Improvise a cowboy song, of cactus and of dew,
And of raging on a mustang across the alkali
To where the snow-bright mountains of new mediation lie,
To the Indian basket-flowers, the ferns, the meadow-rue;—
Sing of beans in the pod, and of wheat in the shock,
Of hay in the stack, and windmills in the air,

# BABYLON, BABYLON, BABYLON THE GREAT

Of castellated silos, and turkeys fat and fair,
Of chickens and of guineas, of pheasants, quails and eagles,
Of the High-School senior boys, foot-ball players, Sheiks
    and swells,
Of Lincoln-highway roses and sweet lovers everywhere:—
And the candies and the vanities of senior High-School belles,
(So, keep going to the sun! So, keep going to the sun!)

Sing a Kansas love-song, modest, clean and true.
Sing a Kansas love-song, modest, clean and true.
*Then lift your psalm of the Manna of our God!*
It is the only way to go into Babylon,
Call down fire from Heaven, and the world renew.

This is the only way a bard is a man.
So lift your proud word against the towers if you can.
Go on, with your guitar, through the Devil's breezy gate.
March on, with simple Lincoln against Babylon, Babylon,—
His dog-eared carpet-bag crammed with state papers,
His sweaty old duster flapping like a rag.—
Go, with prairie Lincoln against Babylon, Babylon,
Go with that tall prophet, again to Cooper Union,
March with mighty Lincoln against Babylon the Great!
(So—keep going to the sun! So—keep going to the sun!)

In this poem I have exhorted Sandburg to improvise, but in a
way the opposite of jazz—for I have always hated jazz, as our
most Babylonian disease. This poem originally appeared in
Christopher Morley's Bowling Green column, in *The New York
Evening Post*, to celebrate a visit of Carl Sandburg to New
York City. Several months later it was printed in Memphis,
Tennessee, by the author, in anticipation of Carl Sandburg's
visit to address Memphis in a recital for the Goodwyn Institute, November 17, 1923. I issued it in a three-foot broadside,
with my picture of Babylon at the top as a kind of hieroglyphic. It was distributed through the kindness of Mrs.
Dicken's Book-Shop.

# PREFACE TO "BOB TAYLOR'S BIRTHDAY"

## A POEM ON "THE TENNESSEE ORPHEUS"

A Rhymed Oration. Being the Phi Beta Kappa Poem, Harvard Commencement, 1922.

ROBERT LOVE TAYLOR, the twenty-seventh and thirtieth governor of Tennessee, was born in 1850, and died in 1912. He was the greatest State governor America has ever had, to me, a great statesman, indeed. This oration is dedicated to the boys and girls of Tennessee. It is intended to be read to a big crowd, out of doors, presumably July 1, Bob Taylor's birthday. If it is read while you sit down, in the house, it means nothing. Please, citizens of Tennessee, and others, assemble a concourse of neighbors with the children at a basket-picnic, on the Mississippi, the Tennessee, the Clinch or the Cumberland rivers, and read it so they all can hear, preferably after it is memorized, and every cadence adjusted and understood, as though they were all syllables of one musical word. After this kind of memorizing, it may be read slowly, as an oration, but not before. At natural intervals in the song, when finally given, let there be good tunes by a good picnic fiddler;—an old-fashioned, barn-dance, log cabin jig fiddler. At the proper moments solemn tunes, like "Old Hundred," and famous dances like "Money-Musk!" Then, after a moment's pause, let the orator resume, paraphrasing and improving on the poem, as he gets the swing. Please let the production be understood by the crowd as oratorical, to be cheerfully filled with local allusions, in the spirit of Taylor's own political speeches, and improvisations on his own fiddle.

We are so choked by the old arts. We need to improvise,

but in the opposite of jazz. Watch Taylor again in fancy, running for governor against his brother, in that famous good-humored campaign, with the Democrats under Bob, using the white rose of York as their emblem, and the Republicans, under Alfred, the red rose of Lancaster, the boys fiddling on the big pine platform draped with flags and bunting. Think of the days when red or white roses were worn by every soul of Tennessee. Those were the days of improvisation.

So this is likewise, of all my productions, the one least intended for cold print. I urge all my friends to amend it as they read it. It is only in this way one can get much out of Bob Taylor's most famous oration—the basis of this poem:—Taylor's own reminiscent "lecture," "The Fiddle and the Bow," delivered from every Chautauqua platform in the United States and printed in his collected works: "The Lectures and Best Literary Productions of Bob Taylor," The Bob Taylor Publishing Co., Nashville, Tenn.

"Practical" people hated Orpheus, Homer, Milton.

Taylor is the livest and greatest new legend in America. As to his charms for "practical" people, I have no doubt some of them foam as they read this. How bankers do hate a poet in office! As to Taylor's actual appearance, mannerisms and quality, I refer you to Taylor's book, the very adequate pictures therein, and several charming school histories of Tennessee, where the tale is told as marvelously as one in any Gilbert and Sullivan libretto. But to this is added an inventive and epic earnestness that is a tremendous sane prophecy for American domestic art and religion and power. Ask the Chautauqua man who met him in his very last days, when he became a national figure in that fashion, and any veteran senator, who met him in Washington, when he became a national figure in that fashion (presumably the supreme fashion). The element hardest to record is the village apocalypse quality, this inventive, epic earnestness.

403

Some of us are beginning to see him the livest and greatest new prophet in America, an unconscious prophet, far closer to the future than Whitman, because actually elected to office again and again. Whitman was a thwarted Tammany brave.

My friend Frank Waller Allen, of Los Angeles, a man of great Chatauqua experience, has talked to me about Taylor at great length, the last few years. And I remember one very pleasant evening with Bishop Gailor of Memphis, and the poet Will Percy, talking about Bob Taylor. This summer while visiting a charming Tennessee county seat, I carried the manuscript of this poem with me, and I heard much gossip of Taylor from fellow-politicians who helped him toward the governor's chair. The *ideal* aspects of a fiddling governor took stronger hold of me. They are now, frankly, the main theme of this song, the *ideal* aspects of the conception of a Fiddling Governor of a state of this Union. We certainly have had enough of utterly sordid "practical" governors, of late. The more Frank Waller Allen tells me about Taylor, the more I feel that the Taylor ideal is a gigantic piece of democratic genius and initiative and, for that mere initiative, that costs so much in vitality—the everlasting glory of his state. Tennessee, and the Union, should, in the end, be held tranced by the ideal. It is as though Tennessee said to the world: "You have business managers. But we have an Orpheus. Unless you also get the immortal soul of a musician, as a governor to rule you, we have put you everlastingly in the wrong. Your business-managers seem to be going to jail, fast." As I read in a Tennessee school-history, a mere primer, the outline of the pretty story, I see the beautiful children of Tennessee huddled together, listening entranced, being made over into artists, poets, musicians, architects. Then I see all the children of America being made over into these, and into statesmen, prophets, saints and sibyls, tranced and listening to "Money-Musk," and looking up at a gigantic figure of Bob Taylor in a great blue rocking-chair in the sky.

Now get the map of Tennessee, and look at the eastern counties. I was begging in East Tennessee, in the log-cabin region about which Taylor was always so eloquent, only a short journey from his ancestral mansion. I was between Flagpond and Greenville. I offered "The Tree of Laughing Bells" pamphlet, in exchange for a night's lodging to a man on the porch of a log cabin, just the sort of cabin Taylor pictured in his orations. The man on the porch welcomed me that night in the name of Tennessee's Fiddling Governor. It was the first time I had heard of Taylor. But it was like coming to the edge of a new, tremendous, eternal tradition. This was about 1905. Taylor had been Governor 1887 to 1891 and 1897 to 1899. In that time he had made himself a part of the soul-fabric of the American people, like Johnny Appleseed and, and—Roosevelt and *such diverse dreamers!* Death and time were no more, and a day was as a thousand years, a thousand years as a day. I had come for eternity beneath the wing of Orpheus. It was there or near there I wrote the Canticle of the Tennessee Rose, which is in "A Handy Guide for Beggars," page 109. The story of "Lady Iron Heels" is an adventure in the same region.

Bob Taylor is worth reading after. *He could teach any man in the world, who would learn how to rule.* Here is a quotation from his famous lecture, "The Fiddle and Bow":

"It would be difficult for those reared amid the elegancies and refinements of life in city and town to appreciate the enjoyments of the gatherings and merrymakings of the great masses of the people who live in the rural districts of our country. The historian records the deeds of the great; he consigns to fame the favored few but leaves unwritten the 'short and simple annals of the poor,' the lives and actions of the millions. The modern millionaire, as he sweeps through our valleys and around our hills in his palace car, ought not to look with derision on the cabins of America,

COLLECTED POEMS

for from their thresholds have come more brains, and courage, and true greatness than ever emanated from all the palaces in this world. The fiddle, the rifle, the ax and the Bible, the palladium of American liberty, symbolizing music, prowess, labor, and free religion, the four grand forces of our civilization, were the trusty friends and faithful allies of our pioneer ancestry in subduing the wilderness and erecting the great commonwealths of the Republic. Wherever a son of freedom pushed his perilous way into the savage wilds and erected his log cabin, these were the cherished penates of his humble domicile—the rifle in the rack above the door, the ax in the corner, the Bible on the table, and the fiddle, with its streamers of ribbon, hanging on the wall. Did he need the charm of music to cheer his heart, to scatter sunshine and drive away melancholy thoughts? He touched the responsive strings of his fiddle and it burst into laughter. Was he beset by skulking savages or prowling beasts of prey? He rushed to his deadly rifle for protection and relief. Had he the forest to fell and the fields to clear? His trusty ax was in his stalwart grasp. Did he need the consolation, the promises and precepts of religion to strengthen his faith, to brighten his hope and to anchor his soul to God and heaven? He held sweet communion with the dear old Bible.

"The glory and strength of the Republic to-day are its plain working people."

I like this better than Whitman's "Song of the Broad Ax" or "I Hear America Singing." It is far nearer democracy, though much farther from the grand style. But it seems to me it will take only one more generation to lift the memory of lives like Taylor's into the real American art. It is nearer to the true beginning.

*Bob Taylor could teach any man in the world who would learn how to rule.* He had no "Bread and Circuses" to bribe the crowd, after the manner of the Roman demagogues who purchased the votes of the Republic. But between fid-

406

dlings, on a thousand platforms, he told stories like this, to people who came a hundred miles afoot to hear him:

## THE CANDY-PULLING

"The sugar was boiling in the kettles, and while it boiled the boys and girls played 'snap,' and 'eleven hand,' and 'thimble,' and 'blindfold,' and another old play which some of our older people will remember—

> 'Oh, Sister Phoebe, how merry were we
> When we sat under the juniper tree,
> The juniper tree Hi O.'

"And when the sugar had boiled down into candy they emptied it into greased saucers, or, as the mountain folks called them, 'greased sassers,' and set it out to cool; and when it had cooled each boy and girl took a saucer and they pulled the taffy out and patted it and rolled it till it hung well together, and then they pulled it out a foot long; they pulled it out a yard long, and they doubled it back, and pulled it out, and looped it over, and pulled it out, and when it began to look like gold the sweethearts paired off and consolidated their taffy and pulled against each other. They pulled it out, and doubled it back, and looped it over, and pulled it out; and sometimes a peachblow cheek touched a bronzed one and sometimes a sweet little voice spluttered out, 'You, Jack,' and there was a suspicious smack like a cow pulling her foot out of stiff mud. They pulled the candy and laughed and frolicked; the girls got taffy on their hair, the boys got taffy on their chins, the girls got taffy on their waists, the boys got taffy on their coat sleeves. They pulled it till it was as bright as a moonbeam and then they plaited it and coiled it into fantastic shapes and set it out in the crisp air to cool. Then the courting began in earnest. They did not court then as the young folks court now. The young man led his sweetheart back into a dark corner and sat down by her, and held

407

her hand for an hour and never said a word. But it resulted next year in more cabins on the hillsides and in the hollows, and in the years that followed the cabins were full of candy-haired children who grew up into a race of the best, the bravest, and the noblest people the sun in heaven ever shone upon.

"In the bright, bright hereafter, when all the joys of all the ages are gathered up and condensed into globules of transcendent ecstasy, I doubt whether there will be anything half so sweet as were the candy-smeared, ruby lips of the country maidens to the jeans-jacketed swains who tasted them at the candy-pulling in the happy long ago."

This was finally crystallized in his formal lecture, "The Fiddle and Bow," into the above form, but not until told a thousand ways a thousand times to a thousand stump-speech audiences.

To tell such stories well is one of what Mr. Gilbert Sedles calls "The Seven Lively Arts."

*Bob Taylor could teach any man in the world who would learn how to rule.*
This "word-painting," just below, was doubtless the final climax of many a stump-speech, and amid the dancing, the devilled eggs and fried chicken, was an outdoor tribute to the abstract qualities of the most abstract art.

#### MUSIC
"The spirit of music, like an archangel, presides over mankind and the visible creation. Her afflatus, divinely sweet, divinely powerful, is breathed on every human heart, and inspires every soul to some nobler sentiment, some higher thought, some greater action.

"O music! Sweetest, sublimest ideal of omniscience—

first-born of God—fairest and loftiest seraph of the celestial hierarchy, muse of the beautiful—daughter of the Universe!

"In the morning of eternity, when the stars were young, her first grand oratorio burst upon raptured Deity and thrilled the wondering angels. All heaven shouted. Ten thousand times ten thousand jeweled harps, ten thousand times ten thousand angel tongues caught up the song, and ever since, through all the golden cycles, its breathing melodies, old as eternity yet ever new as the flitting hours, have floated on the air of heaven, lingering like the incense of its flowers on plumed hill and shining vale, empurpled in the shadow of the eternal throne.

"The seraph stood with outstretched wings on the horizon of heaven clothed in light, ablaze with gems and, with voice attuned, swept her burning harpstrings, and lo, the blue infinite thrilled with her sweetest note. The trembling stars heard it and flashed their joy from every flaming center. The wheeling orbs that course the crystal paths of space were vibrant with the strain and pealed it back into the glad ear of God. The far-off milky way, bright gulf stream of astral glories, spanning the ethereal deep, resounded with its harmonies, and the star-dust isles, floating in that river of opal, reëchoed the happy chorus from every sparking strand."

This is what the old Southern orators used to call "sky-painting oratory." It is indeed that, we confess, and deny it not.

Read indoors, this quotation *is* a bit flowery. But, of course, every one hundred per cent American believes in democracy. Let the reader take it to a county fair, mount the nearest box, wave his hand and read it in competition with every Cracker-Jack seller on the place. Or just read it to himself in that setting. He will suddenly discover it taking on great dignity and proportions.

409

I have tried to write my tribute to Bob Taylor in the spirit of these three quotations. Try the above quotation in front of the grand stand, between horse races, or imagine yourself doing so. Then try my own piece of "sky-painting oratory" given below. I have tried to add a bit more of the pioneer Tennessee County Fair point of view. The third quotation above moves in the other direction. It is a great democratic way of saying that art has some mysterious abstract occult qualities. It is the outdoor or "log-cabin" way of reiterating the dogmas of Walter Pater. I have tried to consider its meaning.

In his school of "The Fiddle and Bow,"
He could teach every man in the world,
Who would learn how to rule.
His was no gladiatorial show,
By tears and kindness he ruled his democracy,
With never a wall flower, never an enemy.
With one bold fiddle, with a heart never cool,
Loving them all, serving them all,
Playing old tunes that conquered them all,
He brought his whole state to one violin school,
He brought his whole marvelling crowd
To one beautiful school.

On his birthday, he teaches his state to flower!
Unabashed orator, dropping his pearls!
To-day, he is shaking the butterflies' thrones!
Orpheus stirs up the squirrels to be barking;
Bee-hives are ringing their phones,
Wasps their razors are honing.
Good wheat ripens, and whistles and drones,
Cotton fields fiddle a tune to the sun,
Cornstalks rustle tassels and ears,
Spiders whirl round with misgivings and fears.

410

Bob Taylor is teaching his crowd to flower,
Shaking the butterflies' thrones!
There are pinch-faced people that snarl and deride,
For a singer trimphant defiles their pride.

Where are the hearts born to power,
My darlings,
Where are the hearts born to power?
You boys and girls
With the frolicsome manner,
From the first and second and third and fourth reader!
Will you lift your conquering Tennessee banner?
Oh, children, born of McGuffey's old reader,
With your new little brothers and sisters,
Will you heed the prophecies,
Mellow and rare,
Of the governing fiddle of Governor Taylor,
As he rocks in his blue rocking-chair,
As he rocks in his blue rocking-chair?

Oh, his giant chair of sky and dreams
Of the Great Smoky Mountains and East County Streams,
Tennessee clover and Tennessee rain,
Mixed with natural laughter and pain,
While Taylor's birthday comes 'round, comes 'round,
As he rocks in his blue rocking-chair, my darlings,
As he rocks in his blue rocking-chair!
As he lends a new splendor to log-cabin hearthstones,
Till the oceans reëcho his violin tones,
Oh, where are the hearts born to power,
My darlings,
Oh, where are the hearts born to power?

Who has the wings of the eagle?
Who has the wings of the lark?

411

Who has the wings of the owlet
As he dives through the twilight and dark?
Who will fly in dance time, in the springtime,
To the Money-Musk of Governor Bob,
As he shouts the new war cry of spring at its height,
And his fiddle gives forth a sweet sob?
As he sits on a cloud in the moonlight,
As he shakes up the world and its bones,
As he shakes up the nations that lie in their ashes,
And his bow sweeps the stars and the zones, my darlings,
And his bow sweeps the poles and the zones?

There are pinch-faced people that snarl and deride,
For a singer triumphant defiles their pride.

But now let us go to each county seat,
Where the old county fairs make the harvest complete,
And friend meets friend with pride.
In the merry-go-round where we will ride
To the music of the far stars' hum,
And the music of the hearth-crickets' drum,
And the tunes of Governor Bob, that will never end,
In the merry-go-round that we will make,
Many queer things we will undertake,
While the children will break ambrosial cake,
Bears will bring us honey-bread,
And the turkeys bring us honey-bread.

In the merry-go-round that we will make,
The cricket will chirp, the bee will hum,
The cricket will chirp, the bee will hum,
While the spokes of the merry-go-round go round.
A world-wide merry-go-round we will make,
With a tall elm tree for the central stake,
(While the spokes of the merry-go-round go round!)

412

The lark will cry the world awake,
The lark will cry the world awake.
Kind hearts will cry the world awake.


And now let us tell just the same child story—
In other terms, and with other glory.


While to-day's young children group around us, clap their
    pudgy hands,
And tell each other tales of beasts of distant lands,
And tell each other stories of sheiks and desert sands,
While they rock in big Grand Rapids chairs, varnished hard
    and slick,
Let flames of his birthday fiddle, coming nearer, make them
    quiver,
Let flames of the Governor's fiddle
Light each spirit's candlewick.
Let there be repeated visions
Of this man in every cabin,
The statesman, the soul's visitor, the mystical vote getter.
Now, just before Taylor finds "you and me,
Behold a young fairy called Tennessee,"
Come to set souls free.
She stands on the nation's hearthstones,
In the homes of millions, debating—
And there for the presence of Taylor waiting,
And chattering there with our tiniest children
As they watch for our man at the window sills,
Stories of hunters and trappers relating,
Martha Washington parties, and Jackson quadrilles.


She is crowned with three burning Tennessee stars,
Her soul is Jackson and Taylor and Boone,
The white far-flaming soul of the West,
For Tennessee once was the world's Wild West,

And is still, in secret, the world's Wild West.
With the eyes of the dawn and the gesture of pride,
And a fairy's heart in her childish side,
A heart for magic—a heart for music,
A heart that will not be denied.
Now Taylor's birthday comes 'round, comes 'round.
He is rocking now, and swaying, and playing,
In this, the millennial hour.
And his fiddle, speaking with tongues, keeps saying,
"Behold, the young beauty, called: 'Tennessee.'"

Obeying the fiddler's merry command,
Tennessee,
In the shining form of a child,
Holds out her white hand.
Then a village Apocalypse indeed!
Taylor's news films of the future,
His merry Orphic games for his every dreaming creature,
Set to the Dixie tunes of "Kingdom Come,"
Tunes for stubborn souls,
No longer blind or dumb.

Threads of incense,
Then log cabins come,
Then Red Indian council halls,
Toys of the past,
Tossed up through the sky's blue walls,
And then,
From the white palm there,
Those toys, and those threads of smoke, become the world's
    World's Fair,
That floats, to merry robin notes,
And goes up, in shining power and authority and worth,
Till there a university of man's whole soul has birth,
From old McGuffey's reader style,

# PREFACE TO "BOB TAYLOR'S BIRTHDAY"

From toy-shop style, and play-room style, and baby Christmas
    mirth,
Spreading in terrible splendor, conquering the sad earth,
Spreading out like a Maytime field,
Coming down like an angel's misty shield,
A fair of the secret spirit, of the proud heart's comforter!

From the fairy comes a cry:
From that strange child comes a cry:
"Our pride is eternal, a tree no worm can kill—
It is older than the old oak trees, deathless like the sky."

And we go with the dream World's Fair,
We walk on its strange wide streets—
And the nation is the child and the child is the nation,
With pride in noble toys—
With the same firm, quick heartbeats—
Old toys grown great, now built anew—
Hilltop sunrise battlements set against the blue—
Set in cloudy streets of giant blue-ridge pines,
Where every kind of dewy flower vine shines.
And yet some childish towers have great pink ribbon bows,
And big bisque dolls,
And Indian dolls
Hold up some mighty roofs in pillared rows.
And jewelled city flags wave high,
And toy-shop mayors bow the knee
To those flags, unstained and wildflower sweet,
And the pouring crowds, set free.

Yet the fiddle cries in majesty of our nation's good and ill,
Great brains work greatly, with a will,
And the trees of pride no worm can kill
Grow stronger still.

While some wireless from Aldeberan
Rolls down from on high—
How democracy has swept the farthest stars—
Broken up Aldeberan's prison bars,
And the shout shakes and thrills
The nation's new-born, dream-born toy,
The Tinselled Oak Tree, priest of Truth,
And the new-born, dream-born toy,
Tinselled Mulberry, priest of Youth,
And the new-born, dream-born toy,
The Amaranth-Apple Tree,
White as the foam of the jasper-sea,
Priest of the Holy Spirit's grace.
And the new-born Golden-Rain-Tree,
Tinselled priest, at our honeyed feast,
Priest of the future Human race,
On our soul-paths set with fantasy,
Where the children of our hearthstones
Find the proud toys of democracy,
Find Majesty and Alchemy,
While Orpheus plays his fiddle there.

And look, there are Maypoles in a row,
And baskets pouring out strange flowers
For all the crowds that pass,
And tiny fairy Maypoles
And roller-skating rinks,
For all the squealing infant class,
In the nation that shall be,
Beginning with this lover—
Of innocent small children,
Beginning with this fiddler
And his fairy Tennessee—
On the borders of our prairies,
Our Middle-Western sea.

And our highest art will come in this Hereafter.
And in all the parks so gay
Sad young Shellys, learning laughter,
Amid High-school yells, and college yells, and adventure yells,
Weird Confederate yells, weird Union yells,
In scandalous music, whispered, hissing, drumming,
While above the skylark flying machines
Of all man's future humming!
Playthings of the fancies of young Shellys that shall be,
And their little brothers and sisters,
And the pouring crowds set free,
By the conqueror of death—
By the great Orpheus fiddler, and his fairy Tennessee.

Oh, the pinch-faced people still think we are drunk,
With this pearl-dropping orator's fair,
With this sky-painting orator's fair.
They call it *the old Buncombe county bunk,*
Deriding our village Apocalypse there,
Our old Happy Valley fair,
Turned to a world's World's Fair,
Though there are the glories of all creation,
Thoughts, from every ultimate nation,
Though the birds and the beasts are there—
Changed from the whimsies of first creation,
To things majestic from Revelation:—
Still, the pinch-faced people think we are drunk,
Curse us, and think we are drunk.

And now let us tell just the same child story—
In other terms, and with other glory.

Obeying the fiddler's command,
Tennessee in the shining form of a child
Holds out her white hand.

From her magic palm, strange doll books come,
Toys tossed up through the wide sky's walls,
They turn to boys' "dime libraries,"
They turn to girls' doll whimsies,
Snark-hunting paper flimsies,
They turn to children's Christmas books,
Alice-in-Wonderland looking-glass books,
And Pilgrim's Progress allegory books,
Singing bolder words as their leaves spread more and more
And up into the sky the flocks of beauty pour—
The flags of imagination on the page of the soul's sky,
Each gorgeous new day's print goes by.

And as the full years sweep along
Each old man reads his patriarch tome,
In the light of his dear hearth home,
And each child follows his new toy book
Though it flies across the world,
For always it returns
To his home-town hearthstone towers and bowers,
And childhood's wildflower banners unfurled.
So, each child keeps his soul alone,
As he keeps his ballot still his own,
True to the stars that gave him birth—
And the dreams he found in the wide earth—
To the Orpheus, to the fiddler and his fairy Tennessee,
And the pouring crowds, set free.

The night rolls 'round, stars light the land.
Obeying the fiddler's command,
Tennessee in the shining form of a child
Holds out her white hand.

And now let us tell just the same child story,
In other terms, and with other glory.

418

Now, hear the cry of all the nations,
Hear the cry of the generations,
Egypt to Utopia,
The hieroglyphic parallel written on the sky—
Following all the way—
The cry of the sun by day,
The cry of the stars by night,
The cry of the deep, deep earth,
The cry of the deep, deep earth.


She holds out her white hand—
From the incense, from the fairy palm,
From the wild cry in the air
White temples and pavilions there
From Adam's day to Kingdom Come,
Tossed up through the great sky's walls,
Petals before a humming wind,
And we watch them spread their delicate eaves
Amid quivering leaves—
Altars—then cathedrals,
Go up in long progression,
Growing greater,
Killing the gloom,
Till we see the white procession
All future forms of holy faith
Stand still and take possession
Of our nation that shall be,
Tremendous white Cathedral ships,
On our Middle-Western Sea,
Whose waves are fields of cotton, corn and wheat,
Orchard paths and boulevards
And pouring crowds, set free,
By the Orpheus, the fiddler, the conqueror of Death,
And his fairy, Tennessee.

ALd now let us tell just the same child story,
In other terms, and with other glory.

Oh, where are the child souls,
With the singers' pride,
Who will wake, refusing defeat and death,
Returning perpetually from the grave,
Generation on generation?
Where are the furious wills of the nation?
Oh, where are the hearts born to power?
"Oh, who is there among us, the true and the tried,
Who will stand by his colors, who is on the Lord's side?"
Who will rise each century, shout once again,
Who will wake in hot faith
With our cavalcade ride?
Send up their American souls from the grave,
And go forth in glory, aspiring,
Breathing springtime breath and noonday fire,
Armed with doll beauty perilous,
Armed with child glory marvellous,
Armed with Southern poems delirious,
Armed with grass daggers
They found in the ground,
Armed with old shields they dug up in the sky,
By the Archangel Mountains high—
Armed with long swords like the young crescent moon.—
Oh, who is there among us, the true and the tried,
Who will ride against Death and his endless cruelty,
However his legions conspire?
Who will ride against all grown-up foes of Democracy?
"To-morrow, to-morrow," their marvelous tune—
"To-morrow," their marvelous cry of desire—
Going forth with pouring armies
Of the deathless young and gay,
Driving Death forever from the way.

# PREFACE TO "BOB TAYLOR'S BIRTHDAY"

Yes, who will sing in the follies of Heaven
To the Taylor-born Tennessee tune?
Who will follow the child Tennessee
Armed with soul-swords like the young crescent moon?
Who will follow her through the twilight,
Or in the morning, by the bright light,
Armed by her music, shouting her fame,
As she rides down the future with her boys all white flame,
As she rides down the future with her girls all white fire?
Just in time to stop the charges
Of Death and all his hosts
That turn at last to beaten ghost.


As she shouts down a thousand long years, my darlings,
Magic to-morrow the best of her tune,
Magic to-morrow her cry of desire. . . .
Her troops dressed in white for the spirits' delight,
She will stand in her stirrups a Torch of White Light,
The fairy child, Tennessee,
The soul of us, hope of us, helper and tyrant,
On her Pegasus horse of thunder and snow,
'Round the merry-go-round she will go.


We dream we will make a merry-go-round,
While Taylor's birthday comes 'round, comes 'round,
A beautiful toy while the daisies laugh—
A picnic place for Taylor's sake
And his lovers, and little brothers and sisters. . . .


We dream we will build a merry-go-round.
Whose root is a flame in the ancient ground,
Whose flagpole is a tree to the sky,
A merry-go-round ten centuries high.

In the merry-go-round that we will make—
Of these Dixie thoughts of Kingdom Come,
In the merry-go-round that we will make—
The cricket will chirp, the bee will hum,
The cricket will chirp, the bee will hum,
The lark will cry the world awake,
Governor Taylor will govern the song,
Ten centuries will sweep along—
And the prairies and mountains will whirl around,
The prairies will whirl around, around.

In the merry-go-round that we will make—
The lark will cry the world awake,
Kind hearts will cry the world awake.
Toys will be men, dolls will be men,
And our sages and saints good dolls again.
Each painted reindeer will be a chum.
Not a single dingo or dog will be dumb.
And the horses will not be horses of wood,
Nor iron nor ivory, nor jewel nor jade,
Not hobby-horses whose paint will fade,
But Pegasus ponies on parade,
But Pegasus ponies on parade,
Whose hoofs are of ice, and whose wings are of fire.
White horses of Hope and the Spirit's desire,
White horses of Hope and the Spirit's desire—
On our horses of fire and thunder and snow
'Round the merry-go-round we will go,
'Round the merry-go-round we will go.

## A SONG FOR ELIZABETH

(Set to music by Albert V. Davies. Sung by Carolina Lazzari)

On the top of my red banner
Is a Psyche-Butterfly,
And I am very proud,
And would lift my banner high,
And march, perhaps, to somewhere,
Or on to splendid nowhere,
Or on to anywhere,
And tell this hour good-by,
And I am in a fidget
To hurry up and get there.

But I must be quite still
Or I will spoil my day.
I do not want my heart to die,
I do not want my soul to die,
I do not want that butterfly
To scare and fly away.

## THE FLYING HOUSE, AND THE MAY QUEEN ETERNAL

Queen Venus, come now, be my heroine,
To form my pictures, and to scan my song,
And dominate that tall, enchanted house,
Invisible house, where I have lived so long.

Fast-flying house, that crosses sea and land.
House, always mine and empty but for me.

423

Fly near me, so your shadow may be near
And fall across my doors, and comfort me.

That house, all lights and shadows and no walls,
Has, for its doors and windows, barriers proud,
Closed wings for doors, or open wings for doors,
And, for its windows, wind-harps, singing loud.

Even your wing-whirr is a comfort there,
Your wireless whisper heard, though far away,
Makes you the heroine in that tall house.
The romance stays, if such fine honors stay.

Here I will live on shadows, if I must,
Kissing one shadow's soft eyes to the end.
I will write out and draw new wind-harp rhymes,
Sons of your shadow's flesh and blood, dear friend.

(First contributed to Christopher Morley's Column in the
*New York Evening Post,* "The Bowling Green," then
reproduced in his book, "The Bowling Green."

# BILLBOARDS AND GALLEONS

(Inscribed to Stephen Graham)

## I

Each day is Biloxi's birthday party,
Splendid with many a sun-kissed wonder,
Splendid with many a swimming girl.
Oh, there is melted the heart of stone,
Fantasy, rhyme, and rhapsody ring.
From street car and Ford and yellow taxi,
Argosies crowded to shrieking capacity—
With moon-struck boy and sun-struck girl.
Tourists, residents, what you please—
From the whirling south, from the whirling
    north,
Bees near the hive,
Or far from home,
Dreaming of love like honeycomb.

*This whole poem is to be read aloud, with great speed, and in one breath, as it were, as though it were one word, rather than one sentence. This, over and over, till the metrical scheme is fluid in the mind, a unit. Then, of course, read very slowly.*

"Barney Google" is what they sing,
"Mister Shean and Mister Gallagher,"
"Black Joe," and "Old Kentucky Home,"
"Swing Low Sweet Chariot," "Maryland," "Dixie,"
"Sometimes I feel like a Mourning Dove,"
"The Pullman Porters on Parade,"
Or hear, now, my "Song of Love."

But storms come down from the soul of the Universe,
Put the long coast in imminent jeopardy,
Despoiling felicity, quenching the ecstasy,
Hide my fantastical town from me—

425

Where every street is a valentine,
The kind we gave to love in youth
Where the lace is deep, three layers deep,
In, and in, and in you look:—
Gossamer book!
Fairy book!

Once, when such a storm was on,
When every spiritual hope seemed gone,
I was burning the world like a bridge, behind me,
I was walking in water so no one could find me—
In the edge of the waves, where the waves meet the beach—
Forest and sea waves, both within reach,
Far from my prairie home,
Far from the old hive, far from home,
Dreaming of love like honeycomb.

Twisted winds, coming down, from Heaven knows where,
Blistered feet were mine, seaweed was my hair.
Dream sea birds flew down on fanatical wings,
Flew down through tremendous red-rainbow rimmed rings.
They were speaking of glory, speaking of death,
Were shrieking creepy, fanatical things.
Many unwritten songs of mine, long forgotten,
And dim resolves, and loves forgotten
Swept in with the driftwood and foamy flakes.
Yet I said: "I will march till glory wakes,
Yet I said: "My brain with marvelling sings
That courage and sleep, courage and sleep are the principal
    things,"

March on, sleep-walkers, till courage comes
With invisible drums,
March, while the sad heart breaks,
Whirl on, like a leaf, then fight again—
Sleep and courage! Sleep and courage! The fate of men!

## BILLBOARDS AND GALLEONS

It was there, on the proud Spanish Trail I was walking,
And I thought of Don Ivan, my Spanish ancestor,
Friend of Columbus, and Isabel's guest,
From the stormy right
Come the green sea talking;
I was walking the Old Spanish Trail toward Biloxi,
So famous for legends of Spanish chivalry!
City of feathers, balloons and confetti,
City of hearties, of birthday parties!
Oh, streets of valentines in long lines,
Great garden of mocking-bird melody,
Oh, filagree city of fogs and mystery!
Far from the old hive, far from my home,
I was dreaming of love like honeycomb.
And startling pathways, starry-white,
Were revealed by the lightning and street light,
Revealed,
Revealed by the lightning and street light.

## II

Buzzing autos, like black bees,
Like black bees,
Hurried through the magnolia trees,
Then billboards, to make nations store,
Come in the vision flashy and vain,
Washed by the midnight sea-born rain,
Washed by the midnight sea-born rain.
They went like cliffs up to the sky,
America's glories flaming high,
Festooned cartoons, an amazing mixture,
Shabby, shoddy, perverse and twistical,
Shamefully boastful,
Shyly mystical.

427

Politics, with all its tricks, both old parties in a fix!
Donkey and elephant short of breath.
La Follette scorning them half to death.


The snappy *Saturday Evening Post*
Displaying, and advertising most
The noisiest things from coast to coast.
Exaggerated Sunday papers,
Comic sheets like scrambled eggs,
And Andy Gump's first-reader capers,
All on those billboards to the sky.
Who put them there, in the way, and why?
Pictured skyscrapers of the night,
Marble-topped, tremendous, white!
There were Arrow-collar heroes proud,
Holding their heads above the crowd,
Looking for love like honeycomb.
There was many an ice-cream vendor,
There were business kings in a daisy chain,
Then movie queens in a daisy chain,
Sugar-faced, unlaced and slender, dreaming of love like
      honeycomb.


Then all the rascals of the land,
All the damned for the last ten years,
Rising from their doom with tears,
Skeletons, skeletons, leather and bone,
Each dead soul chained to a saxaphone—
Watching the roaring storm above,
Looking for honey-dreams and love.
All on those billboards to the sky,
Who put them there, in the way, and why?


Then a railroad map of the U. S. A.
Then a soul-road map of the U. S. A.

Showing all the flowers of the land,
But nowhere, love like honeycomb.
Only signboards, only billboards,
Washed by the midnight sea-born rain,
Washed by the midnight sea-born rain.


## III

There were open boxes of fine cigars,
As big and bold as Pullman cars.
And on the brass-bound lids of these
Old Spain was pictured as you please.
And,
Here's the night's miracle began,
The greatest splendor known to man.

Flourishing masks and cigarettes,
Clicking their ribboned castanets,
Were Gypsies in high back combs and shawls,
Strutting through the Alhambra's halls.

Why were these billboards to the sky—
Who put them there, in the way, and why?

First I thought all the splendor had gone—
I was in darkness—I was in darkness—plunging on.
On the left were summer resort and lawn.
The flash of the trolley car,
The flash of the midnight train.
On the right—little waves, then great waves,
Then masts and shafts, then the wrecks of rafts—
Pirate ships of the Spanish main,
Then the wrecks of the Galleons of Spain.

Red coins, then jewels,
Drowned parrots, drowned peacocks,
Then a tolling sound, a tolling sound,
Then the wrecks of the Galleons of Spain,
Rolling by, rolling on, in the rain!
Rolling by, rolling on, in the foam!

Love calls, death cries;
Drowned pirates, drowned Spanish beauties—
Drowned Incas, then drowned Montezumas;
First friars of Quetzal, then nuns of Quetzal,
Lost faces, sweet as the honeycomb.
First friars of Christendom, then nuns of Christendom,
Lost faces, sweet as the honeycomb.
Then a tolling sound, a tolling sound—
Pirate ships of the Spanish Main,
Then the wrecks of the Galleons of Spain
Rolling by, rolling on, in the rain,
Rolling by, rolling on, in the foam.

And I said: "I will march till my soul re-awakes."
And I said: "My mind with marvelling sings,
That 'courage and sleep, courage and sleep, are the principal
    things,'"

For there came dead eagles, then dead panthers,
Then, millions of men to the edge of the sky:—
Dead Spanish Legions, from the deep-sea regions—
While increasing rain whipped the sea and the air.
Then there came a noise like a vulture crying.
Then there came a cheering, cheering sound—
Bullrings slowly whirling around,
Bullrings, bullrings, 'round and 'round,
Bullrings, bullrings, 'round and 'round.
Then waves like ponies, waves like bulls,

Then waves like Seminoles, waves like Negroes,
Dragging up their chains from the deep,
Singing of love like honeycomb.
Then waves like tobacco fields, waves like cornfields,
Waves like wheat fields, turning to battlefields.
Then
Round-table crusaders, then world-paraders,
Tall kings in shining silver line,
As though for a miracle and a sign,
Singing songs like Spanish wine.

Then I saw the bad Pizzaro,
Then hours of dewy jungle-glow—
Dim Peru and Mexico.
Then the wild seeker, Coronado, singing of love like honey-
    comb,
With all his furious train, foaming by in the rain,
Singing in eternal sleep, lifted, singing from the deep.
Then the tall town of Eldorado,
Passing by, like a fog and a shadow.

And then I saw a girl more pale
Than any fairy ever shone—
A white light in the southern night,
As cold as the north Auroral light
Reigning over the sea alone!
My heart was like a burning world,
I saw it flame above the dawn,
Her robe, her footstool and her throne!
And she was like a moon and pearl,
And like an Alabaster stone!
So far away in the utmost sky!
Her beauty like the honeycomb,
The secret love,
Glory and Fate—

Her wings from the earth to Heaven's gate,
A pillar in the dawn apart.

Then she was gone—the dawn was gone—
Black storm! Black storm!
And I plunged on.

Then lightning bolts across the sky,
Then a great bubble like a dome,
In whirling, whirling, whirling splendor.

Then Sancho Panza! Then Don Quixote,
He who could not know surrender,
Glory's ultimate contender,
Singing in eternal sleep,
Lifted, singing from the deep,
Singing of love like honeycomb!
Then—
Windmills, windmills, 'round and 'round,
Windmills, windmills, 'round and 'round,
Windmills, windmills, 'round and 'round!
Then a great storm, a fearful cry, a bell of doom—
A tolling sound, a tolling sound, a tolling sound.
Then the wrecks of the Galleons of Spain—
Rolling by, rolling on, in the rain,
Rolling by, rolling on, in the foam.

By these ships, on the right, were the red waves cleft,
Then, again on the left, stood the billboards there,
Queerly fine to the zenith line,
Overhead to the zenith line—
Washed by the midnight sea-born rain,
Washed by the midnight sea-born rain,
Gleaming down, as the wrecks went by.
Looking at fair, lost Spain!

## DULCENIA DEL TOBOSO

Between these visions I plunged on,
And straight ahead came to the wonder of dawn,
In that foggy dawn, storm-washed Biloxi!
The piers were wrecks, street cars were wrecks,
Sidewalks were wrecks.
Yet straight ahead arose from the dead,
The valentine, filagree towers of mystery,
The snow-white skyscrapers of new history.

Oh, fantasy, sugar and mockery!
Oh, mocking birds in their whimsy!
Oh, pretty, lazy Biloxi,
City haughty and fair, knowing not why:—
And looking high at the mast-filled sky,
Looking up at the ghost-filled sky,
Looking at fair, lost Spain.


## HOW DULCENIA DEL TOBOSO IS LIKE THE LEFT WING OF A BIRD

My child is like a bird's wing, a bird's wing, a bird's wing.
Slender like a bird's wing, curving like a bird's wing.
Her bones like those that leap and fling,
And make the quick bird's wing,
An elegant
And slender
Fairy-fashionplate design,
Plumed like a bird's wing, steel strong, but very tender,
Every curve of life to render.

And her motion, like a bird's wing, cutting higher,
She spreads above my sky,
A noble, an immortal thing,
A phœnix-wing of fire.

433

She spreads above my sky
An aurora and a sign,
An elegant and slender fairy-fashionplate design.


And then we are timid,
And infinitely small,
Two children playing house
In a pine tree tall.
Or she is then a wren's wing
Hiding a small-boy wren,
Or I am hidden like a hope, tied with a cob-web rope,
Beneath a humming bird's wing, a bird's wing, a bird's wing,
And then she is an eagle's wing, a hawk's wing, a Greek
    god's wing,
Teaching me, her son, to fly where tremendous stars sing.


But I have never gone through clouds that hide her every-
    where,
Have only seen one wing emerge from fog or sea or cloudy
    air,
Her eyes,
Like the fixed eyes
On the butterfly's or pheasant's wing.


I have never seen her young soul's face,
Her hidden eyes, and the other wing,
I have never heard the word of grace
My hawk will cry, my swallow sing.


I have only seen the left wing,
One fair, emerging bird's wing.


My child is like a bird's wing, a bird's wing, a bird's wing,
A dreamy wing, a lone wing.

## THE PEARL OF BILOXI

Proudest pearl of the wide world,
Haughtier than an Inca's plume,
You and I, near this Biloxi,
Long were laid in a shell tomb.
There we slept like white blind kittens
Curled in a warm kitchen box,
While the friendly fist of the sea
On our roof made humorous knocks
Without breaking the shell box.

Grandest pearl of the whole world,
And so vain you are twice dear,
Kin to dragon flies and dragons,
Kin to larks and kin to larkspurs,
Kin to gold and white snapdragons
And hot bees that drink such flagons
You grew whiter year by year,
You grew slender, like a dawn ray
To the plume, and flower, and torch I find you here.

Plume, upon the sunrise crest,
Pride of the beach, and set apart,
Hearing me, if not concurring—
Do we not have one horizon?
Is there not a secret stirring,
Yes, a deep-sea-kitten purring,
Then the slow thump of the ocean,
Deep in your heart, and my heart?

Oh, your heart is sky and ocean!
Each fond heart a world-wide heart . . .
To a new religion set apart . . .
Set apart,
Set apart.

## DOCTOR MOHAWK

### (Inscribed to Ridley Wills)

(A most informal chant, being a rhymed commentary on the preface, "Adventures While Singing These Songs," pages 8 and 14, especially the reference to the Red Indian ancestor. To this to be added a tradition that one branch of my mother's family came of the Don Ivans, of Spain.)

### I

#### BEING A SEVEN-YEAR-OLD BOY'S ELABORATE MEMORY OF THE DAY OF HIS BIRTH

In through the window a sea-mustang brought me,
(Smashing the window sash, breaking the law).
I was tied to his back—I do not know who caught me.

Up from Biloxi, up the great Mississippi,
Through the swamps, through the thaw, through the rains that grew raw,
On the tenth of November (the hail storm was nippy).
Up the slow, muddy Sangamon River—
(While we heard the towns cough and we heard the farms shiver),
The high wave rolled on.  We heard a crow squawk,
With a voice like a buzz saw, destroying the day:
"Caw, caw, you are rolling to meet the tall Mohawk,

*The poem to be read with the greatest possible speed, imitating the galloping of a sea-mustang, each time faster till it is so memorized, all the reptends musically blended, almost as though the poem were one long word, then of course, read very slowly.*

He will burn you to ashes and turn you to clay,
You will burn like a scarecrow with fire in the straw,
You are rolling and whirling on to the Mohawk,
Caw, caw,
Caw, caw."

We sighted and broke the high hedge of Oak Ridge,
We rolled through its tombs.  We saw Incubi walk.
We leaped the snow mounds like a pack of bloodhounds.
Dead lawyers were shrieking: *"You are breaking the law."*
We spoiled and howled down the shrill cemetery sounds,
Swept townward: a green wave, a foam wave, a moon wave,
Up the dawn streets of Springfield, high tide in a cave,
Up to Edwards and Fifth street, and broke every window-
        pane.
They thought we were "cyclone," earthquake, and rain.
We smashed the front door.  We ramped by the bed's head.
On the wall-paper pattern sea-roses bloomed red.

There, for a ceiling bent crab-thorn, hazel-brush,
Red-haw, black-haw,
(And the storm blew a horn,)
There fluttered a carrion crow that cried: *"Caw!"*
A scare-crow so queer, and a crow that cried: "Caw, *Caw!*
        *Caw!"*

## II

*Being my notion, as a Ferocious Small-Boy, of my Ancestral
        Protector.*

The porpoise was grandma.  The Mohawk was doctor:
*"Heap-big-chief-the-Mohawk,"* with eye like a tommyhawk.
Naked, in war-paint, tough stock and old stock,
Furious swash-buckler, street-brawler, world-breaker,

437

Plumed like an Indian, an American dragon,
Tall as Sun-mountain, long as the Sangamon,
With a buffalo beard, all beast, yet all human,
Sire of the Mexican king, Montezuma,
Of Quetzal the Fair God, and prince Guatomozin,
And that fated Peruvian, Atahualpa,
Of King Powhatan and his brown Pocahontas,
And of everything Indian serious or humorous,
Sire of the "Mohocks" who swept through old London,
(Too dirty for Swift and too wicked for Addison;)
He was carver of all the old Indian cigar-signs,
Chief of all the wild Kickapoo doctors,
And their log-cabin remedies known to our fathers,
Sire of St. Tammany, and sweet Hiawatha,
Tippecanoe, and Tyler Too,
He was named Joseph Smith, he was named Brigham Young,
He was named Susquehannah, he was named Mississippi,
Every river and State in the Indian Tongue,
Every park, every town that is still to be sung:—
Yosemite, Cheyenne, Niagara, Chicago!
The Pride of the U. S. A.:—*that* is the Mohawk,
The Blood of the U. S. A.:—*that* is the Mohawk,
He is tall as Sun-Mountain, long as the Sangamon,
Proud as Chicago, a dream like Chicago,
And I saw the wild Star-Spangled Banner unfurl
Above the tall Mohawk that no man can tame
Old son of the sun-fire, by many a name.

When nine, I would sing this yarn of the sea,
With ample embroidery I now must restrain
(Giving the facts and omitting the flowers)
It proved new fantastics were coming to me.
The Mohawk! the Mohawk! the Mohawk! the Mohawk!
Doctor and midwife! ancestral protector!
Breathed Mohawk fire *through* me, gave long claws *to* me,

Told my father and mother they must soon set me free,
Told the dears I had lived with a pearl in the billow
In the Mexican Gulf, in the depths of that sea,
For infinite years. Put the pearl by my pillow.
(It was new as that hour, and as old as the sea)—
The Soul of the U. S. A.—*that* was the pearl.
It became a white eagle I could not understand.
And I saw the carrion crow fly away.
And I saw the boughs open and the sun of that day,
And I saw the white eagle in the clouds fly and whirl
Then soar to the skies to a Star-Spangled Land.

And I cried, and held hard to my mother's warm hand.
And the Mohawk said:—"Red man, your first trial begins."
And the Mohawk roared:—"Shame to you, coward and
    mourner!"
And the Great Chief was gone.

But my life was all planned.

I wept with my mother. I kissed and caressed her.
Then she taught me to sing. Then she taught me to play:—
The sibyl, the strange one, the white witch of May.
Creating diversion with slow-talk and long-talk,
She sang with girl-pride of her Spanish ancestor,
The mighty Don Ivan, Quixotic explorer:—
Friend of Columbus, Queen Isabel's friend,
Conquistador!
Great-great-great-grandfather.

I would cry and pressed close to her, all through the story
For the Mohawk was gone. And gone was my glory:—
Though that white-witch adored me, and fingered each curl.
Though I saw the wild Star-Spangled Banner unfurl,
Though a Spanish Ancestor makes excellent talk.

I was a baby, with nothing to say
But:—"The Mohawk, the Mohawk, the Mohawk, the Mo-
        hawk."
And I knew for my pearl I must hunt this long way
Through deserts and dooms, and on till to-day.

I must see Time, the wild-cat, gorging his maw,
I must hear the death-cry of the deer he brought low,
And the cry of the blood on his pantherish paw,
And that carrion crow on his shoulder cry "Caw, Caw! Caw!"


## III

*One Brief Hour of Grown-up Glory on the Gulf of Mexico.*

Far from the age of my Spanish ancestor,
Don Ivan the dreamer,
Friend of Columbus, and Isabel's friend,
Wherever I wander, beggar or guest,
The soul of the U. S. A.:—that is my life-quest.


Still I see the wild Star-Spangled Banner unfurl.


And at last near Biloxi, in glory and sport
I met Doctor Mohawk, while swimming this morning
Straight into the Gulf of Mexico Sun.
The Mohawk! the Mohawk! the Mohawk! the Mohawk!
From the half-risen sun, in the pathway of blood
Sea-roses swept round me, red-kissed of the flood.
And the flying fish whispered: "the First Trial is done."


Magnificent mischief now was a-borning.
First: I dived and brought up the cool dream called
        *"The Pearl."*

## DOCTOR MOHAWK

As far from the Mohawk as peace is from murder,
As far from the Mohawk as May from November,
As far from the Mohawk as love is from scorning,
As far from the Mohawk as snow is from fire.
Yet, the Mohawk arm lifted me out of that flood
(The blood of the U. S. A.—that is the Mohawk)
And he healed my sick heart where the thunder-winds hurl,
There in the fog, at the top of the sun
Cool were his foam-fins, majestic his graces,
Doctor, and glorious Ancestral Protector,
Exhorter, reprover, corrector.
Then we swam to the sky through crystalline spaces,
The clouds closed behind us, all the long way,
And a rainbow-storm priesthood that hour blessed the bay,
Medicine men, in tremendous array,
While he spoke to me kindly and yet with fine scorning
For hunting for favors with rabbits or men.
Breathed Mohawk fire through me, gave long claws to me
And told me to think of my birthday again:—
How the sun is a Mohawk, and our best ancestor:
I must run to him, climb to him, swim to him, fly to him,
And laugh like a sea-horse, or life will grow dim.
How only the Mohawks will call me their brother,
(We will flourish forever, breaking the law)
They are laughing through all of the lands and the oceans,
(And only great worlds make an Indian laugh)
They are singing and swimming their pranks and their notions
With poems, and splendid majestical motions,
And they will stand by me, and save and deliver,
With the pearl near my heart, they will love me forever,
An eagle, a girl, then a moon on the sand,
The bird of the U. S. A.—that is the darling—
Whirling and dancing, swimming with awe
In the light of the sun, in the infinite shining
Of the uncaptured future:—that is the darling.

COLLECTED POEMS

The infinite future, that is the eagle,—
An eagle, a moon, a girl on the sand,
The Soul of the U. S. A.—that is the pearl,
Without flaw.

Note:—For the "Mohocks" read Gay's Trivia iii, 325; Spectator
Nos. 324, 332, 347; Defoe's Review, March 15, 1712; Also Swift's
Journal to Stella.

A SONG BASED ON EGYPTIAN
HIEROGLYPHICS:

THE TRIAL OF THE DEAD
CLEOPATRA

# THE TRIAL OF THE DEAD CLEOPATRA IN HER BEAUTIFUL AND WONDERFUL TOMB

The trial opens B.C. 29. This is the date of the death of Cæsarion, shortly after the suicide of Cleopatra. Cæsarion, natural heir to the empires of Egypt and Rome, son of Cleopatra and Julius Cæsar, was assassinated by his cousin Octavian. This made Octavian Augustus Cæsar sole heir of Julius Cæsar, made him ruler of the known world.

(Inscribed To Elizabeth Mann Wills)

## I. SHE BECOMES A SOUL, FLOWERING TOWARD EGYPTIAN RESURRECTION, B.C. 29

Said Set, the Great Accuser: "You poisoned your young
    brothers."
But the mummy of Cleopatra whispered: "These were the
    slanders of Rome."
"You poisoned your faithful servants, you sold the Nile
    to Cæsar."
But the mummy of Cleopatra whispered: "These were the
    slanders of Rome."
"You gambled with Marc Antony for the last wheat in Egypt,
And for the last blood of Egypt."
But the mummy of Cleopatra whispered: "These were the
    slanders of Rome."

\*    \*    \*    \*

And Set, the soul defiler, the hyena, the tomb-violator,
Yet Prosecuting Attorney of gods and stars,
Eternal in the eternal judgment room,
Said: "Antony is again my witness
Again to declare this woman vile."

445

For the ninth time Thoth drew him on the wall,
Again, that ink was a green and sulphurous flame,
And Antony was pictured in his armor:—
Bacchus, turned soldier, painted on the stone.
For the ninth time Thoth gave that ibis cry,
And called forth that traitor from his tent.
He stood, a pillar of flame and smoking gold,
And spoke, but as the puppet speaks in shows.
Ancestral enemy of Octavian—
He took Octavian's part before these gods,—
Every praise of the Italian city
For Julius Cæsar's nephew on the throne:—
Flattering that crowned Augustus in his seat
With all the slanders against Cleopatra
Invented by Rome's poets and her priests!
And slandering Cæsar's child Cæsarion,
Killed by Augustus' sword in Alexandria.

\* \* \* \* \*

A speaking mummy, neither living nor dying—
A human log, held upright by Anubis,
Once the goddess high priests make of girls
The queen was more than mortal in her sorrow.
More than her thirst and hunger, was deeper still
A memory like old poison in deep wounds—

She whispered again, in the face of Set, the deathless:—
"Cleopatra, the young girl, died when Cæsar died.
Only my shadow revelled with Antony,
Coming forth by day from this dark hall
To win the empire for Cæsarion.
Coming forth by day to make my boy
The heir of Egypt, Rome, and the purple seas—
As all you high gods knew from the beginning.
Only my shadow revelled with Antony,

He was the plume of Cæsar, nothing more.
Half-republican, then half-Egyptian,
Half-clay—half-god—the Rome clay prevailed,
He turned against his prince, Cæsarion. . . .
Then lost at Actium the purple seas.

Held in a spell by Set, the god of evil,
In a drunkard's dream, Antony chanted then
Forgetting his life-hatred of Augustus.
He who had called himself before the Senate,
"Champion of Cæsar's widow and her son."
There on the terrace of a million years,
In a big doll's-voice, Antony chanted then
A song the Swan of Avon yet should sing,
That all the poets of the world should know.

\* \* \* \* \*

Her eyes were like two rays of the great moon,
When Mediterranean storms destroy the ships.
She looked at him. And the eyes of Antony,
Became the idiot eye-holes of a helmet,
The visor down. And his world-flashing sword
Was smoke and dust—his face a wavering flame.

In that dim court there stood the great iron scales;
"Scales of Justice," known to souls to-day,
In one side, the Feather of Perfect Truth,
In the other—the heart of the waiting dead.

\* \* \* \* \*

Appointed to devour all hearts rejected—
The crocodile called Ammit glowered and waited.

Then Thoth gave Cleopatra "Words of Power."
And Cleopatra called through the dusty court,

With the musical voice of all the women of time—
And the flaming heart there on the iron scales cried:
"Cleopatra died when Cæsar died.
I am the heart of Cæsar, nothing more."
And the Apes of the Dawn beside the scales gave tongue:
"She is the heart of Cæsar, nothing more."


And then Cleopatra spoke alone:
"I have knocked at this inner door of my own tomb,
Waiting patiently for this my judgment,
As all you high gods know, since Cæsar died.
We crossed the purple seas for Alexandria
Two clouds, blood-red, two storms against the moon.
He brought me here, that day, and you judged him.
Queens have been crowned, have reigned, and have grown
      old,
Have been sealed in holy tombs with 'Words of Power':
Have come to judgment and to resurrection
Since Cæsar knocked with me upon this door,
While his body lay in blood in roaring Rome.
You set him free, you sent him to the skies!
Give me my throne today, beside his throne.
When Antony turned against Cæsarion
I put the Asp against my naked breast;
My *Mummy* joined my *Shadow* at this door,
My *Heart,* and *Soul* and *Name,*
Came to one place.


"Why should the gods keep Cleopatra waiting,
A first, and then again a second time,
Suffering the mummy's peril and thirst and hunger,
Suffering the mummy's fear and hell-fire flame?
I, a dead log, cry to be made a god,
Above all memory and all forgetting.

448

# THE TRIAL OF THE DEAD CLEOPATRA

I, Cleopatra, defy Set, the Accuser,
And I stake all on Cæsar and our son.
I have called those witnesses now nine times nine,
Let Set prevent their coming nevermore!

"Why should this violator of the dead,
He who would tear the precious mummy-cloth,
He, to whom only mummy-thieves will pray,
He, who would rend the helpless flesh and tendon,
Stealer of vases of most precious ointment,
Counter of beads of lapis-lazuli,
Hyena-souled, small-minded, jackdaw-king,
Stealer of mummy-crowns and mummy-sandals,
Tearing them from the flesh of long-dead men :—
Be the wrecker of tombs of gods—stealer of suns?
Why should this mole steal heavens and suns from me?

"Why should this one defiler of the earth,
Prevent the coming here of Julius Cæsar,
Egypt's dazzling Bird of Paradise,
The great cock-pheasant and peacock of the world,
And the beautiful young prince, Cæsarion,
Heir of Egypt, Rome, and the purple seas?"

The silent gods half-opened their dull eyes,
Isis, in mercy, lifted one slender hand.
So, at last, the deathless prayer seemed heard.
Thoth, with his chisel, cut in the wall before them,
Then painted, Rome's giant hieroglyphic—
Dead Cæsar, with his deep red flowing wound—
Then Cæsar's boy,—Horus Cæsarion,—
An exquisite god-prince, naked and fair.
Yet patience! Oh, mummy and prisoner, Cleopatra,
For that slow, cruel, humorous artist, Thoth,
Tantalizer of the souls of men,

Painted and carved, for many a racking day,
Sword-waving hieroglyphics, that, marching, sang
Only at the end: "Come shining forth,
Come forth, oh, deathless sons of Amon-Ra."

\*     \*     \*     \*     \*

Cæsar and Cæsarion at last,
Stepped from the wall to the side of Cleopatra
And the great queen fell there, like a speaking log,
Touching their feet.   Her mummy case was wrecked—
A scattered, shattered chrysalis, and tomb.
But Cleopatra called through the dusty court,
With the musical voice of all the women of time—
And the flaming heart, there, on the iron scales, cried:
"Cleopatra died when Cæsar died.
I am the heart of Cæsar, nothing more."

B.C. 20. *Nine years later.*

But what then of the flame called Antony?
It merged into the majesty of Cæsar,
Walked with his stride, the shadow of his shadow,
Hid in his robe, lost itself in his wound.
Had neither vanity nor purpose of its own,
Was seen no more.   And Cæsar stood there, waiting.
Only his crown was brighter now: his whip
Shone like a torch above the dusty floor,
The light from his eyes like two rays from the moon,
When Mediterranean storms destroy the ships.

Then Set, the beautiful, the hard, and proud,
Ignoring Cæsar and Cæsarion,
Called again to the old Egyptian gods,
Pointing at the high-throned Alexander,
Still the new-comer in that pantheon,
Pointing long fingers at the fallen queen—
The mummy cloth, still binding her dead knees,

450

Dried mummy wreaths fallen from her hair:—
"These are invaders, like the Hyksos kings!
What have the Ptolemies to do with Egypt?
What right had the Macedonian phalanx here?
Why are Roman legions on the Nile?
Are they enthroned by ancient Amon-Ra?"

Then to those gods, the golden Cæsar spoke:—
"Oh, grief of Cæsar in the heaven of heavens!
Without her, thrones are dim and lights are vain!

"She set me on my horse, to win the Parthian crown,
We were resolved to conquer utmost Asia,
Build again the empire of Thutmose Third,
And send the ardent arrows of Amon-Ra,
To ultimate Britain and ultimate India,
Win new empires for Cæsarion,
Heir of Egypt, Rome and the purple seas.
But Cassius, Casca and Brutus struck too soon.
Cæsar they could endure, but not his heir.
They could endure a king, but not a god.
They could endure a queen, but not a goddess.
And they hated my queen-goddess, Cleopatra.

"No blood was in her veins, but the sun's blood.
Sweet Hathor lived in her eyes and her dimpled knees;
And here, with open wounds, I praise her yet.
I was weary and old, with shadowy ambition.
She kissed me into pride and power again.
She was the Isis nations make of queens.

"She made me into a son of Amon-Ra,
Into Egypt's dazzling bird of paradise,
The great cock-pheasant and peacock of the world.
With one kiss of her girl-lips, long ago.
We dreamed of the Terrace of a Million Years.

"There on the island, where I met her first,
This priestess taught me the wisdom of old Thoth,
Who hears the wit, and even the sweet singing,
Uttered among the humorists of the moon.
And when she bore my son Cæsarion,
We sailed with him on all the purple seas,
We climbed with him to every earthly throne,

"Thinking of things beyond all human speech.
We chanted 'The Chapters of Coming Forth by Day,'
Till Thoth, himself, flew in from the wide sea
(The ibis with the rakish wing and stride)
With the great chapters marching after him,
The hieroglyphic soldiers of his heaven,
That will go marching, flying and glittering,
In all the tombs and capitals of men
In all inscriptions of papyrus rolls,
In many languages, in picture-plays,
Waving stone wings through men's minds forever,
When all Rome's regions are but dust and bones,
When every arch of triumph has fallen down,
When men will fly with iron wings, and speak
Across the sky in words that bind the world,
And light can shine through earth, through steel, and granite.
Those hieroglyphics still will march and sing,
Defending gods and all the tombs of gods,
From Set and his innumerable train,
And all who violate your judgment hall."

The heart of Cleopatra in the balance,
Neither rose nor fell, and not one breath
Overthrew the Feather of Truth, in the scale.

\* \* \* \* \*

# THE TRIAL OF THE DEAD CLEOPATRA

The god of spices, and incense, and embalming, B.C. 11. *Nine*
God of the body's dim eternity.                 *years after.*
Anubis, the faithful jackal, kept the scales,
And warded off the wicked hands of Set.
The Feather of Truth, and the heart, kept balance, still.

But Set, the hard, the proud, the confident,
Set, with the crocodile, Ammit, at his side,—
Set, the beautiful, the hard and proud,
The devious, the diabolical postponer,
Tried, still to outwear her heart, till it fall from the scales
Into the monstrous jaws to the second death.

He said: "Your fable is yourself in truth,
Your rumour is your soul, your name is you
To the secret caves of long reëchoing time."

Set, the Accuser, lifted his hand of stone
And sounds came up from the darkness under the sea
And the bones in darkness under all the sands:—
"She poured us out like water and like wine,
She wasted us in battle, let her die!
She wasted us in battle, let her die!"

But what have the gods to do with such complainers?
They love the beautiful, the hard and proud—
Only these can wake them from the night.

*The law's delay among the gods is great.*
*They sleep on shadowy thrones. Their words grow gray.*
Their ribs are basalt and their faces basalt
Cut by the hardest chisels of proud priests,
There on The Terrace of a Million Years.

High above in the light of each changing year,
Priests of the jewelled temples of Abydos,

Thinking not of forgotten Cleopatra,
Of Cæsar, Cæsarion, or Antony,
Sang their sweet songs of the soul's resurrection,
Songs to Osiris, "First of the Westerners,"
Thinking only of their unburied dead,
Of mummies to be sealed in their holy tombs.

\* \* \* \* \*

With quiet gesture and tremendous mien    B.C. 2. *Nine*
Set still held the gods' too-sleepy eyes.      *years later.*
He pointed there to the pitiful prostrate one,
Half-mummy, and half-living girl. Her lips
Had called in vain for water and for food
For years and years, for moments like centuries.
More than her thirst and hunger was deeper still
A memory like old poison in deep wounds,
Antony's treachery to Cæsarion.

\* \* \* \* \*

Anubis, the faithful jackal, fed her smoke,
There with iron paws, beat down the snakes of death.
Unnoted and unknown to gods or ghosts,
To Set or to his suffering prisoner,

\* \* \* \* \*

Strange winds from the uttermost heavens   *Anno Domini* 1.
     swept the tomb.

\* \* \* \* \*

Said Set, the torturer, the king of hell-fire:—
"If you are the daughter of a god,
If you would change your name and take your throne,
Command these grave-stones to be made your bread
454

In my great name, proudly defying them.
I am the light-god, I am the king of the skies."

Her one virtue, a transcendent scorn,
Her one virtue: supernatural pride,
Thirst and hunger had made the great queen mad.
But still she cried and sang through the dusty court
With the musical voice of all the mothers of time,
And the flaming heart, too, on the iron scales cried:—
"Cleopatra died when Cæsar died.
I am the heart of Cæsar, nothing more."
Then, then, she was given in mercy The Wisdom of Thoth.
Then, though her mummy-face was in the dust,
She whispered against the tempter one last spell—
And the pride that would not break conquered the stars:—
"Must Set still violate the judgment hall?
Let the cold scales be the sole judge of my heart.
And as for the kingship of the universe
Hail to the true light-god, Amon-Ra,
And his Roman son, Caius Julius Cæsar—
Egypt's dazzling bird of paradise,
The great cock-pheasant and peacock of the world!
Oh, wings of Cæsar, high above all mountains,
Wings of Cæsar above the purple seas."

\*     \*     \*     \*     \*

Strange winds from the uttermost heavens swept the tomb,

\*     \*     \*     \*     \*

Now the steady hand of Thoth was trem-
    bling—
The artist, king of magic and miracle,—
Physician, healer, merciful, at last.
He touched her shrivelled hands with reverent love.

*Anno Domini
10. Nine years
later.*

455

He touched her gilded eyelids and strained arms.
He loosed the mummy bands from thigh and heart.
Singing from the ancient Book of the dead,
"Lift up thy head, oh thou who liest prostrate."

And she was again held upright by Anubis,
A speaking mummy, transfigured, and not dying.
And she stood pitifully by Cæsar, there,
Half-mummy, but half-god: and beautiful—
A soul indeed—a human soul at last—
The Macedonian glory in her face,
Flowering toward Egyptian resurrection.


## II. She Becomes a Goddess.

Strange winds from the uttermost heavens *Anno Domini*
    swept the tomb,        19. *Nine years*
A mystery and a mercy, still unknown.   *later.*

*　　*　　*　　*　　*

The ghost of Cæsar swayed like a weed in a storm.
And his flaming wound was great in his shadowy side.
Still the steady hand of Thoth was trembling
Amid his proud, unfaltering picture writing.
He shook his Ibis-wing, nodded his head:—
For the log had well-nigh changed into the goddess.
And the wisest woman of all the mothers of time,
Still the secret favorite of shrewd Thoth,
Heard now with him the rumours of all nations.
(For these two could apprehend and prophecy
Further than all those basalt gods there brooding,
Further than Set, the accuser of gods and stars.)
Strange winds from the uttermost heavens and uttermost
    tombs!

456

Dim dreams on the march above the universe!
Miracles on the edge of the Dead Sea!
The little river Jordan roared like doom!
There were shoutings and hosannahs among small peoples!
Wild fishermen on the Sea of Galilee!

Even Anubis lifted his jackal head.
There was the incense of a more merciful empire,
The beginnings of terrible justice, in the air,
Greater than the mercy of Osiris!
His power was waning in the Universe,
A power was gathering from the deeps and the heights.
As a great storm, this power was whirling down,
Blowing through mountian ribs, as through silk veils,
Potent to make real gods, even of these:—
*Who sleep on shadowy thrones, whose words grow gray,*
*Whose ribs are basalt and their faces basalt,*
Cut by the hardest chisels of proud priests.
Their hearts were softened while their thrones were shaken,
There on The Terrace Of A Million Years.

And the cry of Anubis came like a temple gong.
And the cry of the woman rang through the dusty hall,
With the musical voice of all the mothers of time:—
"Oh gods of mercy and of majesty,
Oh gods of softening hearts and trembling thrones:—
When first I came to this my dark tomb door,
When I came clamoring for my goddess throne,
And Cæsar knocked with me, a suppliant here,
You set him free, you sent him to the skies,
To mourn for me, to wait for me in vain,
Through years and years, and moments like centuries.
Give us our thrones to-day beside your thrones!"

Still Set was opening his mouth in scorn,
"Your rumour is your soul, your name is you,"

She stretched frail arms toward all the gods and thrones
Arms at last unwrapped from mummy bands,
And sang above Set's accusing voice
With the voice of a child arising from long sleep,
"Why should the gods of Egypt believe the eternal Accuser,
Or the lying poets of Rome?
These were the slanders of Rome."

\*    \*    \*    \*    \*

Still Set cried on with his eternal spell,
With the old charge that would not be put
        down:—
"Your granite hieroglyphic, still is you!
The written rumour of your name is you,
To the farthest caves of long reëchoing time."

*Anno Domini
28. Nine years
later.*

\*    \*    \*    \*    \*

The forty-two assessors and the twelve great gods of Egypt
Were growing very old.  And their daughter, the pale queen,
The last of royal Egypt, was thwarting the Great Accuser.
They watched with increasing flame in their vague, hot eyes
(Flame like the goldsmith's furnace melting brass)
Her still uplifted arms, her advancing step,
Her gentle increasing strength, as the years rolled on,
The years and years, the moments like centuries.
They saw from their rocking thrones, unafraid, unsmiling,
That the Feather of Truth fell not from the balance,
The flaming heart fell not.  But it whispered still:—
"I am the heart of Cæsar, nothing more."

Privileged doubter of all gods and stars!
Privileged prosecutor of gods and stars!
Privileged scourge of men, and gods, and stars:—
Set cried boldly: "Still you are Cleopatra!

# THE TRIAL OF THE DEAD CLEOPATRA

Still mongrel in Egypt, like yonder Alexander!
Upstart! Parvenu! Usurper!
You are shamed in the eyes of all the women of time.
Gambler, Thief, Poisoner and Betrayer!
The world will believe my word in the mouths of the poets,
And these gods will believe all the golden slanders of Rome!"
Barking his terrible bark, he waited and harried,
With his ravening hungry monster at his side—
Set, who had broken the heart of holy Isis
Once, in the far beginning of the world:—
Set, who had murdered, then tried the good Osiris,
Before this very court of the basalt gods
Still stood unsmitten in the Osirian court
Though The Merciful King, now at the top of his stairway,
Ruled, and justified all the pure of heart.

\* \* \* \* \*

Strange winds from the uttermost heavens swept the tomb
Blowing through mountain ribs as though silk veils,
Then all the old years fell from The Merciful King,
New youth came with new mercy to Osiris:—
He, First of the Westerners, lifted his shepherd's crook,
Isis, The Mother, lifted one slender hand,
Thoth, the Great-hearted, lifted his Ibis wing
To the very roof of the black basalt hall.
And the walls were as the walls of the great full moon.
And that Macedonian Cleopatra
Glorious as Hera, blazing like Psyche the bride,
Was dressed now in strange spiritual snow-white.
And so, transfigured, and with power transcendent
In her arms, the little child, Cæsarion:—
She fixed her eyes on mighty Alexander,
With the gods, a stone-carved son of Amon-Ra,
On the Trembling Terrace of a Million Years.

She prayed, with Cæsar there by her snowy shoulder:—
"Oh son of Amon-Ra, called the Macedonian,—
Oh one man Cæsar envied, Oh, Alexander!
Oh conqueror, your great mother bore you
To Egypt's golden sun-god long ago.
And so it was you came to take your kingdom
In our beautiful oasis, Sekhet-Amit,
And there it was that Amon-Ra came down
To claim you, and my father, Ptolemy,
As Egypt's kings his Macedonian sons!
You set my fathers on Egyptian throne,
Giving, in love, their queens to Amon-Ra."
Then Cæsar, Cæsarion and the queen
Prayed toward the basalt throne of Alexander:—
"Give us our thrones to-day, beside your throne."

He stretched his priest carved arms in miracle,
Stepped from the swaying terrace in strange might,
Stepped from the terrace with that wild assurance
He once rode trembling lands and fearful seas,
A blazing sun, hidden within that tomb,
A god and king and peacock of the world,
Unshaken, though the heavens and earth were shaken,
Cæsar, his brother, there, eternally.

He gave into each right hand the terrible lotos,
That sends forth stars and suns in yellow pollen.
He gave them on their foreheads, holy seals
From the lotos cup of the Egyptian heavens.
The God-cup there ended the thirst of the dead.
And the flaming wound in Cæsar's side was healed.
And the terrible lotos blooms dropped stars like jewels
Gone was the hieroglyphic of Cleopatra
From the tomb-walls and from the coffin-lids.
Gone was the fabled wife of Antony.

Gone was all former meaning of her name.
The blood of Mecedon had left her veins.

All the goddesses there on their thrones,
Shook sweet Hathor's sistrum like soft bells.
And they called her: "Hathor's-body-and-heart-and-soul."
And they called her: "Hathor's-laughter-and-true-name."

Her ears became the tiniest humorous calf's-ears,
Like sweet and humorous Hathor's masquerade,
When she dances among the half-grown girls and boys.
Then her white robe fell like snow blown from a cliff.
She stood there the brown Hathor, Queen of the Nile!
An airy, girl-Egyptian, full of whims,
Tender, innocent, marvellously young—
A black-eyed girl with body of tawny gold.
But still she cried, and her heart from the iron scales cried:—
"Cleopatra died when Cæsar died."

Leaving the scales, where for long years it had waited,
Her heart flew back to her breast forevermore,
Justified! Justified! Before the good Osiris.
The Name, "Osiris," now blazing on her breast,
As on the breasts of Cæsar, and her boy.

Leaving the scales, where for long years it had waited,
The Feather of Truth flew to the forehead of Isis,
Plume of the mother, the merciful mother, Isis,
Plume of the Queen, whose victory is the Truth.

Thoth cut the great verdict on the wall,
And the new names of the Queen, that the great gods cried,
Picture-names they invented each new hour:—
"Eyes-of-Love," "My Lady-Is-As-Gold,"
"Beautiful-Kitten," "Little-Wild-Lion-Girl."

461

The law's delay among the gods was ended.
Cæsar, with the perfect eye of the elder Horus,
Wearing the ancient crowns of the south and the north,
The Queen, clothed in the ravishing form of Hathor,
And their beautiful son, the heir, Cæsarion,
Heir of Egypt, Rome, and the purple seas;—
These three, the last of the Egyptian Triads—
Flamboyant, triumphant, magnificent,
Chanted "The Chapters of Coming Forth by Day,"
As in old days, chanted the golden chapters.

The "Words of Power" swept through the dusty hall,
Fulfilling there all the magic of Thoth,
The love of Osiris for the wise and just,
The love of Amon-Ra for his little children,—
Vindicating that strange wind from heaven
That still as one more mystery, shook the tomb.

There, there, was more than Egyptian resurrection.


### III. SHE IS LIFTED WITH THE OLD GODS INTO THE WESTERN SKY

The walls widened, and were the horizon's rim.
The roof arched up, and was the infinite sky.
Where were those gods, who had lived in priest-carved stone?
Their souls were high above the universe.
Their outspread plumes now filled the uttermost heavens
In the marvellous west, where all our dead have gone.

Cæsar, Cæsarion, and the Queen,
(She was no longer Cleopatra),
The last to be raised to heaven through heathen pride,
Wearing sandals of lapis-lazuli,

# THE TRIAL OF THE DEAD CLEOPATRA

In a moment were one flash of ascending light.
They climbed blue steps, and sat with the good Osiris,
At the top of his stairway, "First of the Westerners,"
Bowered in the flowers of the deep western heavens,
There where the terrible star-lotus blooms.

They took their thrones with the forty-two assessors,
With the four sons of Horus, and with Sekmet,
With Thoth and Maat, and the Memphian Chivalry,
Anubis and King Menes and his train.
They took their thrones with Isis and with Nepthys,
Hatshepsut, Tiy and the strange Ikhnaton,
With Alexander, with the Ptolemies,
With Amon-Ra, and his Macedonian sons.

She stood with young Cæsarion in her arms,
She stood with shadowy Cæsar in that sky.
She kissed him into pride and power again.
Beneath their feet were every sun and star,
The Thrones and The Terrace of a Million Years,
And time, and fear, and the whirling universe.

And the Book of the Dead was rolled up for that day.
The judgment scene was ended.  Far below
The priests of the jewelled temples of Abydos,
Thinking not of the forgotten Queen,
(She who was no longer Cleopatra),
Of Cæsar, Cæsarion, or Antony,
Sang their sweet songs of the soul's resurrection,
Song to Osiris, "First of the Westerners,"
Thinking only of their beloved dead,
Of mummies newly sealed in their holy tombs.

* * * * *

Set, the beautiful, the hard and proud,
Stealer of vases of most precious ointment—
Stealer of red, pitiful, human hearts—
Determined still to win the universe,
Set, the Accuser, victor in his fashion,
Since, to accuse, to him was victory,
Insulter of judges and stars to the highest sky,
He, who accused Job long ago,
In the judgment hall of Jehovah of the Jews,
Then laid his hand upon him through long years:—
Set, the Accuser, resuming his name of Satan,
Wearing sandals of hell-fire, laughing, not smiling,
Barking his terrified bark, marched far to the north,
There to accuse and tempt in the Dead Sea Desert,
And on a pinnacle of King Herod's temple,
And on a flower-decked mountain of meditation:—
The son of a girl, fairer than Cleopatra,
A son of Amon-Ra, prouder than Cæsar,
And lovelier than the young Cæsarion.

On reading the latest proof of this poem, I have found a book that elaborately confirms the political hypothesis:—"The Life and Times of Cleopatra, Queen of Egypt—A Study in the Origin of the Roman Empire," by Arthur Weigall, published by Thomas Butterworth, Limited, 15 Bedford Street, London W.C. 2; and G. P. Putnam's Sons, 2 West 45th Street, New York City. But the same idea may be found in Ferrero's "Greatness and Decline of Rome," in all the comment on Cleopatra. I have outlined this poem of mine as a possible photoplay in "The Art of the Moving Picture," pages 254-260.